About the Author

Catriona Rainsford was born in Cambridge. After leaving school she travelled to India but was forced to return to the UK when she broke her leg in a fall. A promise made in a pub at closing time then took her to Mexico, where a chance meeting began her two-year journey with the *malabaristas*. Catriona currently lives in London while she studies for a degree in politics, economics and anthropology. She has won prizes for her travel writing in the Bradt/ *Independent on Sunday* travel-writing competition in 2010, and the *Guardian* travel-writing competition in 2009.

The Urban Circus

TRAVELS WITH MEXICO'S MALABARISTAS

by **Catriona Rainsford**

First published in the UK in February 2013 by

Bradt Travel Guides Ltd
IDC House, The Vale, Chalfont St Peter, Bucks SL9 9RZ, England
www.bradtguides.com

Print edition published in the USA by The Globe Pequot Press Inc,
PO Box 480, Guilford, Connecticut 06437-0480

Text copyright © 2013 Catriona Rainsford
Maps copyright © 2013 Bradt Travel Guides Ltd, drawn by David McCutcheon FBCart.S
Edited by Jennifer Barclay
Typeset from the author's files by Artinfusion
Cover design: illustration and concept by Neil Gower,
                   typesetting by Creative Design and Print

ISBN: 978 1 84162 444 0 (print)
e-ISBN: 978 1 84162 778 6 (e-pub)
e-ISBN: 978 1 84162 652 9 (mobi)

British Library Cataloguing in Publication Data
A catalogue record for this book is available from the British Library

With thanks to the Nobel Foundation for permission to quote from Octavio Paz's acceptance speech,
© The Nobel Foundation 1990.

Production managed by Jellyfish Print Solutions; printed in India
Digital conversion by Scott Gibson

A la banda
Sin ustedes, no habría una historia
(Without you, there would be no story)

and to Mum, Dad and Julia
Without you, there would be no book

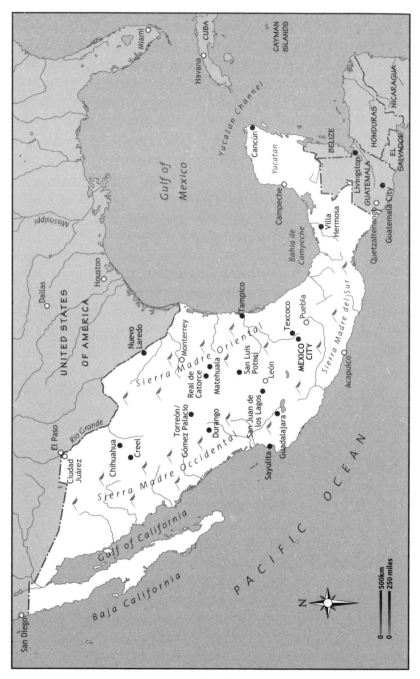

Contents

'Our art movement is not needed in this country.'

French surrealist André Breton, on visiting Mexico in 1938

'A man who is without polis, by reason of his own nature and not of some accident, is either a poor sort of being, or a being higher than man... clanless and lawless and heartless is he.'

From Aristotle's 'The Politics', quoted by Spanish bishop Bartolomé de las Casas in reference to the nomadic lifestyles of some of the indigenous peoples of the newly discovered Americas

1
Millionaires

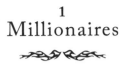

We watched the second Creel massacre on a grainy surveillance video replayed in a truck-stop diner somewhere in Jalisco. I'd been facing the other way, gazing idly at the truck driver we were hitching with as he stirred tablespoons of instant coffee and sugar into his mug of boiling water. A surly waitress clattered crockery at an adjoining table. Trico jerked his head at the news bulletin playing on the TV screen above my head.

'Hey Cat, look,' he said. 'It's where we met.'

I craned around to watch as the cameras followed the men's progress through Creel. The footage had been taken at dawn, the men's long black shadows etched across the gold of the streets. They snorted handfuls of cocaine from clear plastic bags before approaching a house, firing several rounds through the front windows and then crashing through the front door with AK-47s tucked under their arms. We sat and looked until our driver heaved himself to his feet, brushed off his moustache, and lumbered out towards the truck with a sigh of *'De verdad, Mexico está perdido.'* Truly, Mexico is lost.

We drained the last of our coffees and followed him outside. And I thought of Creel the way I had seen it, seven months before, the day I met Trico.

The first time I saw him, he was riding a unicycle along a wall. This was not unusual for Trico; he saw the entire world as a complicated arrangement of surfaces to ride unicycles on. But at the time I didn't know that, and stopped walking for a few seconds to watch him.

The wall marked the edge of a raised plaza in the centre of Creel – a village tucked between the mountains of the Sierra Madre Occidental, just before they fracture into a labyrinth of yawning canyons that make the territory all but impassable and conceal any number of people who don't wish to be found. The street alongside the plaza was wide and lined with low-slung buildings, revealing a fringe of pine trees above the line of rooftops. It was the sort of street that looks lonely without horses in it. There were no horses in it – only a couple of parked pickups with cold sores of rust over the wheels and a few men in shapeless brown trousers wearing the expressions of people who didn't know the time, and rarely needed to.

Behind the unicyclist, his companions milled around in the dappled shade under the trees on the plaza, idly twirling juggling clubs or beating slow rhythms on djembe drums, their belongings in tattered bundles at their feet. It was the final day of a small festival that had been held in some caves nearby, in that after-party hour that hangs heavy with spent adrenaline, when those that have homes hurry back to them, leaving those that don't to linger dazedly behind. Like them, I was adrift and disoriented after the festival, and perhaps my lost expression invited a gesture of solidarity. Calling me over, they offered me a swig of their beer.

They were travelling *malabaristas* – itinerant circus performers who wandered the streets of Mexico, hitchhiking from town to town and surviving by whatever donations of spare change or food the local people would give for their impromptu shows. You'd see them at traffic intersections all over the country – strange, jester-like figures who would skip out in front of the vehicles as they waited at the red lights, give a quick display of juggling or fire spinning, then collect any coins the drivers handed them as the cars moved off on either side.

I had seen them before, and pitied them. Not *them* precisely, but others like them, drowning in the flood of seething city traffic, gasoline-stained hands thrust out for a couple of spare pesos. I had read about them as well, never more than a couple of sentences in the middle of some rumination on Mexican poverty: another symbol of desperation in a country where almost half the urban population worked on the black market and men joined the drug gangs because they saw no other way to make a decent living. They would be grouped in the same category as the boys who jumped on car bonnets as they waited at traffic lights and started frantically cleaning the windscreen, hoping that guilt or gratitude would inspire a tip. Or the children with huge black eyes like Japanese animations who wandered between the lines of cars, choking on exhaust fumes and reaching up to the windows to hawk small plastic packets of chilli peanuts. Just more impoverished kids trying to scrape a living off streets that were already overworked.

I might have gone on believing that, if it hadn't been for Trico.

Trico was one of those born showmen whose star turn is themselves. Possessed of a frenetic energy, he did everything with quick, jerky little movements, like a clockwork toy wound up too tight. The vibrantly clashing colours and patterns of his clothes and chiselled planes of his face were crowned by a topknot of wild black dreadlocks, exploding with multicoloured braids. Sawn-off bits of plastic tubing kept the piercings in the lobes of his ears stretched to a width of several centimetres. Taken as a whole, the effect was one of carefully calculated insanity.

There on the plaza, he was the only one not limp with fatigue. Perched absurdly atop a unicycle with coloured beads on the spokes of the wheel and a tyre that appeared to have come off a mountain bike, he rode round and round us in dizzying circles. Weaving between the trees and even attempting the few steps down to the main road, he called out to the near-empty square –

'*Arre arre arrrrre!!! Bienvenido-o-o-s aaal spec-tac-ulo-o-o!*'

Glancing around to assess his potential audience, he caught sight of a couple of Tarahumara girls, about six years old, watching wide-eyed from under the trees. Their feet were bare and they clutched bundles of bracelets made from grubby twisted string. The Tarahumara of the Sierra Madre are among the poorest indigenous peoples of Mexico, and often young children are expected to help bring home a few extra pesos by selling handmade trinkets to the tourists in the villages. The little girls wore dresses with the unique shabbiness of hand-me-downs, stained with elder sisters' accidents and elder cousins' dinners. Pedalling the unicycle over to come to a rocking equilibrium in front of them, Trico drew three fluorescent orange juggling clubs from the bag on his back and pointed exaggeratedly to his eye to indicate that they watch. He delivered a brief but enthusiastic display, embellishing the basic juggling patterns with tricks and flourishes. On finishing he gave them a bow, and they giggled in delight and hid their dirt-smudged faces behind their hands with childish coquettishness.

When he pedalled back over towards us, I complimented him on his performance and his unicycle.

'Thanks', he said. 'It's been with me two years. Good model. Terrain unicycle.'

'A what?'

'A *terrain* unicycle.' He spoke with the laboured patience of one sadly accustomed to such ignorance. 'Thicker tyre, better grip. Good for off-road riding. Mountains, deserts, that kind of thing.'

'Your whole life is a circus, isn't it?' I asked. He laughed. His features were dramatic and clearly defined, as in carvings of the Aztec warriors, and deep dimples bored into each side of his face when he smiled.

'The whole *world* is a circus,' he said, riding a further circle around us in reverse. 'And all of us are the clowns.'

Despite his exuberance – or perhaps because of it – there was something curiously unreadable about him. It left you wondering what was spontaneous and what was rehearsed, how much was personality and how much persona. He embodied what captivated me most about Mexico: the impossibility of knowing where reality ended and fantasy began.

ψ Ψ ψ

Malabarista. Most dictionaries will tell you it means 'juggler', but it's broader than that. It describes a specific type of circus performer: one whose skill lies in the manipulation of objects. And beneath that it carries a note of ambiguity, a hint at something darker. I have heard that in Chile, it can also mean 'trickster': one whose skill lies in the manipulation of people.

Although I had always loved the fluid syllables of the word, it had never occurred to me to become a malabarista. It wasn't an obvious career choice for someone with little natural coordination. But that day was one of those aimless ones when, freed from the blinkers of any particular plan or direction, you see the world as a kaleidoscope of possibilities fanning out around you. On such a day, just as a newly hatched duckling will adopt the first thing it sees as its mother, any chance encounter can lead you into an unexpected and unlikely future. I had been planning on leaving Creel later that evening. Instead, hearing that Trico and his friends intended to stay on to explore some of the surrounding area, where the road west led into the rugged backcountry of the Sierra Madre, I checked into a hotel room on the outskirts of the village and promised to see them again the next day.

One of their group had unearthed some distant relative who had a house in the village, where they set up camp on the veranda using a couple of elderly tents and a large sheet of tarpaulin. By about 11 every morning they would be on the plaza, and over the following days I got to know them a little better.

There was Sandra, tall and dreadlocked, with a childlike vulnerability in the way her lips parted over two buck front teeth. She was originally from Ciudad Juárez, the crime-torn border town to the north, notorious at the time for being the most violent city in the world. She had been living on the streets around Mexico for the last two years. When I asked her why, she said simply, 'Because it's better than living in Juárez.' She told me a story of having gone once to a party at the house of a man she didn't know, an acquaintance of a new friend. A man had welcomed them on arrival, offered them a drink, and informed them offhandedly that they should stay away from the locked room at the end of the corridor as he had a kidnapped man in there. There was no knowing if it was true or not, but it was the sort of thing that in Juárez was well within the bounds of possibility.

Sandra appeared to have no need for food as long as she had a continual supply of beer, which she had come up with an ingenious method of obtaining. She would search in rubbish bins until she found an empty aluminium can, which she would take a pair of scissors to and, with a complicated system of folds and cuts, turn into a pretty little model flower with tear-drop petals and a fringe of silver curls. '*Arte reciclado*', she called it. She would then go to the nearest shop that stocked alcohol and swap the flower for a can of beer. When that can was finished, she would use it to make a new model flower, which she would take to a different shop and swap for another can of beer. It was an impressively self-sustaining system. The only trouble with it, she conceded, was that it forced her to constantly keep moving, as she could never go to the same shop twice.

'Are the shop staff always willing to swap a beer for an aluminium flower?' I asked.

'Oh yes,' she assured me, 'almost always. The women because they like the flowers, the men because they understand the need for beer.'

Then there was Luis, who was toned and coffee-coloured with a sensitive mouth and stiff little curls on his brow, like a carved hero on the centrepiece of a Renaissance fountain. He would have been extremely good-looking if it weren't for the pitted chickenpox scars up the side of his face and a wolfish way of looking people up and down, as if deciding where to take the first bite. Bernardo warned me about him that first day on the plaza, indicating him with a slight inclination of his head and whispering in my ear:

'Don't trust him.'

'Why not?'

'He's crazy. He stabbed a guy a few days ago, after a party in a town not far from here.'

'Really? Why?'

Bernardo shrugged.

'He said that he had a good reason.'

He gave no indication whether the good reason was defence of his life, or revenge for some imagined insult.

'Was the guy alright?'

He shrugged again and gave that most Mexican of answers, that could mean 'yes', or 'no', or 'I don't want to tell you', or 'I don't know', or almost anything else. It's the equivalent of the famous head wobble in India: a nationally recognised code laden with delicately nuanced meaning to those who have grown up with it but infuriatingly, almost maliciously incomprehensible to anyone else.

'*Quién sabe?*' Who knows?

Bernardo was tall and seemed to walk with his centre of balance located somewhere behind his feet, as if his upper body were leaning back against a wall even as his legs kept striding forward. It suited him well, as he also looked out at the world with a wall-leaner's air of ironic detachment. As far as I could tell, he had only one goal in life, which took up so much of his mental energy that he had little time to think of anything else. This was to make hair braids. Specifically, to make a hair braid for every woman he came across, in every place he went. Hair braids were Bernardo's way of marking his territory, of establishing himself as the alpha male of the surrounding area. He kept a careful mental list of women he had braided, in the way that lesser men might collect notches on their bedposts, and every time a sweep of black hair crossed the street tagged with one of his signature flashes of colour, he would smile to himself with a little nod of satisfaction. The first time he spoke to me it was to ask if I wanted a hair braid, and when I declined he promptly offered to make me one for free. This was about more than money; this was about conquest.

Only I called Bernardo by his real name. I never heard anyone else call him anything but *chilango*, the generic name for anyone from Mexico City. This was always spoken in a tone that hovered between affection and mockery, the non-chilangos' contempt for chilangos being matched only by the chilangos' contempt for *them*. Luis had warned me about him, later that day on the plaza, indicating him with a slight inclination of his head and whispering in my ear:

'Don't trust him.'

'Why not?'

'He's a chilango.'

'What's wrong with that?'

He looked momentarily confused, having apparently expected the statement to require no further explanation.

'They... they think they're better than everyone else. But they're sneaky. They...' He seemed to be struggling to find the right words to impress on me the full sneakiness of the chilangos and finally gave up with a small shake of his head. 'When you've been in Mexico longer, you'll understand.'

For a brief moment, I considered asking him about the alleged stabbing, but thought better of it. I had a feeling this would turn out to be another one of those things that until I had been in Mexico longer I just wasn't going to understand.

ψ Ψ ψ

At the time, I wasn't intending to stay in Mexico much longer at all. After several months of travel through Mexico and Central America, my bank balance was dwindling rapidly. I had come up through the northern Mexican state of Chihuahua on my way to California, from where I was to fly home, find a job, and consider my next move. I was unsure what the future held, but I imagined the next few months of it would include morning alarm clocks and presentable shoes and subservience to the whims of shift supervisors and assistant managers and (worst of all) those belligerent 9 a.m. customers who don't quite know what they want, but know it's your fault they didn't get it. The thought gave me no pleasure.

Travel is an addiction. Anyone who has been on the road for an extended period of time knows that. Freedom is a drug. But as with any drug, the doses that got you high at first come to feel rather tame after a while. And as with any drug, a hardcore freedom addiction can end up enslaving you more effectively than your old life ever did.

First you become a slave to the calendar, compulsively checking how many days you have left until your return ticket and wasting hours, pencil in hand, working out how you're going to fit in everything you want to do and see before that dreaded day comes. Then, once you take the addiction to the next level and no longer buy return tickets, you become a slave to the budget. Now the pencil is dealing not with dates but with figures, as you start penny-pinching ever more stingily and chastising yourself for your every unnecessary expenditure. Eventually, you start taking odd jobs along the road in bars and restaurants and, although you congratulate yourself on having found a way to never have to go home, a treacherous voice in the back of your head keeps whispering that if you wanted to spend all day working in a boring job, you could do it in your own country, where at least the wages would be better. At this stage, the 'freedom' of long-term travel can start to feel a little hollow.

'Freedom costs money,' my father would sigh when he was in one of his more cynical moods. 'In this life, there is always someone trying to control you. Employers, banks, politicians… they all have the power to tell you what to do, how to live. Freedom is having enough money to tell all of them to fuck off.'

Slowly, reluctantly, I had started to suspect he might be right.

This was the stage I had reached at the time I met Trico and his friends. Over the following days in Creel, I watched them with increasing interest.

They had arrived at the festival with very little money and left with nothing at all, yet through a combination of street shows, selling hand-made jewellery, and good old-fashioned opportunism, they always seemed to have enough to eat and – more importantly – to be at least slightly drunk. This, it seemed, was their definition of freedom.

After a few days, they announced they were going to camp for a night in Recowata, a series of hot springs nestled in the mountains about 20 kilometres to the west. I checked out of my hotel room and joined them for the trip.

We hitched a ride in a battered pickup to where the track to the springs forked off the main road, our jackets pulled over our heads to shield us from the cold drizzle that had been falling all afternoon. From the turning, we carried our packs several kilometres through the pine forest, emerging on the lip of a canyon from where a steep track zigzagged down to the cluster of volcanic pools at the bottom, cradled in the rock above a narrow river which lay grey in the dusk rain.

As night fell, the rain eased off. By the time we got down and set up camp on the edge of the pools the sky had cleared enough for tiny stars to start struggling through the clouds. Fireflies flashed like spells among the trees. Before long Sandra had a small fire going, coaxing a sulky lick of flame out of the damp wood and poking with a stick at a pot of coagulating rice. Up to his neck in the steaming water and swigging from a plastic bottle of Flor de Caña, Trico gazed around him in beaming satisfaction.

'*Ay, qué rico,*' he announced to no one in particular, leaning back to survey the sweep of star-speckled sky framed between the walls of the canyon. '*No tenemos ni un peso, pero somos milionarios.*' We don't have a single peso, but we are millionaires.

It was that sentence that made me go with them.

2
The Disappeared

'Light me.'

Sandra dangled two arm-length chains in front of Trico's crouched figure, each chain ending in a wick made of tightly rolled strips of denim soaked in petrol. Cupping a hand behind the wicks to shield them from the wind, Trico struck a lighter. There was a faint whoosh as the gasoline ignited.

She straightened and moved away a few paces, a fire-tipped chain clutched between the fingers of each hand. As Luis and Bernardo struck up a tribal beat on the djembes, a tiny flex in the muscles of her wrists set the balls of fire swinging backwards and forwards, finding the rhythm of the drums.

Her cue was played into the music: a sharper, more insistent note cutting three times through the others. In answer, she threw her right arm above her head in a soaring arc, a comet of flame streaking behind. The movement swept her into the dance, the undulating motions of her wrists and arms weaving the chains around her body. I watched the burning wicks trace spirograph patterns of fire through the air, encircling different parts of her body in turn, their paths constantly changing direction to merge and then divide, carving fresh circles through unsuspecting patches of darkness. Shadows flickered across the contours of her figure.

During her performance, Trico crouched over the cut-off bottle filled with petrol, dipping the ends of each of his fire clubs in turn and shaking off the excess liquid. As the fire on Sandra's wicks wavered and started to fade, he approached her from the side, clubs in hand. Slowing her dance to a graceful stop, Sandra touched a dying flame to one of them and his figure was suddenly illuminated, his features cast into sharp relief by the flare of the fresh gasoline. He moved to the point where she had stood in front of the drummers and began to juggle. The torches rose and fell in ever-changing patterns, his hands deftly manipulating them in swirls, arcs and pirouettes. His eyes, dark and unblinking, were transfixed upwards, reflecting the spinning points of fire.

Finally, those flames too began to flicker and pale. With a last flourish, he caught each of the torches as they fell and, one by one, blew them out. The djembes rapped out a closing salute, and then fell silent.

There were a few scattered claps. The street was almost deserted.

'Go, Cat,' Trico hissed. 'The *charol*.' Collect the money.

I passed around the spectators, proffering an upturned hat and smiling to cover my embarrassment, feeling awkward in the unfamiliar and unglamorous role. Some merely shrugged, but most fumbled in their pockets for coins. By the end of the round the hat was jingling, but still light. Luis peered into it and sighed.

'Enough for a beer. Let's go.'

The gasoline extinguished, they shivered in the cool mountain air, drawing jackets around their shoulders as they gathered their equipment under the jaundiced glow of a single street lamp.

Then, there was a shout from the other side of the road. A woman beckoned from a shop doorway. Setting down his drum, Bernardo ran over to her and was ushered inside. Emerging a minute later and crossing back to the group, he carried a steaming polystyrene tray in each hand. In one, a thick slop of beans, smelling richly of onions and garlic. In the other, a stack of tortillas and a mound of white rice, with a tied plastic bag of green salsa perched on top. He grinned triumphantly up at us.

'*Comamos.*'

Let's eat.

ψ Ψ ψ

In the heavy, pine-scented mist of a Creel dawn, Luis sat knotting macramé bracelets on the veranda, his fingers still nimble despite the morning cold. He sang softly to himself a tune that I recognised as the Doors' 'Riders on the Storm', but with the words replaced by a semi-phonetic approximation in colloquial Spanish.

> *Chale, dónde estoy?*
> *Dónde amanecí?*
> *No tengo pa'l camión*
> *Ni por mi caguamón*
> *Chale, ya me voy.*

Which translates roughly to:

> Fuck, where am I?
> Where did I wake up?
> I've got nothing for the bus
> Or even for a beer
> Fuck it, I'm off.

In front of him, a few threadbare chickens pecked disconsolately among the puddles on the dirt road. Behind, an earthy scent of coffee wafted from the open front door.

On returning from Recowata, I had moved into the camp on the veranda. People were always coming and going in their lives, and an extra person was easily accommodated. Space was made for me in one of the tents, where I slept with my head squashed against the djembes, and no more was said on the matter.

The veranda was a rickety but spacious wooden structure with a corrugated iron roof, protected from the wind by the single-storeyed concrete house built in an L-shape around it. The house had no internal doors. One entered through the veranda into a bedroom which merged into the kitchen, from which the master bedroom was partitioned off by a pink floral curtain. The bathroom, which appeared to have been added as something of an afterthought, was tacked on behind that. The interior was painted white and decorated with dried flowers and images of Jesus, the Virgin of Guadalupe, and assorted Catholic saints.

Its owner had been introduced to me as Sandra's aunt, although I suspected from the way in which Sandra, like the others, addressed her respectfully as *señora* that their true relationship was rather more remote.

Mexicans tend to have little concept of varying degrees of distance when it comes to blood ties – family is family, and must be treated accordingly. Round-faced and motherly, with wispy black hair tied in a ponytail on the nape of her neck, the señora seemed cheerfully unfazed by the unexpected occupation of her veranda. By the time the first rays of the sun had started to brush away the mist that settled over the pinewoods during the night, the front door of the house would be set invitingly open, and we would be woken by the smell of fresh coffee brewing on the stove. This was our cue to enter and sit at the hospitably large dining table while she bustled around serving coffee and regaling us with friendly chatter.

Widowed several years before, she shared the house with one plump and pretty grown-up daughter and two young granddaughters. Of the granddaughters, only one shared her burnt-toffee skin and wide, almost Oriental features that are a hallmark of indigenous blood. The other was sandy-haired and grey-eyed, with a strikingly pale face in comparison to the other women of the family. Every time the little girls entered the kitchen, the señora would sweep them into her arms and exclaim to us with exaggerated delight:

'See how lucky I am to have two such lovely granddaughters – one *güera* [fair], and one *morena* [dark]! Such a blessing, don't you think, to have one of each! And both from the same father! I know it seems strange that two such different girls have the same father, but such things are possible, you know.'

Such things are indeed possible, due to the entwined streams of Spanish and indigenous blood which run through most Mexican families and can occasionally throw to the surface the face of a long-lost ancestor generations later. The señora, however, seemed to be struggling harder to convince herself with these declarations than she was to convince any of us. The plump daughter would inspect her nails. The whereabouts of the father was never mentioned, and none of us ever asked.

Aside from her sensitivity regarding her mismatching grandchildren, the señora was the sort of woman who put you instantly at ease. That morning, finding myself alone in the kitchen with her while Luis and Sandra sat outside and Trico and Bernardo had gone to buy eggs, beans and vegetables to prepare for breakfast, I inquired cautiously about the first Creel massacre, which had taken place the summer before. Even one massacre gives you pause in a town of around 6,000 inhabitants. I saw her stiffen slightly, before answering with uncharacteristic brevity:

'Thirteen dead, all from one family. One of them was a baby. But it's better not to talk of these things... This is a small town, you understand?'

She turned hurriedly back to the stove, hands flurrying around a large silver pot that seemed to be taking frustratingly good care of itself.

'More coffee?'

I understood, at least enough to take the mug of grainy black coffee she ladled me from the pot and ask no further questions.

It looked an unlikely scene for a massacre. Spread out along a fold between forested hills and watched over by a white stone Jesus perched on a high rock amidst the trees, Creel faced the world with an air of cheerful dilapidation. It had been built as a depot on the railway linking the state capital of Chihuahua to the Pacific Ocean, and for many years had stood at the end of the line as the engineers struggled to find a way to continue the track through the rugged series of canyons beyond. Since the completion of the railway it had become the main hub for trips into the spectacular Copper Canyon region, attracting a modest but steady inflow of tourist dollars. Testament to this was the crooked row of gift shops along the main road past the plaza, decorated in a jumbled selection of bright, paint-box colours.

Yet something was amiss in the atmosphere of the town. Despite it being midsummer, the main street was eerily quiet. The array of trinkets in the gaily painted shop fronts attracted few admirers. Neither the little Tarahumara girls nor Sandra and Luis were having much success selling their handmade jewellery and would pass the days sitting dejectedly on the wall that separated the pavement from the raised plaza, occasionally tensing with excitement at the sight of a foreign face. The village seemed to be waiting, with diminishing hopefulness, for days that had passed, like a movie set abandoned at the end of filming.

For years, Creel had been living a double life. On the surface it had been an island of rural tranquillity in an increasingly troubled region, the draw of the Copper Canyon railway allowing it to establish itself as a picturesque tourist haven. But, as some of the grander, white-columned houses on the edge of town hinted, its situation in the heartland of one of the world's most profitable drug-growing regions, and its potential as a money laundry, had also attracted business of a murkier kind. In the end, the slow, steady trickle of tourist dollars had proved to be no match for the big, fast bucks to be made through drug-trafficking and extortion. Creel was no longer an enchanted bubble, safe from the devastation that had swept through the Sierra Madre and out across northern Mexico. With the massacre, the illusion had been shattered, the dark underbelly exposed. The tourists stayed away.

Ironically, they were the ones with the least to fear. Although there has been a smattering of incidents in which foreign visitors have been kidnapped or murdered in Mexico, in general there is little incentive to target tourists, as long as they keep their heads down and don't meet the wrong people or find out too much. For locals, it is not so simple. As the señora had implied, in a small town it can be frighteningly easy to meet the wrong people and to find out too much. It can be as easy as being born into the wrong family. The significance of blood ties in Mexico does not apply only to hospitality, it also applies to revenge. In the massacre of 2008, gunmen opened fire on a family party held by relatives of the town mayor. What he had done to incur the gang's wrath has never been made clear.

The empty streets of Creel and the señora's fear were my first glimpse into the full scale of the human tragedy unfolding across northern Mexico.

My second came later that evening.

The señora allowed us use of her kitchen, as long as we bought the food and made contributions towards the gas, and Sandra and I were chopping vegetables for a soup. On the far end of the kitchen table, a piece of paper caught my eye. It was a single sheet, folded over into an A4-sized pamphlet. On the page facing upwards were several rows of black-and-white photographs, each the grainy image of a female face. At the base of each photo, like epitaphs: name, age, physical characteristics, date last seen. At the top, the heading: '*Ayúdanos a Localizarlas*'. Help us find them.

Sandra had seen me looking.

'*Las muertas de Juárez*,' she told me.

In her mind, at least, the heading was meaningless. They had already joined the ranks of the dead women of Ciudad Juárez.

Women had been disappearing from Juárez since 1993, long before President Felipe Calderón's declaration of war on the drug cartels in 2006 sparked the rapid escalation of violence across northern Mexico. Some of their bodies had been found, discarded on rubbish heaps or decomposing in the surrounding desert, many showing signs of rape, torture and mutilation. Others had simply vanished. Exact motives for the killings were still unclear. Some believed they could be an initiation test for criminal gangs. But the prevailing theory was simply that on the Mexican border life is cheap, and female life is the cheapest of all. The term sometimes used in academia to describe the killings perhaps captures best their cold brutality: systematic sexual feminicide. Statistics are vague due to the inadequacy of official investigations, but estimates of their numbers range from three hundred to over a thousand.

I looked carefully at each face in turn. Many of them were in their late teens, some as young as 15. From the girls' dimpled shoulders exposed in grown-up ball gowns and jewellery a touch overstated for true sophistication, I imagined that several of the photographs must have been taken at their *quinceañeras,* the extravagant coming-out parties thrown for girls when they reach their fifteenth birthday and are officially welcomed into the Catholic Church. The receptions following the church service are their Cinderella moment, when for the first time they are allowed to present themselves as women and dance with a man, the eyes of everyone upon them. Long before that time, many Mexican girls are using stubby pencils to draw their fantasy dresses on scraps of paper, awaiting the occasion with the breathless anticipation with which they are later expected to await their weddings. At the event, they pose for commemorative photos which are then displayed proudly on mantelpieces: treasured mementos of the transition from girlhood to womanhood. On the smudged photocopied sheet, in neat rows like tombstones, their eager smiles looked more like a reproach. Other faces were older, their eyes already saddened by experience. Some smiled, others stared blankly at the lens, presumably for their passports or (more likely) their *credencial de elector* – the Mexican identity card. Some were beautiful, others less so. All were under 40.

Sandra was watching me.

'You understand now? Why I don't live in Juárez?'

I nodded. There was a long silence as we both stared at the files of women gazing back at us.

'His mother was one of them, you know.'

I looked up at her. 'Whose?'

She jerked her head towards the open door, from where Luis's voice was audible, explaining a particular macramé knot to one of the other boys outside.

'About three years ago now, I think. They never found her body. One of *las desaparecidas*.'

The disappeared.

'I didn't know...' I tried to say some appropriate words, and found there were none. 'What did he do?'

She shrugged, then smiled a tight and humourless smile.

'Disappeared.'

I remembered Luis' voice, singing softly in the morning mist.

Chale, dónde estoy?

3
Aluminium Flowers

꧁꧂

A couple of days later Trico announced that, if I were to travel with them, it was imperative that I learn some form of *malabares*, or circus skill. The available options were poi, staff or juggling.

'Poi', the form of malabares that Sandra played, are two balls at the end of chains which are spun in patterns around the body. When the balls are replaced by wicks soaked in gasoline and set alight, the poi 'spin fire'. Staff follows the same principle, but with wicks on each end of a rigid staff rather than chains. These toys, Trico explained, rely on fire for their effect and are popular among southern Mexicans. The northern malabaristas tend to dedicate themselves to *malabares puros* – *pure* juggling. His tone left no doubt which he considered the superior art form. Put like that, my choice seemed obvious: I would learn to juggle.

However, on realising very quickly that I had startlingly poor coordination, Trico adjusted his expectations accordingly and decided that, for now, it was sufficient that I should be able to spin poi. To his dismay, I turned out to have startlingly little ability at that as well, and we took a short break from the lesson so that he could soothe his rattled nerves and have a much-needed *caguama* (the large bottles of beer that are shared communally at almost any Mexican gathering and take their name from giant sea turtles). We climbed the hill behind the señora's house to sit on a rock amidst the pine trees, looking out over the valley.

Over the previous days in Creel, Trico had become the member of the group I would talk to most. The knack, with Trico, was to catch him at the right moment. At times, he would be possessed by, in his own words, '*Tricopsycho-o-o – el payaso-o-o – mas loco-o-o – del mundo-o-o*' (the craziest clown in the world), an alter-ego which I assumed he had developed for street shows but would surface, apparently unbidden, at frequent and unpredictable intervals. Tricopsycho was loud, obnoxious, and almost impossible to communicate with, merely gesticulating wildly and talking in rhymes and ridiculous catchphrases. After initial amusement at his first few outings, I found Tricopsycho frustrating and rather irritating and would avoid him as much as possible. As soon as Tricopsycho retreated and Trico returned, he would become calmer and more pensive, and proved to be an intelligent and surprisingly patient conversationalist. Patience was necessary with me back then, as although my understanding was good, my spoken Spanish was still very hesitant.

Having caught him in one of these moments out on the hillside, I took the opportunity to ask him the question that had been bothering me since my conversation with Sandra: whether the malabaristas, particularly those from Juárez, did it in order to escape. He considered the question carefully before answering.

'I suppose there are more travellers from Juárez than from other places because they want to get away. And street performance gives them a means to do that. But it's not just a means to escape; it's more than that. Some of the best jugglers I know come from Juárez, drummers as well. And the things they learn in their travels, they take back to Juárez. They play music in the street; they juggle and spin fire at the *semáforos* [intersections that have traffic lights]. And they are some of the bravest people in Mexico; you know why?'

'Why?'

'I'll tell you a story. I first went to Juárez about two years ago. Only a couple of days after I arrived, I was walking in the street with two friends, looking for a good semáforo. We found one and were walking towards it when a police car pulled up at the red light. There were two policemen in the front.

'As we approached the semáforo, a suburban-style pickup came up in the lane next to the police car. It was slowing down a bit, but still seemed to be going a bit too fast, and I remember wondering if it was going to stop. Then we heard three shots *bang bang bang* – it's so loud, you know, louder than you would imagine – and people started screaming. We threw ourselves behind some parked cars, hearing more shots from the intersection, and more screams. By the time we came out from behind the cars, the pickup was gone, the windows of the police car were shattered and its interior was covered in blood. The driver was dead. They got the other man out alive, though very badly injured. I don't know if he survived.

'That experience made a huge impact on me. It was the most horrific thing I had ever seen. After that, every time I went to a semáforo in Juárez I would be shaking so much I could hardly catch the clubs. If I saw a police car I would run and hide in the nearest shop, even if I was in the middle of a show. There in the semáforo... you're so exposed. If I had already been there when that shooting happened, one of the bullets could easily have hit me. And shootings like that happen all the time. Juárez is a warzone. El Chapo and La Linea have been fighting for control for years.' ('El Chapo', or 'Shorty' is the nickname for Joaquín Guzmán Loera, the infamous leader of the Sinaloa Cartel who once ranked 41st on Forbes' list of most powerful people in the world. 'La Linea' is the armed wing of the rival Juárez Cartel, whose members include various corrupt officers of the Chihuahua state police.)

'Every day there are assassinations. And so many of them happen in the semáforos. It's easiest to get a good shot when a car is stationary. So the malabaristas... they are putting themselves in the front line of that war, you understand? Yet still they go back, still they keep doing it. It's not just about the money. It's about showing that you don't have to live in fear. That you can still make people smile, even in a place like Juárez. I think it gives people hope. That even in the middle of all that destruction and violence, it is still possible to make something beautiful.'

ψ Ψ ψ

We stayed in Creel for 10 days after the return from Recowata, which was at least eight days longer than any of us had intended. It was important, Trico explained to me on the first day, to leave with some money, as there were few people and no traffic intersections in the Sierra's backcountry and we would need at least 100 pesos a day for beer.

'How many days will we be in the Sierra?'

He shrugged.

'*Quién sabe?*'

'Then how will we know how much money we need?'

'You worry too much,' he told me sternly. 'Calm down.'

I calmed down. *Quién sabe,* I realised, was the trump card of any conversation. Once it had been played, the game was up; there was no point in persevering. I resolved to use it more often.

He said nothing about food, and I didn't ask. The other conversational trump card I was becoming familiar with was the word '*fresa*', which literally means 'strawberry', but is used in Mexican slang to refer to members of the cosseted richer classes or anyone spoiled and soft. With the malabaristas, I had discovered that this was a relative concept. In Mexico City, the word was used jokily to describe the sort of gaudy socialites who drank champagne at breakfast and spent the average Mexican monthly salary in getting their nails done. Among Trico and his friends, it was applied to anyone who fussed over such luxuries as a bed to sleep in or more than one square meal a day and was invariably uttered with an expression of icy, curled-lipped scorn. Of all the wide and imaginative selection of Mexican insults this, for them, was the worst. It was acceptable to be a large goat (*cabrón*), or even, on occasion, a pubic hair (*pendejo*), but to be a strawberry was unforgivable. On discovering that half of the things I had always considered essential were in fact things that only a strawberry would need, I decided that for now, it was safer to keep quiet.

Beer, however, was one requirement that was never questioned. Far from being a luxury, it was just about the only necessity of the malabarista lifestyle.

'*Pan líquido,*' Trico explained once as he took his first quenching gulp of the day, many hours before anyone had begun to think about food. Liquid bread.

I had spent the last of my cash, and although I still had some money left in the bank, I had left my bank card with my things at a friend's house in Chihuahua, back when I had intended to return there soon after the festival and leave for California. This put me in an awkward position, as the group worked together and pooled all their earnings to buy food and drink communally, and I was aware that my contributions were embarrassingly small. I was useless for anything more complicated than passing the hat at street shows, had only mastered the most basic of macramé knots, and showed dispiritingly little potential as a drummer. I wasn't even much of a cook (which, in rural Mexico, equated to not being much of a woman). During my English upbringing, I had always done reasonably well at the things that were considered important, chiefly writing essays and passing exams. But here, those skills were useless. The fact that I could write competently in a language that none of them understood (and, it being the language of *gringos*, had no particular desire to learn) did not impress anyone and, more to the point, didn't get us anything to eat or drink. I was in desperate need of a re-education.

The only thing for which I showed any aptitude was making Sandra's aluminium flowers. We exhausted the possibilities in Creel's alcohol dispensaries fairly quickly, but discovered that the flowers could also be swapped for food, and occasionally even sold. Approaching people in the street with them rarely brought much success, but I found that if I sat on the plaza and allowed people to watch me make one, the transition from empty can to flower would sometimes charm them enough to pay 20 pesos for it. This fact gained more meaning for me after my conversation with Trico about Juárez. I reflected romantically that perhaps the true social role of the malabaristas was to give hope that beauty could be found even in things that were normally considered ugly and worthless. Of more immediate relevance was the fact that 20 pesos was one caguama. I was just about redeemed in the eyes of the group.

But even with my contributions, the continual need for beer meant that we were spending money as fast as we could earn it, and with each passing day the problem got worse. The lack of tourists meant that there was little turnover of people in Creel, and the interest and generosity of the locals could only last for so long. After a week, the village was thoroughly bored with fire shows, macramé and aluminium flowers, every woman remotely amenable to braiding had been braided, and even the señora was starting to make the odd murmur of impatience. Like wandering entertainers of old, the main currency of the malabaristas was their novelty. Once that was exhausted, they had no choice but to move on. They were free to travel wherever they wished, but never free to stay.

Having made the decision, it took us a further three days to put it into action, and when we did leave it was at five in the afternoon with 45 pesos among us, 20 of which we spent on a caguama on the road out of town.

We hitched a ride to San Juanito, a town about 30 kilometres to the north. It was a shabby place, built entirely of concrete and corrugated iron. Despite also being a station on the Chihuahua-Pacific line, it had failed to rival Creel as a tourist destination and now slumped sulkily among the hills, dwelling on its ugliness with an air of sullen resentment. It was an unprepossessing place to arrive, homeless and broke, just as dusk started to usher in the chill night air from the mountains. There were a few semáforos, but mostly of the forlorn kind where single cars wait for nothing in deserted streets, shuttered shop fronts frowning at them on either side. Trico and Luis muttered half-heartedly about buying gasoline and trying to earn some money, but the dispirited atmosphere had drained the energy out of all of us, and nobody responded with much enthusiasm. Instead, we spent our last pesos on corn chips, a couple of tomatoes and a tin of refried beans, which we ate standing on a street corner, hunched and huddled together against the cold.

'What now?' Sandra asked.

'Find somewhere out of the wind to sleep,' Trico replied. 'Maybe on the outskirts there'll be a *terreno* where we can put a tent.' He turned on his heel and walked off without waiting for a response. Trico did most things on the assumption that other people would follow. For lack of a better idea, we obediently trotted after him.

At the railway lines we considered scouting around for empty carriages that might provide some shelter, but a filthy, skull-faced little man appeared from between the wagons and accosted us with such hostility that we all took a step back.

'What are you doing here?'

'Only looking for a place to sleep, brother,' Luis assured him. 'We're travellers; we don't know this town. Do you know if there's a *terreno* nearby, somewhere we can put a tent?'

The man relaxed slightly, but his eyes continued to flicker between us with the vicious defensiveness of a feral animal.

'No. Not here. There's nothing here. There is an *albergue* though, if you follow this road. You can sleep there. Go there.'

We thanked him and retreated.

'*Piedra*,' Trico muttered under his breath as we walked away. For a moment I was confused; 'piedra' means 'stone'. Then I realised he meant the man was using crack cocaine. Although cocaine is not produced in the Sierra, it is still rife there: around 90 per cent of what ends up in the USA is trafficked through Mexico, supplementing the Sierra Madre's own exports of marijuana, opium and methamphetamine.

We found the *albergue* 10 minutes down the road. From the outside, it looked like a cross between an army barracks and a primary school. It was a low, white-painted building in three narrow wings around a concrete yard. The entrance to the road was shut off with a high fence of vertical black bars. A solitary man sat in a plastic chair outside. Luis whistled through the bars to attract his attention.

The *albergues comunitarios* are among the few publicly funded services for the down-and-out in Mexico, set up to provide basic accommodation and health services for the desperate. Need for these services far outstrips their availability, and I felt uncomfortable even asking there. At the same time, I was intrigued to see what the last resort looked like in an area where deprivation and lack of opportunity had already forced a large part of the population into drug production, living in constant fear of the *narcos*, the army and the Drug Enforcement Agency.

Men and women were housed in separate wings, on opposite sides of the yard. As far as I could tell, the main job of the guard sitting outside was to make sure they didn't mingle. Faces appeared at the windows on either side, pointing at us and making inaudible comments as the guard unlocked the gate and we trooped uneasily into the forecourt. A second member of staff came out and hurriedly ushered Sandra and me over to the women's block, as if scared of the impact we might have on the tranquillity of the place if allowed to remain in full view. She chivvied us inside and shut the door behind us.

The room we had been led into was low-ceilinged and harshly lit, with mattresses in closely spaced rows across the floor. There were perhaps 20 women in there. Half of them looked pregnant, some quite heavily. They sat on the mattresses or stood in small groups, whispering to each other behind their hands. On the mattress closest to the door was a tiny, fragile-looking girl, who I guessed couldn't be older than 18. Her lip was swollen and an angry purple bruise swelled around her left eye. She stared up at us as we walked in, but looked away quickly as soon as I tried to meet her gaze.

Before we'd rallied from the awkwardness of our entry, one of the women broke away from her group and marched over to us. She was thick-set and square-jawed, with the officious manner of a self-appointed leader.

'What are you doing here?' she demanded.

'We're travellers,' Sandra explained. 'We arrived this evening; we have no money. We don't know anyone in this town. We were hoping to stay here, just for one night. It's so cold outside.'

The woman folded her arms over an ample but shapeless bosom, surveying us with the haughty condescension of an old-fashioned schoolmarm.

'You shouldn't have come with men,' she told us. 'They will wonder why *they* aren't looking after you.' Her voice carried a note of disapproval, as if to imply that she was wondering exactly the same thing.

I felt a surge of irritation, but a glance at the girl with the black eye, who was now staring intently at her feet, killed my urge to ask sharply how well their men were looking after them.

'Try saying you're pregnant,' she advised, relenting slightly. 'That usually helps.' She inspected each of our stomachs – Sandra's board-flat, mine slightly rounded by several months of grease and tortillas – before adding, pointing at me: 'Probably better that you do it.'

I had a growing feeling that I would rather sleep outside. And as it turned out, the cause had been lost anyway. When the member of staff returned, it was to inform us that there was no chance of Trico, Luis and Bernardo being allowed to sleep there. They were healthy young men, in no need of charity. Their (not entirely untruthful) protests that they were alcoholics had fallen on deaf ears.

'I suppose we should take it as a compliment,' mused Luis, as we were shepherded out onto the road and the gate was shut behind us. I said nothing. Although definitely better than no social services at all – which is still the case in many of the more remote parts of the Sierra – the regimented, dehumanising conditions of the *albergue* had been sobering.

It started to rain.

We were still standing there dumbly when a police car drew up. Police vehicles in the Sierra have a brutish look: hefty 4X4 pickups with bars round the back and truck-sized wheels. The men inside it looked similarly brutish, all meaty jaws and thick black moustaches, reeking of competitive masculinity. I wondered vaguely if they were going to arrest us, and whether it would really be such a bad thing if they did. The fact that standing in the road in the rain isn't illegal didn't occur to me – by all accounts, the letter of the law is not a primary concern in the Sierra. Besides, a strange consequence of homelessness is that you always feel as if you're doing something wrong, even when you're not.

Instead, they turned out to be surprisingly good-humoured, their tempers no doubt sweetened by the Sierra's speciality mood-altering produce. They drove us to the municipal council building, which was under renovation, and told us we could sleep there for the night as long as we left by the time the workmen arrived the next morning. It was a grim shell with bare concrete floors and no glass in several of the windows, but at least it was inside. We found some scattered sheets of cardboard and laid them on the ground to keep out the worst of the cold. Having expected to be sleeping outside in the rain, we were elated with our good fortune. This, I was learning, is one of the joys of this mode of travel. It destroys all expectations to the point where everything short of disaster comes as a pleasant surprise and you finish each day with a rush of delight at simply being alive.

'*Buena onda* [good vibe], these police from San Juanito,' Bernardo commented as we settled down for the night. We all murmured our agreement, although I later wondered whether they were the same police who, after being informed of the first Creel massacre in a desperate phone call from the village priest, did not arrive on the scene until several hours later – so long afterward that the *padre* had to beg the grieving mothers not to carry away the bodies of their murdered sons themselves.

4
The Patron Saint of Lost Causes

Morning arrived sulky and cold, creeping in under a pewter sky. The building that had seemed palatial when it had welcomed us in from the rain the night before now looked dismal and smelled of urine. A change of plan was called for.

'Cuauhtémoc,' was Bernardo's opinion. 'A proper city, where we can work. Then come back to the Sierra when we have some money.'

He looked from Sandra to Luis. They nodded slowly, turning to Trico.

'You can do what you like,' he said, rolling his sleeping bag with an indifferent air. 'I'm going to Basaseachi.'

Trico, I had started to realise, was defiantly not a pack animal. He was with the group but not *of* it, and as soon as a difference of opinion arose he was open to neither persuasion nor compromise. He had come to the Sierra with a wish to see Basaseachi, the highest permanent waterfall in Mexico (Piedra Volada, the highest, only flows during the wet season), and he would not leave without fulfilling it. He announced his plan without reproach, but with a finality that precluded further discussion.

Bernardo shrugged. Three pairs of eyes turned on me. Trico started folding and packing the bundle of clothes he had been using as a pillow without looking up.

I thought about it. I could go with the group to Cuauhtémoc. But I had no skills to perform in the semáforo, and imagined Cuauhtémoc (perhaps unfairly) to be just another unappealing grid of concrete. The crevassed mountains and brooding forest of the Sierra whispered at my back on a breeze spiced with pine resin.

'I'll go to Basaseachi,' I said.

Fleetingly, almost imperceptibly, I thought I saw Trico smile.

ψ Ψ ψ

The first man who gave us a lift out of town was a plump little fellow with a sweaty collar and a sticker of a saint on the dashboard. He chatted amiably about nothing in particular as we left the tired environs of San Juanito and ascended along a sinuous mountain road, the forest a shadowy tunnel around us.

The road was sprinkled with tiny clusters of houses, most of them boasting no more than five lopsided shacks and little evidence of inhabitants. Despite this, each was served by a little white cart selling burritos or tacos, standing in the rutted mud at the side of the road with a poignant eagerness which, as hitchhikers, we recognised all too well. When the sweaty-collared man dropped us off we waited half an hour for the next lift, for want of traffic rather than want of generosity. Trico filled the time by doing a juggling show for the señora serving burritos, who watched beaming from behind her rows of silver dishes and seemed genuinely delighted at the disruption of her lonely roadside vigil. She then proceeded to ply us with tortillas and lukewarm beans with such heartbreaking enthusiasm that one would have thought it was we who were doing her a favour, urging us on with encouragements of *'coman, hijos, coman!'* ('eat, children, eat!') any time we showed signs of flagging. At our next stop along the road we were obliged to eat still more, despite already being uncomfortably full, for fear of hurting the feelings of an equally maternal señora in an equally desolate little outpost.

The next driver was a leathery, taciturn man with a wide-brimmed hat and a fiercely drooping moustache which he displayed like a warning over a grim mouth. He smelled of tequila, and made no effort to hide the gun handle that poked out of the storage compartment above his head.

'Do you think he was a narco?' I asked Trico, when he let us out at the turn-off to Basaseachi.

'No. A grower, maybe, but not a narco. His pickup was far too old and rusty. But the first guy probably was.'

'Really? How do you know?'

'Didn't you see the sticker? *San Judas de Tadeo.* Patron saint of lost causes. All the narcos love him.'

I remembered, months before, visiting the church of San Judas in Mexico City. For one used to the scattering of grannies that form the average congregation in English church services, it had been an interesting experience. The church was packed, and a large proportion of the worshippers were young men with shaved heads and tattoos, several of whom trailed a lingering fragrance of marijuana as they approached the altar to pay their respects to the saint. In 2008, the Archdiocese of Mexico had released a statement clarifying that San Judas was not intended to be the patron saint of criminals or drug dealers, but it didn't seem to have had much effect. (On the contrary, they now seem to be placing more faith in him than ever. In January 2012, a man was stopped at the Reynosa-Hidalgo border carrying two suspiciously large statues of the saint which, on inspection by the border police, turned out to be hollow and stuffed with $233,000 worth of marijuana.)

Saint Jude has always been a popular figure in the Catholic Church, but in Mexico he inspires unparalleled levels of devotion. There is something very Mexican about the concept of a patron saint of lost causes: something that neatly captures the paradoxical mixture of hope and despair with which the Mexicans view themselves, their lives and their country.

Mexico revels in its ambiguities. A *mestizo* nation whose blended Spanish and indigenous bloodlines make the ancestry of most people impossible to discern with any degree of confidence, the Mexican character is also famously contradictory and indefinable. Those who have tried (notably Octavio Paz in *The Labyrinth of Solitude*) describe it as outgoing yet reticent, optimistic yet fatalistic, proud yet self-deprecating. '*Los Mexicanos son los chingones*' is a much-expressed sentiment. 'The Mexicans are the fuckers' – the best, the top dogs. Yet they are also '*los hijos de la chingada*', 'the sons of the raped mother', a nation descended from raped indigenous women and a raped civilisation. The legacy of this 'rape' of Mexico's native peoples by the Spanish *conquistadores* remains strong in the national psyche and is frequently cited as the root of both the drive for macho dominance and the weary feeling of persecution that permeate Mexican society.

The way the Mexicans view their country is similarly ambiguous. Many openly express the belief that Mexico is beyond salvation, and when you read the newspapers it is tempting to conclude that they're right. Hopelessly ensnared in webs of corruption, poverty and violence, it has come close to being declared a failed state, and each passing year brings little relief – merely spiralling death tolls and further tales of horror. Yet despite everything, the sense of despair is never absolute. Lurking beneath the surface is a feeling, faint but still just discernible, that here, even lost causes deserve a saint. The Mexicans always manage to draw on some hidden reserve of optimism, despite often being the first to say that they have precious little to be optimistic about.

The placid face of San Judas de Tadeo, piously displayed on the back or bicep of many a petty thief or small-time narco, seems on closer inspection to have a slight smile playing around the corners of his mouth. Whether it is a smile of sympathy or derision is hard to tell. He is as enigmatic as Mexico itself.

ψ Ψ ψ

Basaseachi towers at the head of a majestic, red-walled canyon, the water storming down from the upper reaches of the Sierra to blast furiously over a sheer cliff of 246 metres into the tangled forest below. A spindly waist-high fence of buckled metal has been erected around the drop, about 30 centimetres from the edge. As we stood there it seemed as if the earth had split before us and I felt an irrational rush of power, like Moses parting the Red Sea. The feeling lasted until I realised that Trico's attention had wandered from the view to the fence, and my heart sank as I realised what he was thinking.

'Trico, no. Please?'

Really I should have been grateful that, at about five centimetres in width, the top bar of the fence was too narrow even for Trico to attempt on the unicycle. As it was, he had to be content with walking along the top of the fence, arms outstretched, a slight quiver in his fingers the only indication of any nerves as he came right up to the point where the fence ended over the raging water, and then walking backwards away from it again. By the time he got down I was almost in tears. He looked at me in genuine bewilderment.

'What's wrong?'

I shook my head. There was nothing to say. It was a childish thing to do, of course. But a certain type of childishness, in the malabarista world, was an essential survival skill. To live hand-to-mouth, as they did, it wasn't enough to see only what things were, but also what they could be. The childish imagination that turned empty cans into flowers and pieces of fruit into juggling balls couldn't resist also turning safety fences into tightropes. The whole world was a circus. It wasn't as if I hadn't been warned.

We spent the day at the waterfall, trekking down beside it through shaded bowers smelling of moss and rotting wood to sit for a while in the spray-chilled cave at its base. On the way back up we found a gorged rattlesnake, too bloated by its recent meal to even raise its tail in warning, and a plastic bag containing half a loaf of damp white bread, a few slices of rubbery cheese, and half a pot of mayonnaise. In reactions which, Trico informed me gravely, were indicative of our respective levels of *fresa*-ness, I was more excited by the first find, Trico by the second.

In the late afternoon we washed in an ice-cold stream nearby and then sat outside the little huddle of shops and *comedores* (eateries) at the top of the path that led to the waterfall, surrounded by empty cans we'd dug out of the rubbish bins. Bored with flowers, we started developing the technique to make new and more complicated forms, each trying to outdo the other with increasingly elaborate creations. Before long, we sat within a little circle of butterflies, strange insects, curved vases spilling over with different types of flower, and even – my proudest achievement – a soaring bird, with outstretched wings and a fanned tail. Trico, determined to make a unicycle, spent half an hour with his eyes crossed and tongue stuck out in concentration, a growing pile of rejected prototypes at his side. Two teenage girls and their mother came out of one of the *comedores* to squat next to us, their long coloured skirts flowing over the pavement as they laughed at our efforts and tried to guess what the latest work in progress would be. After about their tenth hopeful suggestion that maybe *this* one was the Virgin of Guadalupe, Trico finally gave up on his unicycle and I found myself marvelling, not for the first time, at the extent of the Mexican ability to find the demurely praying form of their national icon in just about anything. (The first time had been on hearing of the decision of the Mexico City authorities to remove a section of the floor of Hidalgo metro station and transfer it to a specially created shrine after the volume of pilgrims flocking to a suspiciously Virgin-shaped water leak had proved impossible to reconcile with the tempers of rush hour commuters.)

At dusk, the mother retreated into her empty *comedor*, emerging 20 minutes later with a frying pan in each hand, one containing the ubiquitous refried beans, the other *huevos a la Mexicana* – scrambled eggs cooked with green chilli, white onions and red tomatoes, reflecting the colours of the Mexican flag. She shooed one of her daughters inside to fetch tortillas and salsa (without which no Mexican meal is ever complete) as she laid the pans on the ground in front of us.

'*Coman, hijos, coman!*'

The best thing about hand-to-mouth travel is also the worst: the feeling of being constantly humbled by, and undeserving of, the kindness of people around you. Even in a place like the Sierra Madre.

We left vases of flowers, bizarre aluminium animals, and anything Trico deemed to have sufficient Virgin potential on every table of her little *comedor*.

The night crept in cool but clear, and we made a bed for ourselves in a sheltered corner behind a burrito stand, as neither of us had a tent. The space was cramped and we found ourselves nose to nose, grinning at each other a little awkwardly.

'So – tell me your story,' I said.

'My story? I have many stories.'

'The first story. How you started living like this.'

He thought about it, unconsciously protruding his lower lip and wrinkling his forehead into a maze of deep furrows. He had a habit, especially when deep in thought, of screwing up or stretching his features in the experimental way babies have when they're just beginning to learn the use of their facial muscles, resulting in a face that was constantly on the move between strikingly handsome and (as my father later described one of the less flattering photos of him) fascinatingly ugly.

'Did you know how to juggle before you started travelling?' I prompted.

'No, I knew nothing when I left home. Not even poi!' He gave a little snort of derision. 'The only skills I had were to do with trucks. Fixing them, taking care of them... I could even drive them, although I didn't have a licence. It was the only thing my father ever taught me – he's a truck driver, you know. He used to take me with him on journeys sometimes, so I could watch him and learn. I remember the first long trip he took me on, all the way to Cancún. I was about ten. I don't think I'd ever realised before how big Mexico was, or how varied. I grew up in San Luis Potosí – on the *altiplano*, the high plateau on the edge of the desert. It's beautiful there, but the landscape is so hard, and dry, and it feels like it must go on like that forever. The route I took with my father went past Mexico City and along the motorway past Puebla, where you can see Popocatépetl so clearly, a perfect cone tipped with snow. You cross the plains and go through the pine forests, then there is this long, slow descent all the way down into Tabasco. As you go down you can feel the temperature getting warmer, see the vegetation changing. I was so excited I couldn't sit still. Down past Villa Hermosa and finally onto the Ruta Maya – the big highway that crosses the Yucatán Peninsula, where you feel sticky with the heat and see palm trees and banana palms and finally the Caribbean Sea and the long, white beaches. I loved it. I wanted to go with him all the time, but usually he preferred to take my brother, Marco. Marco was more interested in learning how to drive the truck, but I was always too excited by everything outside to concentrate properly, so my father would get angry.

'I'm glad he made me learn though, because when I left home it was the only thing I knew how to do. I hitchhiked out of San Luis and the first ride I got was with a truck carrying fertiliser. The driver was young, about thirty, and he was going all the way to Manzanillo, on the Pacific Coast. I was useful to him, because I could help take care of the truck. He even let me drive it for a short way, when he got tired. He didn't care much that I didn't have a licence. It was more important to get there on time. In return he bought me food, and beers. We got on so well that he took me with him on his next journey, back across the country to Aguascalientes. I didn't really care where I was going. Everywhere there was so much to see. In Aguascalientes I fell for a girl... she was so pretty, a *morenita* with such beautiful eyes! I wanted her to come with me, but then I found out that she didn't eat eggs or beans, which obviously would have made her impossible to travel with. You can't live off just rice and tortillas.' He paused, seeming to be thinking back over long years of experience before adding: 'Well, you can, but it gives you a terrible stomach ache.'

'So I left her in Aguascalientes and headed south to Cancún. Always with truck drivers, asking for food from the *comedores* on the way. People are generous in Mexico, and usually they will give you a little bit of rice and beans with salsa, or even eggs and sometimes meat, if you're lucky. But if nothing else, you can always get a couple of corn tortillas, a pinch of salt and a fresh chilli. It's good to eat fresh chilli if you have little food, you know. You take a bite of the chilli after every bite of food, and the heat fills you up, makes you feel as if you've eaten three times as much. Then there is other food that you can find along the road. Around the desert there are the *nopal*es – the cacti with many round, flat sails, you know?'

'The ones that look like Mickey Mouse?'

He laughed.

'Yes, those ones. They are good to eat. You have to be careful, because dotted over the surface are little clusters of spines. The worst are the tiny hairs that get under your skin like splinters and are almost impossible to get out. But if you cut all of the spines off with a knife then you can eat the flesh of the cactus. It's best grilled over a fire, with salt and a squeeze of lime. Then further south, once you come down towards the tropics, you start to find other trees. Avocados, oranges, tamarinds... there's always something to eat, if you look. So that way I arrived in the Caribbean.

'It was in the Caribbean that I learnt malabares. First poi and staff, then devil sticks, and finally juggling. It was easy to learn because there were so many malabaristas there. Fire jugglers, acrobats, stilt walkers... organised collectives doing choreographed shows, with proper costumes and painted faces and girls in bikinis spinning fire. I couldn't believe it when I saw them. Back then there were fewer malabaristas and a much lower standard of performance in the north than there is now. But in the south the standard was amazing, better than you see in a lot of official circuses. And you could earn good money, especially in places like Cancún and Playa del Carmen, because the big hotels and bars were always looking for performers to put on shows for the tourists. Often they would give you free meals and drinks, as well as your fee. Sometimes we would get lobster for dinner – imagine!' He smiled at the memory. 'You can have a good life down there.'

'So why didn't you stay?'

'I did stay. I was in the south for two years, mostly in Cancún. But... I don't know... It wasn't good for me to be there too long. Cancún is fun, but it's a crazy place. So many people are there on holiday, in clubs all night, drinking tequila and vomiting in the street. And if you do a performance you're full of adrenaline afterwards so you go to find a party, and you have money so you buy drink and drugs, and there are drunk girls all over you... Well, it's brilliant, right? Of course it is! But when it's every single night and you start to think it's normal to live like that... you go a bit crazy. And Cancún can be so sleazy. I remember walking through town after shows or parties and having to step over topless foreign girls, passed out in the street. And although it's nice to be able to do proper, well-organised shows, it's sad that they're always for foreigners, not for your own people.

'So I left, and started to travel again. Playing in the semáforos, or outside *comedores* in return for food. You don't make so much money, of course. In Cancún I would earn 500 pesos for one show. At least! Here, maybe one plate of rice and beans. The people here don't have so much. But what they do have, they share. Like the señoras today. You share your art with them, and they share their food with you.'

'How long have you been on the road now?'

'Six years. I was seventeen when I first left home. Still in the *preparatoria*.' He laughed. *Preparatoria* is the final level of education before university: the equivalent of British sixth form, though it tends to have a more specific subject focus. 'A month before my final exams.'

'What were you studying?'

'Electrical engineering.'

'Really?' I was taken aback. It wasn't quite the answer I had been expecting.

'Don't you believe me?'

'Of course I do. It's just... Why did you choose to leave rather than take your exams?'

He shrugged.

'I wanted to see something different. To get out of San Luis.'

I had been hoping for more than that: stories of family conflict, maybe, or some existential crisis. But I didn't want to sound like a psychologist, and figured that the most honest answers are usually the ones you have to wait for.

'Do you ever go back there?'

'Sometimes I go back to see my family. And to go to the desert. San Luis is on the edge of Wirikuta. The sacred land of the Huichol people. The heart of Mexico. It's good to go back. To remember where you came from.'

'How long is it since you were last there?'

'Six months, maybe.' He thought for a moment. 'You've never seen the desert, have you?'

'No. Not properly. I came directly from DF to Chihuahua.' (DF, standing for Distrito Federal, is how most people refer to Mexico City.)

'Do you want to go?'

'Now?'

'Why not? We can go to Chihuahua, to pick up the stuff you left there, then south to Durango. I left some stones there, and silver wire and pliers, stuff to make proper *artesanía*. I can teach you – maybe you'll like it better than malabares. And then south to San Luis, and the desert.'

'And then?'

'*Quién sabe?*'

I laughed. I had come to think of '*quién sabe*' as an evasion, a conversational dead end. But now it struck me that it could also indicate an infinite world of possibilities.

5
Señor Talón

'So, how's it going with your new boyfriend then?'

'Since when is he my boyfriend?'

'Since you disappear for two weeks and then turn up with him on my doorstep in the middle of the night, looking all flushed and excited.'

There had never been any point feigning innocence with Hele. Ten years my senior and already with a gloriously colourful life history behind her, she viewed me with the gently patronising affection of an older sister and had always found me amusingly transparent. Trico and I had arrived in Chihuahua late the previous night in a groaning timber truck descending from the Sierra Madre, to rap on the door of the house where I had been staying with her and her boyfriend's family before leaving for the festival in Creel. She had surmised the situation with a sly flicker of her cobalt eyes and I could tell she had been waiting for a private moment to question me ever since.

I had first met her in Mexico City, where I had been staying in the house of a friend of hers, who I had contacted through an online hospitality network. I was fresh off the plane from England and still barely over my jetlag at the time Hele swept onto the scene, heartbroken but defiant, accompanied by several trunks of books and vast boxes of clothes spilling tantalising wisps of lace and leather.

She had arrived in Mexico two months previously on the invitation of a Mexican photographer with chin-to-toe tattoos who had seen her in a bar while visiting Estonia and, captivated by the angles of her striking cream-skinned face, resolved to win her as his girlfriend, muse and model. Enthused more by the prospect of fresh experience in a faraway land than by the man himself, she had seen out the end of her contract as a social policy researcher, moved to his house in Mexico City and starred in his latest photographic project alongside the dismembered body of a dead goat. On discovering shortly afterwards that he took Satanism and alcohol considerably more seriously than he took household responsibilities or her happiness, she had promptly moved out and found herself alternative accommodation while she considered her options. She reacted with baffled exasperation to her family's assumption that she would return to Estonia and gather the scattered pieces of her previous life and career. Hele was not of the temperament to give up that easily. Having paid for the ticket to Mexico and even gone to the trouble of moving her wardrobe over, she'd be damned if she was letting all that effort go to waste.

Shortly after I left Mexico City she had met Jorge, an easy-going and good-looking Chihuahuan whose languid company she found soothing to her broken heart. The fact that she knew only ten words or so of Spanish, roughly equal to what he knew of English, did not strike her as a significant obstacle to the relationship. She already spoke seven languages – she would soon learn. And in the meantime, at least when addressing Mexican men, French spoken with a Spanish accent and come-to-bed eyes was perfectly sufficient. When I next contacted her six months later, I was amused and impressed in equal measures to learn that she had not only stayed with Jorge, but moved into his family's house in Chihuahua, an unprepossessing desert city in the heart of north Mexico's narco country.

A less formidable character might have been shaken by such a series of upheavals, but Hele had handled it with near-total composure (punctuated by the occasional bout of screaming fury – she was not the sort of person who did anything in moderation). In the grand scheme of her life, the Mexican episode did not strike her as particularly unusual. Although possessed of a fierce intellect, she had always suffered from an irresistible attraction to the unexpected and the bizarre, which would frequently win out over basic common sense. Possibly it was this latter characteristic that had formed the basis of our friendship, despite the gap in age and experience.

'Well?' she demanded now.

'He says he wants me to go south with him. To San Luis Potosí.'

'And? Will you go?'

'I think so.'

'That's a yes, then.'

She looked down the road in the direction Trico had gone on his way to the semáforo, considering judiciously before delivering her verdict.

'I approve,' she decided. 'He strikes me as an artist, not a bum.' She spoke with the measured authority of one with enough experience of both to be confident in her ability to tell the difference.

From inside the shop behind us, we could hear Jorge's voice, badgering staff and customers alike for five pesos each for a caguama. Hele sighed.

'Mine, I'm afraid, is a bum. But he can be rather sweet.'

She had met Jorge while travelling in Oaxaca. He was also nominally a malabarista and drummer, though not of a terribly proactive variety. In fact, I had yet to see him perform in public. He had long limbs, soulful brown eyes, and a gaggle of confused teeth which crowded into the front of his mouth as if jostling to get out. These, like those of so many of the younger generation of Chihuahuans, were discoloured a mottled brown. This was not due to poor hygiene, but rather to the dental fluorosis that has afflicted large swathes of the population ever since the salt fluoridation programme implemented across Mexico in 1991 failed to make adequate provision for the fact that several states, including Chihuahua, already had excessively high quantities of fluoride in the water supply. Hele, correctly observing that Jorge's teeth were the one thing that marred his good looks, had attempted to put him on an expensive course of dental treatment. Jorge, however, was deeply suspicious of the dentist, and had so far contracted a severe case of flu every time an appointment had been booked.

Jorge's height and fair skin sometimes caused him to be mistaken for a gringo, much to his irritation and disgust. He had spent eight months illegally in the States as a teenager, mowing lawns for wealthy Texans, and the treatment he had received there had not left him well-disposed towards those from north of the border. I thought at times that he must have managed to make as substantial an impression on the States as they had on him: he was the epitome of the stereotypical – but actually very rare – 'lazy Mexican'.

Two Spanish words I had learnt specifically in connection to Jorge were '*hueva*' and '*talonear*'.

I learnt 'hueva' the first time I was staying with them, when around mid-morning each day Jorge would lean back on the sofa/bed/chair/ground, stretch himself with a luxurious, cat-like sense of entitlement, and announce:

'*Tengo hueva.*'

'What does that mean?' I had asked Hele.

'He says he's tired.'

'Hueva' actually has a more nuanced meaning than simply 'tired', as shown by its close relationship with '*huevón*', which means 'lazy' or 'slacker'.

'But he only woke up half an hour ago,' I pointed out.

A meaningful shrug, an eloquently raised eyebrow. Over a six-month relationship with someone whose language she didn't speak (although she was learning fast), Hele had become a master at expressing herself without words.

'*Talonear*' means 'to hustle', which was something Jorge did compulsively, and for which he had a rare talent. Something about his beseeching eyes, the foal-like gangly elegance of his long limbs, the musically nasal drawl and softened 'ch' sounds of his Chihuahuan accent (Chihuahua in Chihuahua is called 'Sheewaawaa') made him instantly likeable and impossible to refuse. He exploited this shamelessly. He was all but incapable of walking past a food stand, market stall or pedestrian without begging something, whether or not he had any immediate need of it. I could only assume that he was stockpiling to protect against the threat of ever having to work in the future. The practice was doubly baffling, as he was a talented drummer and fire-staffer, but although he would happily practise these skills alone or with friends, he seemed to find the idea of doing them for money undignified. Trico, who approached street performance as seriously as a religious vocation, soon conferred on him the affectionate, though slightly scornful nickname of 'Señor Talón' (Mr Hustle).

'I'm hoping Trico will be a good influence on him,' Hele went on. 'He always works more when there's another man around to encourage him. I think it's a competitive thing. He used to go and work with Javi, but now Javi's moved in with his girlfriend, so he prefers to work alone and not have to split his earnings.'

'Javi's paying the rent from what he earns in the semáforos?'

'Oh yes. He's very dedicated. Out in the semáforo*s* for morning rush hour, drumming on the plazas during the day, another semáforo shift for afternoon rush hour, then often fire-spinning during the night as well. Rotates where he works so each set of commuters doesn't get bored with him. He knows average traffic density at every time of day for all the big semáforos in Chihuahua. It's very impressive.'

Jorge came bounding out of the shop, grinning broadly.

'What are you talking about, *chicas*?'

'We were *saying*,' Hele told him pointedly, 'how *impressive* it is how hard Javi is *working* these days, since he moved in with Lupita.'

'Oh yes. Hah! That's how it goes with the old *esposas*, eh?!' He laughed happily at the pun. '*Esposas*' means both 'wives' and 'handcuffs', a fact I have always found rather telling. 'You don't have a *colaboración* [contribution] for a caguama, do you?'

We trailed in our pockets for a few coins. It would be the height of bad form not to. The drinking of a caguama is such an important communal activity that it is practically a rejection of friendship to refuse. And admittedly, we were hardly averse to beer drinking ourselves. Jorge headed triumphantly off to the nearest shop stocking alcohol. Hele shook her head, with an expression that dithered between affectionate exasperation and outright annoyance.

We were sitting outside a friend's shop on the edge of Chihuahua's central plaza. A few doors down was a restaurant where local mariachi bands played, the singers in enormous sombreros and braided black jackets wailing in glorious anguish over a backing of violins and sobbing trumpets. Between the shows, gangs of off-duty mariachis, resplendent in their gleaming silver buttons and sharply creased trousers, would spill out into the street and hang around the lines of parked cars, furtively glugging beer from fat brown bottles. These they wrapped in sweatshirts or plastic bags to conceal them from the watchful eyes of the police, who do next to nothing to check the dominance of the drug gangs but are ever-vigilant when it comes to enforcing the law that prohibits drinking on the streets. In Mexico you can break any law you like as long as it's a *big* law and you do it with a bit of aplomb. In general, the more minor your crimes, the more likely you are to get punished. Although to an extent this is probably true in all countries, Mexico is undeniably more flamboyant about it than most. In a country where El Chapo, the most notorious drug baron in the world, 'escaped' from maximum security prison in a laundry cart, most of the police cells are full of men serving their compulsory 36 hours for public drinking.

In the plaza opposite, a young couple canoodled self-consciously under a bronze statue of a man in a 10-gallon hat being bucked off a horse, and cheerful, bun-faced men in the *elotes* stalls sold steaming cups of sweet corn mixed with cream, cheese, chilli and lime. Above them all, the *Angel de la Independencia* spread its wings in triumph atop its soaring white column. It was a little smaller and less impressive than the grandiose cousin in the centre of Mexico City on which it was modelled – a fact that Chihuahua had compensated for by arming its angel with a poison-green laser beam which it would fire at random around the city in a casually threatening manner.

Chihuahua sprawled across the arid plain of north Mexico in the easy way that desert towns have: a city that had nothing to hem it in and could allow itself all the space it needed to get comfortable. Its wide streets all ended in views of the surrounding mountains, and it was a rare building that rose over two storeys high. Lines of houses sagged gently along the sides of the roads, painted in sun-faded colours that chipped off around the corners and door frames to reveal the crumbling concrete beneath. To a newcomer, the whole city had a sleepy feel, as if it were permanently three o'clock on a Sunday afternoon and it had slunk off between the rounded brown hills to doze in the sun.

But like so much of northern Mexico, its relaxed appearance concealed a darker reality. Chihuahua was one of the main hubs on the drug-trafficking route that led from the growing areas in the Sierra Madre to the Juárez border four hours' drive to the north. And although Chihuahua had nothing like Juárez's bleak, warzone atmosphere or level of senseless brutality, it too was hopelessly tied up in the escalating carnage of the cartel wars. It had a reputation as a lawless, Wild West kind of place where you could be shot on the whim of a bored 15-year-old and local police chiefs crawled obsequiously for the favour of the drug lords.

Despite this, there was something curiously likeable about Chihuahua. The city was well aware of its own reputation and seemed to be constantly acknowledging it with a nod and a sly wink, turning everything about it into a sort of crude parody of itself. Chihuahua was a city with a very Mexican sense of humour.

ψ Ψ ψ

The door of Jorge's house was always open, in the welcoming manner of houses where there is nothing to steal. Local landmarks included the gloomy hulk of a disused factory, a pole-dancing club, and a restaurant where six men had been machine-gunned down a few months previously. It was a fairly representative Chihuahua *barrio*.

The house was a squat grey building. As you walked past it, the pavement started heading uphill but left the house behind on the level below, giving the disconcerting impression that the whole structure was leaning sideways. It had five tiny rooms, a clutter of dusty furniture, and a floating population of inhabitants that ranged from three to however many it was possible to squeeze in.

The first of these was Jorge's mother, Elena. She rarely spoke, and would shuffle through the house in apathetic silence, avoiding eye contact with those around her. She had a short, shapeless haircut, a shapeless body, and always dressed in shapeless tracksuits in dark colours. The impression was that of a woman who wanted nothing more than to become invisible. Most of the day she sat at the kitchen table, drinking from two-litre bottles of Coca-Cola and drawing on endless cigarettes. Every few hours she would swallow a huge, capsule-shaped pill.

Then there was Gabriela, the eldest of Jorge's sisters. She was 20, slender and pale, with a quiet manner and sorrowful grey eyes. She had recently gone back to school and was studying hard, but was frail and constantly tired, and when at home would spend most of her time asleep.

Last of the permanent residents was Laura, Jorge's youngest sister. Only 17 but of formidable stature and hefty build, she was as robust as her sister was delicate and as loud as her mother was silent. One of Hele's favourite stories of life with the family was of one evening she had been walking home with Jorge and they had bumped into one of his friends, a local guy of about 25, sprinting towards them in a state of wide-eyed terror. Alarmed, they had entreated him to tell them what was wrong, but he had barely managed to stutter a couple of words before hiding behind Jorge in panic as Laura came storming around the corner in pursuit, swinging her sizeable fists and bellowing, '*CHINGA TU PUTA MADRE, CABRÓN!!!*' ('Fuck your whore mother, asshole!') In a region where machismo and *marianismo* – the idea that a woman should be as subservient and compliant as the Virgin Mary – were still accepted as a matter of course, Laura was a refreshing, if rather intimidating, character.

The occasional residents of the house were an ancient grandmother, who every now and then would materialise in the bed that stood in the darkened recess between the living room and the kitchen, and then vanish a couple of days later as mysteriously as she had arrived; Jorge and Hele, whenever they returned from their frequent travels; and finally, the drunk uncle. He wasn't, strictly speaking, an inhabitant as he wasn't allowed in the house, but he spent all day, every day on the pavement outside, drinking relentlessly and accosting anyone who went in or out with interminably long and completely unintelligible rambles.

Some form of drunk uncle was a common feature of the poorer barrios of northern Mexico. Employment opportunities and average wages were so low that many families were forced to function on a trickle-down of wealth. There would be one family at the top (often long-since emigrated to Houston or San Diego or some other city in the southern United States), who would be helping to support the more respectable of their relations south of the border. These relations would have a car, and a house with carpets, and a front door that they closed when not in use. They, in turn, would be helping to support their struggling cousins in barrios such as this one. At the bottom of the pecking order were the drunk uncles, who would loiter outside the houses of their extended family, in the hope of food, or company, or possibly just the reassurance of still having family, even if they were no longer welcome in their houses.

Trico and I stayed in Chihuahua for about a week. As all of the house's occasional occupants were currently in residence, we made a bed for ourselves on the floor in the front entrance (a tiny space of about two square metres) which we would fold away during the day. Trico would work every day in the semáforos and I had been reunited with my bank card and the last of my money, so we were able to make contributions. Still, I felt awkward intruding upon the already overcrowded household. It was Elena who worried me. She showed no sign of either noticing or caring about our presence, but there was no way I could be sure. She was completely unreadable.

One day, when we were alone in the kitchen, I expressed this worry to Hele.

'I don't know how to act around her. I feel rude ignoring her, but I don't want to pressure her to communicate if she prefers to stay silent. How can I tell whether she's happy for us to be here or not? It's impossible to know what she's thinking. She just seems so... blank.'

Hele paused, her knife hovering over the glistening back of the onion she had been slicing. Then, she set it down on the table.

'Let me show you something. I'm sure Jorge won't mind.'

She went into the adjoining bedroom, and I heard her rummaging through some drawers. When she came back, she handed me a photograph.

The photograph was of a woman. She was young, laughing open-mouthed at the camera. Her long hair framed her face in thick dark waves. A simple cotton shirt showed off her slim figure and narrow waist, without straining too hard to emphasise it. The whole image had a free, un-posed quality to it, as if she had just been caught by surprise in a moment of mirth.

'Is that...?'

'Mm-hm.'

I looked at the woman again, trying to see something of the Elena I knew in her, but drew a blank. Her eyes were dancing while Elena's were dull. Her lips smiling while Elena's were slack. Her face sculpted while Elena's was puffy. There was nothing I could recognise as belonging to the same woman.

'She was beautiful.'

'She was, wasn't she?'

'What happened to her?'

'Jorge's father. That's what happened. I think this photo must have been taken in the early years of their marriage, when Jorge was still very young.

Not long after that, he started to beat her. Jorge remembers it. His father, raging drunk, shouting. His mother screaming. When he was a bit older he would try to intervene, but his father would only throw him aside and hit him as well. She couldn't go to work anymore, because she was always covered in bruises. So there was very little money coming into the house, and his father drank most of what there was. That's when Jorge learnt to hustle. He would beg whatever food he could from around town and bring it home so they had enough to eat. I guess old habits die hard, eh?'

'Where's his father now?'

'Jail. Two years into a fifteen-year sentence. Double homicide. He only got fifteen years because it was a bar fight, so they said it was unpremeditated. And of course, they didn't charge him for what he'd been doing to his wife and children for years. Round here, what a man does in his own home is considered his own business.

'I think Jorge hoped that, with his father gone, he could have his mother back again. But she'd already had most of the life knocked out of her. I don't know how long she's been taking the sedatives. Whether she started before he went to jail or after. Either way, I guess she just doesn't want to feel anything anymore. Like you said: to be blank.'

'Do you think she'll ever come back?'

Hele shrugged, in imitation of the fatalistic Mexican manner. '*Quién sabe*? But I'll tell you one thing. When I first moved here, I felt the same as you. Didn't know how to act around her. Didn't feel comfortable being here. I thought she was just an empty shell. Even when she did speak it seemed mechanical. Like a robot. But when I stayed here longer I realised that every now and then... you see a glint of something in her eyes. At first, I thought I might have imagined it. Just because I wanted to see it so much. But then one day, I was feeling really low. I'd had a terrible argument with Jorge and I'd been crying. I was sitting outside on my own, and I was really debating with myself whether I should just leave. Then, she came outside. And you know what? She had brought me a cup of coffee.

'I know it's just a cup of coffee. But for her, that was like a miracle. She saw that I was upset, and she wanted to help. So she did the only thing she could think of.'

She paused thoughtfully, looking down at the photograph. Elena laughed back at us. When I studied it again, I thought that maybe I saw something I recognised. The shape of the eyes, perhaps. I might have imagined it. Just because I wanted to see it so much. But maybe that's the first step.

'I guess what I'm trying to say,' Hele continued, 'is that when you're around her, try not to see her how she is now. See *her*. The woman in the photograph. She's still in there, somewhere.'

ψ Ψ ψ

As Trico and I walked out towards the motorway to hitch a ride to Durango, there was a volley of sharp cracks, and I suddenly found that I was the only person still standing. Trico and everyone else in sight had immediately thrown themselves to the ground to crouch behind the nearest car or taco stand. Before my woefully slow reactions had time to catch up, they were already getting to their feet again, brushing themselves off and grinning at each other in slightly sheepish relief. It wasn't this street. Not this time.

Trico shook his head resignedly as we started to walk again, just as the first of a stream of police cars flew by, sirens screaming.

'Bloody Chihuahua's getting almost like Juárez. The price you pay for being on the road to El Chuco, eh?'

'El Chuco' is the slang name for El Paso, Juárez's luckier twin on the northern side of the Rio Grande. As the entry point for an estimated 70 per cent of North America's cocaine, it stands on the front line of the US government's Canute-like battle to hold back with walls and patrols the tide of drugs and cheap-to-hire illegal immigrants washing northwards from over the border. For a country that prides itself on being the flag-bearer for market capitalism, the approach shows ironically little consideration for the laws of supply and demand.

6
The Five Rules of Master

The Durango sky dwarfs the earth. Against a background of deep, saturated blue, white clouds rise in soaring formations, as flat-bottomed and clearly defined as those in a cartoon, turning their backs on the weathered landscape as if considering it unworthy of their attention.

'You know,' Trico shouted, over the rush of the air and vibration of the engine, 'there are films shot in other parts of Mexico that have the Durango sky superimposed over the sky of the real setting. Gives them more of a feeling of grandeur.'

We were lying on our backs in the bed of a pickup, hurtling south along an open highway. The number of pickups on the roads of Mexico makes it the perfect country for hitchhiking. Not only is it possible to travel in large groups and with considerable amounts of luggage if necessary, but it also gives a spice of adrenaline to the journey that is completely lost behind the glass of a windscreen. Colours look brighter. The horizon looks wider. The slipstream whips your hair back and sweeps old worries behind you as a new direction unfolds ahead. We had slept for a few hours in the truck that had carried us from Chihuahua, and in the morning hitched a ride out into the mottled Durango plains towards a skyline patrolled by serrated mountain ranges, softened and stained blue with distance. Durango State is cowboy country, the archetypal Western landscape. John Wayne spent so much time filming in it he bought a ranch there.

'In Durango,' Trico went on – as with many states in Mexico, Durango's capital city shares the state's name – 'I will take you to meet Master.'

'Who's Master?'

'You'll like him. He can even speak to you in English. Used to live around

San Diego, helping people get established after they'd crossed the border. Now he has a house in Durango. All the malabaristas and *artesanos* stay there when they're in town.'

'Will we stay there?'

'I'd rather not. It gets quite crowded. I have other friends in Durango we can stay with. But we will definitely go there. Master is sure to tell you some interesting things. He's been around, you know? Once you get to know him a bit, you must ask him about the five rules.'

'What are the five rules?'

Trico laughed.

'Better you ask him. He gets quite excited about them.'

I was intrigued to meet this 'Master'. I pictured him as a sage, a man of incomparable wisdom. From him, I was sure, I would learn the gospel of Mexican street life.

ψ Ψ ψ

It was several days before Trico fulfilled his promise. First, there were various other friends to be visited, stories to be exchanged, caguamas to be drunk. And he owed some money to another malabarista staying at Master's house, so it was necessary to play a few days of semáforos before going there. He asked me if I would help him with the charol. I was reluctant.

'Surely people would give more generously to the person who actually does the performance? Besides, they can see that I'm a foreigner. They will probably think I'm a *gringa*. Won't they question my right to be there, taking money from Mexicans?'

But the Mexican mind, apparently, didn't work that way.

'Don't be silly,' Trico retorted. 'People always give twice as much to a girl. And what's more, a *güera* [fair-skinned girl]! We'll make a fortune!'

Although most Mexicans are mestizo, there is a broad spectrum ranging from dark and stocky, with the glossy black hair and wide features of the *indígenas*, to comparatively tall and pale, with the narrower faces and limp hair of Europeans. Those of a more European aspect are popularly considered to be better-looking, one symptom of the discrimination against Mexico's indigenous peoples which persists to this day. Güeras, therefore, tend to be subjected to more than their fair share of male attention.

Trico's prediction turned out to be correct. In fact, the only disadvantage of my doing the charol was that certain men had a tendency to wave a coin out of the window as bait, wait until I came over, and then hold it just out of reach while they attempted to engage me in conversation. The majority were polite, but seemed not to realise that when I only had 30 seconds or so to go round up to 20 cars, it was not the most convenient moment to answer a barrage of questions about where I was from and whether I had any sisters.

Trico was less forgiving.

'*Pendejos*,' he snorted. 'Of course they realise. They just want you to stand there so they can leer at you. Ignore their money and go on to someone else.'

The novelty also caused quite a sensation among the other semáforo workers, the salesmen and windscreen-washers, although their attentions were considerably more helpful. I had feared that, as a foreigner, my presence would be resented. But on the contrary, they never treated me with anything other than the irreverent camaraderie with which they treated each other. I think their easy acceptance of me stemmed half from genuine friendliness and half from glee at seeing a foreign güera brought down to size, sweating in the midday sun and choking on car exhaust alongside them. In particular, they delighted in laughing at my ineptitude and giving me advice.

'Hey, güera, you should start with the cars on the far side of the road and work back towards this pavement! Otherwise you'll be stuck on the wrong side when the lights go green!'

'Hey, güera, why did you stand there waiting for that woman to fumble through everything in her wallet? When they do that you can be sure they're only going to give you a handful of *centavos* they want to get rid of! Go to the other cars first and come back to that one if you have time!'

'Hey, güera, borrow my hat! See how burnt your face is; you look like a tomato!'

At first I bristled at being addressed as güera, but soon realised that it was not intended to be objectifying. Mexicans are not known for their tact, and tend to simply describe what they see. Being a güera was actually quite an advantage in this respect, as having such an obvious distinguishing characteristic distracted from other, less inoffensive observations. The largest of the sweet-sellers at our regular semáforo was known simply as *gordo* – fatty.

The other semáforo workers were more territorial than the malabaristas, whose itinerant lifestyles and reliance on novelty prevented them from staking a claim on a particular location. The windscreen-washers tended to be most defensive of their patch. They usually worked in groups of two or three, and as each one could generally only wash one windscreen per semáforo, the wider semáforos could easily have accommodated several groups. I never saw it happen, though, and Trico claimed to have witnessed some vicious fights when a rival group intruded onto another's semáforo. There could, however, be two or three separate vendors, as long as they were all selling quite distinct categories of things. For instance, a vendor of *mazapanes* (round sweets made from icing sugar and crushed peanuts) could usually tolerate a vendor of electric fly swats, but would take greater issue with a vendor of *chupitas* (flavoured lollipops, often spiced with chilli powder).

Despite their relative tolerance, there was some form of hierarchy among the vendors, in which the dirty-faced boys selling single roses were quite definitely on the bottom. But it was an amiable, boisterous hierarchy, rather like that between brothers of varying ages. The older ones teased and bossed around the younger, but through it all there was a definite feeling that in a tight situation, they would be there for each other. Between semáforos, in the down-time marked by the green lights, we would gather together in the largest patch of shade, sifting through bags of small change and using the smallest coins to stock up on water or (if trade was good) beer. In a beneficent mood, a peanut seller might open a bag to share, and the older vendors would order one of the younger over to the nearest taco stand to ask for a splash of *salsa valentina* and a wedge of lime to squeeze over the top.

The older vendors in our regular semáforo dressed in wide-brimmed hats and baggy shorts, the waistlines tucked snugly under their rounded bellies. Their indigenous features and nut-brown skin indicated that they, like many semáforo workers across Mexico, were likely to be migrants from rural areas. Since the North American Free Trade Agreement (NAFTA) of 1994 liberalised the markets of Mexico, the US and Canada, eliminating almost all trade barriers among the three countries, Mexican farmers have struggled to compete with cheaper US agricultural imports, particularly those of subsidised US corn. Although some sections of the economy have benefitted, the effect has been hardest felt by rural smallholders, who lack the economies of scale enjoyed by US agribusinesses. Many have been driven out of business and forced to migrate to the cities in search of employment, swelling the already sizeable informal urban economy.

The industrial cities of northern Mexico appear at first to be somewhat charmless. In the city centres, the elegant pretension of the colonial architecture sits uneasily alongside the brash commercialism of the advertising hoardings and the chain stores, neither quite seeming to belong there. The true spirit of these cities, to me, lies in the semáforos. It is there that the gritty vitality of Mexico asserts itself, with resilience, impetuous flashes of generosity, and a casual disregard for the letter of the law. Over those days, and the months to follow, I developed a deep respect for the initiative and solid work ethic of those who make their living there.

Trico was in his element in the semáforo, whistling piercingly through his teeth, winking at pretty girls crossing the road, occasionally climbing on the bonnet of cars and waving a club over the windscreen in clownish imitation of the windscreen-washers, and generally revelling in the attention. As soon as he mounted his unicycle and started to juggle, however, his whole demeanour would change. His face would become a mask of concentration as he stared at the coloured clubs spinning and swooping in front of him. The expression of meditative calm blended with wonder had a strange piety about it, like the face of the Virgin Mary in religious paintings as she gazes, humbled and awestruck, into the heavens. For 50 seconds or so, he seemed to leave this reality and enter another. Then, as the lights turned green, he'd be back, bowing extravagantly and pulling faces at children who never seemed quite decided whether to laugh or cry.

After a few hours we'd finish up and count our coins, placing them in 10-peso piles and lining them up in ranks across the pavement. We would swap the majority for notes in the Oxxo corner shops that are ubiquitous in Mexican cities, and then head to a small restaurant Trico knew, where 16 pesos would buy a burrito so large that it would satisfy you for the rest of the day. It was a dingy place, smelling of smoked *chile chipotle* and onions. The owner must have been a keen follower of current affairs, because the walls were plastered in newspaper clippings and a small television in the corner was permanently set to a news channel.

As we sat there eating lunch the day Trico took me to meet Master, the television news bulletin was covering the latest revelation in Mexican politics: that then-President Felipe Calderón was earning more than US President Barack Obama. Their salaries at the time were similar but, in relation to the economies of their respective countries, Calderón's was significantly higher. A later study by the Centro de Investigación y Docencia Económicas in 2011 showed that he was earning 32.7 times the average national income, compared to 9.8 in the case of Obama.

'Felipe *Raterón*,' Trico declared, between mouthfuls of his burrito, jerking his head at the television. *'Ratero'* means 'thief', *'raterón'*: big thief'. 'Stole the election, and now he's stealing the money.'

It was commonly believed that Calderón had taken the closely fought 2006 election by fraud, although nothing had ever been proven. Disillusionment with politics in Mexico was profound. After 71 years of authoritarian single-party rule by the Institutional Revolutionary Party (which has the acronym PRI in Spanish), a hope for true democracy had briefly bloomed in 2000 when an alternative candidate, Vicente Fox of the National Action Party (PAN), was finally elected. Nine years later, with PAN still in power and Fox replaced by Calderón, many ordinary Mexicans felt worse off than ever as the carnage of the drug wars swept the country, and their sense of bitterness was deep. (So deep that the 2012 election placed the PRI back in power, only two terms after they were so triumphantly dispatched. Once again, fraud was alleged, but not proven.) Widespread corruption throughout government has always been not so much suspected as assumed. The news report about Calderón's earnings came as no great surprise. He was simply following a long tradition of Mexican politicians, expressed most succinctly by Carlos Hank Gonzalez (the late billionaire businessman, politician, and one-time powerbroker for the PRI, notorious for his money-laundering and dealings with drug-trafficking organisations) in the maxim:

'A politician who is poor is a poor politician.'

ψ Ψ ψ

Master's house consisted of three small rooms, lined up like stables along one side of an enclosed concrete yard. In the corner of the yard, a muscular boy in his mid-twenties was kneeling over a bucket of soapy water. He had a scrubbing brush in one hand and a sopping green T-shirt in the other and was receiving detailed instruction from a girl in a bowler hat on the removal of stubborn gasoline stains. There were about a dozen other people in the yard, and more could be glimpsed sprawled on mattresses through the open doors of the rooms. Those outside were sitting with their backs against the wall, leaving the central space free for two boys and a girl, who were passing nine clubs between them in a complicated three-way juggling pattern. Every now and then there would be a murmur of approval for a particularly good trick, or a chorus of disapprobation when one missed and a club would go flying past to knock over an empty beer bottle or hit an unsuspecting person in the face.

Next to me, two boys were deep in a serious and involved conversation about juggling. To the uninitiated, translating literally from the Spanish, it sounded at times like coded orders in a guerrilla war, and at others more like instructions for knitting patterns.

'...What I'd go for is a four-four-one going behind then returning to the waterfall with machetes. It's simple but really effective.'

'A two-two-one would make it tighter, no?'

'It would, but then you would have to wait in the waterfall before going in with the machetes, unless you can come up really quickly from the back pass...'

'...What would you add here?'

'Maybe just a few rounds of back-cross in single turn. Or double, if you prefer. Or a Mills' Mess, then maintain the columns on the right-hand side and add a flower on the left...'

They discussed juggling the way politicians discuss politics or priests discuss religion: with the single-minded earnestness of people who know that there is only one thing of true importance in this world, and its fate is in their hands.

The boy on my other side leaned over to me.

'Do you know how to juggle?' he asked.

I confessed that I didn't. It was a question I was starting to dread. Every social group has their own criteria by which they judge others. Among the malabaristas, you earned respect through your juggling prowess. As my inferior level of Spanish made it harder for me to redeem myself through conversation, I felt my lack of circus ability even more keenly.

'But you know how to play poi?' he pressed.

'Not really. Trico's tried to teach me, but I'm not very good.'

The boy looked appalled.

'I want to learn, though,' I added hastily. His expression softened slightly.

I was sure what was coming next: the procurement of makeshift poi made out of long socks stuffed with bags of rice at the toes, closely followed by the humiliation of being watched repeatedly hitting myself with them by a circle of people to whom circus was one of the key expressions of beauty in this world. But this boy had a different strategy.

'The most important thing,' he told me, 'is that you *understand* malabares.' He pointed at the wall. 'Do you know what that is?'

The grey walls of the yard were brightened up with images, symbols and slogans daubed in coloured paint. The one he was pointing at centred on an eye, with four rectangular wings in a cross shape around it, a point at the top, and two rounded shapes like ears on either side.

'It's an Aztec symbol, isn't it?'

'It represents *ollin*, which in Nahuatl means "movement".' Nahuatl was the language of the Aztecs, and varieties of it are still spoken by an estimated 1.5 million people across central Mexico. 'In Aztec mythology, we are now in the fifth age of the earth. The previous four ages were the ages of earth, air, water and fire, but they were all destroyed. Now we are in the *Nahui-Ollin* – the age of movement.'

I nodded, wondering where this was going.

'What is the basic shape of most forms of malabares?'

I stayed silent, hoping the question was rhetorical. The boy used his index finger to sketch a sideways figure of eight in the air in front of us.

'Think about it. In the basic movement of poi, each poi must make a circle on either side of your body. In the basic movement of staff, each end of the staff makes a circle on either side of you. In the basic movement of juggling, you throw each ball or club diagonally across your body, and it falls straight down into the opposite hand. If you drew its path in the air it would make the same shape. What does that shape mean?'

This one I knew.

'Infinity.'

He nodded excitedly.

'Exactly! Like the *ollin*. Perpetual movement. Just think of that and it will all flow from there.'

He wove his two wrists through the air in front of him, manipulating a pair of invisible poi. The figure wasn't quite a figure of eight, as an extra beat was added on each side, but I found that conceptualising it in that way helped my hands understand the movement, the wrists continually crossing and re-crossing in the centre. After a couple of minutes of watching me, he nodded in approval.

'Yes. You understand the feeling now? You can use the same wrist action over the head, or behind the back as well. It's the fundamental movement of poi.'

I continued to weave my hands through the air, thinking of the *ollin*. I could understand why the legend of the age of movement was something that the malabaristas had seized upon and used as a building block for their own philosophy. They were bound together by perpetual movement: that of their art and that of their lives. Through their own movement, and the influences they picked up on the way from disparate cultures across their country, they were creating a mythology of their own. Circus had a deeper meaning to them than I had realised. Juggling was more than just a pastime, and more than just a means to earn money. It was something they believed in, a metaphor for their own lives, which gave those lives shape and meaning, and to which they attached a quasi-mystical significance.

One of the purposes of circus has always been to create an illusion of magic. The earliest records of juggling in indigenous American cultures suggest that it was once performed only by shamans in order to convince others of their supernatural powers. In medieval Europe, wandering jugglers were frowned upon by the clergy and sometimes accused of practising witchcraft. Jugglers and jesters have often been looked down on throughout history, and the practice of juggling has been seen as something subversive, childish, or both. But then, that's exactly what appeals to me about it. In centuries past, the court jester was the only person allowed to mock the nobility and the king without facing severe punishment. He was a critic and satirist, whose childish guise belied his dangerousness. And, as with malabaristas and clowns to this day, his rejection of accepted rules of behaviour was not only tolerated but to an extent celebrated, and even supported, by regular society. He represented an important social safety valve: a form of escape from social convention, available only to those prepared to embrace madness and ridicule.

ψ Ψ ψ

Master himself was a slender man with a gentle, almost Oriental face, and a soft velvet fuzz of hair across his scalp. He was one of those people who look curiously ageless, and I found myself struggling to guess whether he was closer to 30 or 50. His English was ungrammatical with a thick Mexican-American accent, but had an ease and flow to it which my over-meticulous Spanish lacked. He was sitting at a plastic table at the far end of the yard, whittling a rattlesnake out of a curved piece of wood. The wood was fibrous, greyish in colour, and riddled with holes like Swiss cheese. He held it out to me.

'Cactus wood. The holes are where the spines were.'

I took it and ran it through my hands before handing it back.

'It's a good carving.'

'Gotta look out for these in the desert. Move slowly away soon as you hear the rattle. They won't bite unless you scare them. But one bite will kill you in hours if you don't get treatment. I used to work in San Diego y'know, hooking up new arrivals with safe houses and contacts to help them move north. Met a few that had lost people to these mothers on the way.'

He went back to whittling the ridges on the warning rattle on the end of the snake's tail. I thought of the harsh expanse of desert stretching across the northern border. Many would-be emigrants pay *coyotes*, or guides, to lead them through the hidden tunnels running underneath the Mexico-US border, but those who can't afford the *coyotes'* exorbitant fees will sometimes risk the long and treacherous overland route: a week's walk through the desert, far out of reach of any medical assistance.

'Do you ever find them in the city?'

'Nah. You find these little bastards though. Durango is famous for them. They're one of the symbols of the state.'

He showed me a model scorpion, twisted from thick pieces of rust-coloured wire. Master was a passionate collector, maker and hoarder, and his hunting ground for both materials and inspiration was always the desert. His corner of the yard was strewn with dried snake skins, bones or skulls of small animals, little models made from wood or wire, crystals, fossils, twisted dry wood and potted cacti. With its scorched air and sun-bleached concrete, it felt almost like a little corner of desert itself.

'I'll show you how to make them if you like. They're easier than they look.'

He cut eight lengths of wire for each of us from a tangled coil of it under the table, and started to guide me through the series of plaits, twists and curls necessary to make the scorpion, pausing occasionally when he was passed a fat, scruffy joint. He talked all the while about the desert, and the objects he collected there.

'See these fossils? Ammonites. You know the whole *altiplano* used to be sea? Strange, to be walking through the desert, hundreds of metres above sea level and be finding fossils of sea creatures. You find them round Monterrey as well. I'm planning another trip soon to bring back more.'

'Do you leave the house open when you go?'

'What? Oh yeah, yeah, the kids look after it.' He waved a hand vaguely around the people in the yard. 'They just have to promise they won't bring anyone back who's not *banda*.'

'*La banda*' is an important concept in Mexico. Meaning literally 'the group', the word is also used in a wider sense to mean 'one of us'. To be told you are '*la banda*' or, if truly honoured, '*la pura banda*', is a high compliment.

Master thought a moment.

'And that they'll follow the five rules.'

I saw my chance.

'What are the five rules?'

'The five rules!' he switched abruptly into Spanish. '*Las cinco reglas!*' A mixed chorus of laughs and groans went up around the yard. Master ignored it.

'The five rules,' he announced, in a tone of utmost seriousness, 'are really only one rule. They are five things, and you must do at least four of these things each day if you wish to live a happy and fulfilling life.'

'OK,' I said. 'What are they?'

He paused for a moment, his eyes boring into mine, his eyebrows lowered. 'They are: eat, sleep, work, exercise, fuck.'

A wide smile spread across his face and he sat back, grinning triumphantly, waiting to see the effect his words had had. Around him, the same smile was mirrored on the face of every person in the yard as they all stared at me, as if expecting me to fall to my knees and be dramatically converted. I wasn't quite sure what to say.

'OK,' I stuttered finally. 'It seems very, um, simple.'

'Exactly!' He seemed delighted that I had managed to grasp the concept so quickly. 'Exactly!'

'Exactly,' said one of the boys, sarcastically. Master rounded on him.

'You say that, Mario, yet you sit on your arse all day with your little pliers and I can't *remember* the last time I saw you with a girl. When was the last time you fucked, Mario, eh?'

'More recently than *you*,' Mario muttered.

'I,' Master retorted, with considerable dignity, 'have been exercising.'

He turned back to me, and asked in English: 'How old do you think I am?'

I decided to go for my lower estimate.

'Thirty-five?'

He beamed in satisfaction.

'I am forty-five years old. And I was a junkie for fifteen years.'

'Really?'

'I remember times when I wouldn't eat or sleep for days. That's when I made the five rules. To keep me sane. It wasn't until I stopped doing all that shit that I realised how many 'normal' people don't keep the five rules either. How do I look? Not bad for a forty-five-year-old ex-junkie, eh? Here, give me that.'

I handed him my completed scorpion. He twisted its pincers together with those of his, bent the two into a large bangle shape, and then slipped it onto my upper arm, between the elbow and shoulder.

'There you go. A souvenir of Durango for you.' He laughed.

ψ Ψ ψ

Trico and I moved on the next day, hitching a ride east across the plains to Zacatecas, a maze of tangled alleyways and Baroque architecture famed for its silver production and colonial charm. We stayed for a couple of days with a drumming collective Trico knew from his travels (Trico, it seemed, knew half of Mexico from his travels) before continuing the journey, mostly by pickups, across increasingly arid stretches of semi-desert to San Luis Potosí. I later found out that, shortly after we left him, Master had taken a deep gulp from a caguama, a deep drag on a *toque*, and then keeled sideways off his chair to land heavily on an unfortunately placed rock. He broke two ribs and nearly punctured his lung, although he didn't find that out until he sobered up enough to get to hospital the next day. The banda occupied the surrounding semáforos for several hours to pay for his treatment. He didn't work, exercise or fuck for several weeks afterwards, but I am assured that he ate and slept twice as much to make up for it. The banda made sure of that. Perhaps Master's most important rule was the one thing he considered too obvious to mention: always look after your own.

7
The Wheel of Fortune

In Doña Maria's house on the outskirts of San Luis Potosí, they were throwing a party for the washing machine. It stood in the middle of the yard, a great hulking beast with a wrinkled grey tube like the trunk of an elephant protruding from the back. It had stopped working a couple of days previously and Doña Maria, in what struck me as a delightfully Mexican approach to the problem, had promptly stocked up on food and beer, placed the ailing machine in the most conspicuous possible location, and invited all the family over in the hope that someone, in a moment of drunken inspiration, would have a brainwave as to how to fix it.

By mid-afternoon little progress had been made, except that a thicket of wires was now protruding from the back along with the tube, but Doña Maria was unperturbed. She was with her family, and her family gave her more pleasure than even a functioning washing machine. She sat in the corner of the yard, resplendent in a demurely pretty lemon-yellow dress, shaking her head affectionately at the efforts of a rat-faced man who Trico had introduced to me as Tio Loco (Crazy Uncle), apparently on account of his crack cocaine habit.

Doña Maria was a beautiful woman, with high cheekbones and lively eyes. The only signs of her advancing years were her silver hair, which she tied in a sleek bun on top of her head, and a mesh of delicate wrinkles across her face. These were so fine as to be barely noticeable, as if someone had removed the skin, lightly crumpled it, and then smoothed it gently back on. When we entered Trico had done an exaggerated double-take on seeing her, proclaiming, '*Ay, abuela* [grandmother], you get more gorgeous every time I see you! You better watch out, *abuelo*, all the men in the barrio must have their eye on her!'

'Eh?' her husband shouted back, grinning vaguely. He was a straight-backed gentleman with a magnificent silver moustache, clearly deaf as a post but with the tolerant air of a man so used to his family's antics that he scarcely needed to hear them anymore. Trico grabbed Doña Maria and swept her into an energetic salsa across the yard. She squealed in mock horror at this affront to her matriarchal dignity, but even to imaginary music her little feet found all the steps.

A couple of hours later we sat on plastic chairs around the yard with an assortment of uncles, aunts and cousins in varying stages of drunkenness, empty beer bottles at our feet and plates of *enchiladas potosinas* – a local speciality of deep-fried pockets of spiced corn dough, stuffed with cheese and chilli – perched on our laps.

Trico winked at his grandmother.

'Hey, *abuela*. Tell Cat how you and grandfather met.'

'Oh!' She exclaimed, clearly delighted. 'Not that old story again!'

I recognised my cue.

'Please, Doña Maria? I've never heard it.'

Doña Maria needed no further encouragement.

'Oh, very well. When I was a girl, more than anything else I used to look forward to when the fair came to San Luis. Such fun it was! My mother would give me time off my chores so I could go down to the fair with my siblings, with a few pesos for the rides and games. One of my favourite things was always the Wheel of Fortune. How wonderful to be up high like that, with a view over the whole fair! To see all the children running around down below, the pens where the animals were kept, musicians playing and people dancing! Every time the fair was in town I would ride it at least once.

'When I was eighteen, the time of year came when the fair was in San Luis, and as usual I went over to ride the Wheel of Fortune. The moment I saw the young man operating the wheel, I fell in love. Such a handsome man! Such a splendid moustache! All the time the fair stayed in San Luis I went back there every day. After the ride I would find an excuse to talk to the handsome operator, if he had the time, and such stories he told me! He was only a few years older than me, but already he had travelled with the fair to every corner of Mexico. I could happily have spent hours there with him, but of course I couldn't stay for too long, or my parents would get angry, wondering why I hadn't come home. But I knew from the way he looked at me that he felt the same way as I did.

'On the final day before the fair left San Luis, I went back to the Wheel of Fortune one last time. Both he and I knew that the next day the fair would be gone, and all that remained would be an empty field and flies fighting for the scraps of food left behind. He would be far away, turning the Wheel of Fortune for strangers in Morelia, or Querétaro, and we would never see each other again.

'I walked straight up to him, and held out my coins for one final ride. But he didn't take them. Instead, he took my hand in both of his.'

'And what did he say to you, *abuela*?' Trico asked. They had clearly told and retold this story a thousand times; they each spoke their lines with the immaculate timing of well-rehearsed actors, and delighted in the performance.

'He looked straight into my eyes without letting go of my hand, and he said to me – *Vámonos*. [Let's go.]'

'And what did you say to him?'

'I looked back at him, and I said – *Vámonos*.'

She laughed gleefully. It was a typical Mexican story, suspiciously laden with romance, destiny and symbolism. But the beauty (and at times the curse) of Mexico is that all stories are entwined with sparkling threads of fantasy, so delicately interwoven with the truth that it is impossible to disentangle the two. To fully appreciate such stories, one must learn to suspend disbelief.

'Where did you go then, *abuela*?'

'To a party!'

'And then?'

'To another party! Everywhere there were lights and music and dancing, and it seemed as if every day there was another *fiesta*. I was swept off around Mexico, and everything was so exciting and so new to me that for weeks I barely felt my feet touch the ground or remembered where I was. It wasn't until three months later that I wrote home and told my parents where I had gone! I knew they would have stopped me leaving, you see, so I gathered only a couple of my things and left without telling a soul. Such a bad girl I was! Oh, my poor mother!'

She rolled her eyes in a melodramatic imitation of remorse, which fooled no one and was not intended to. Trico shouted with laughter.

'She's a rascal, this one, isn't she?' he asked me proudly.

'*Ay, madre,*' Trico's mother tutted, bustling out of the kitchen with a tray of fresh *enchiladas*, still glistening with oil. 'You really shouldn't encourage him. He only appeared again yesterday, after six months of no word from him. Didn't even tell us he was coming!'

Doña Maria beamed. 'He has my blood in his veins, this boy.'

'What happened next?' I asked. 'After you wrote to your mother?'

'Oh, she wanted me to go back, of course. As if I would have left Fernando and gone back to face the anger of my father! Such a beating he would have given me! But by then Fernando and I had married anyway, when we passed through his home town of Puebla, so there was nothing she could do. We stayed with the fair for the next ten years – until we had seven children and couldn't all fit in the caravan anymore.'

ψ Ψ ψ

Trico's mother Elvira was the eldest of the seven, and had the meticulously dutiful nature of a woman who had been a mother all her life. She would be up at dawn every day, tidying the living room, sweeping the floors and mopping the bathroom. By the time anyone else began to stir she would already be sifting through the piles of washing. Her house was her domain, and she liked to keep it immaculate.

It was a constant battle. With stoic determination, Elvira held out against an onslaught of muddy boots, empty beer cans, splotches of sauce on floors or clothes (often the result of careless grazing from her lovingly prepared dishes as they simmered on the stove), scattered toys, cigarette butts and countless other minor affronts to her standards. The house was a thoroughfare of friends, neighbours and relatives, who floated in and out as comfortably as they would in their own houses, perhaps to borrow a spanner, prepare themselves a snack, or deposit a small child into Elvira's competent hands while they dashed off to perform some urgent errand. She never uttered a word of complaint, merely fluttered around behind them, clearing up in their wake.

She treated her son with a lovingly bemused patience, which did not so much as waver during the Tricopsycho phases which seemed to have become more frequent and more pronounced as soon as we had arrived in San Luis. Her tolerance held out even when frequent invasions of Trico's friends, including me, were added to the mêlée.

Chino, so called for his curly black hair, was one of Trico's regular semáforo partners. He had startling blue eyes and a smile that involved his whole face – raising the cheeks, sharpening the chin, and putting quotation marks around the mouth and eyes. His short stature and permanent good humour made him a favourite target for affectionate teasing, and Trico would often address him either as '*pendejín*' (little pubic hair) or '*mil amores*' (thousand loves), on account of his tendency to fall sweetly and dreamily in love with whichever woman he had most recently been introduced to. Trico and Chino would spend many hours practising two-way juggling patterns in the courtyard together, developing experimental new tricks and occasionally knocking over the pot plants or dirtying the hanging washing with an escaping club. Whenever this happened, Trico would turn on Chino and scold him fiercely.

'*Concentrate*, Chino, look what you've done now! My mother only just washed that sheet and now it has a dirty great club mark on it.'

'But it was you who missed it, Trico!'

'That's because you threw it wrong, Chino. It was much too high.'

'It wasn't as high as the one you threw that you said I should have stretched for.'

'But that one was *supposed* to be high, Chino. It was part of the trick. I quite clearly indicated with my eyebrows that you would have to stretch.'

'How am I supposed to notice what you're doing with your eyebrows? Couldn't you just have said something?'

'Now that wouldn't look very professional in a show, would it Chino? You will just have to concentrate more in future. You would be a very good juggler if only you were more focussed.'

Similar experiences had put off several of Trico's closest friends from juggling with him too regularly, although they would still pass by the house to cook a communal meal or share a caguama. One of these was Güera, who explained her reluctance to play semáforos with Trico with the logic that she loved him dearly and would be very sad if she had to kill him. She made her living primarily as a macramé artist, was irrepressibly excitable and approached every task, however minor, with a sort of urgent enthusiasm. With her snubbed nose set in a beaming moon-shaped face, she reminded me of a Dr Seuss cartoon. The effect was completed with a rainbow-striped hat, stretched to a bulbous sausage over the crop of dreadlocks piled on top of her head.

Another frequent visitor to the house was Oscar, Güera's sometime boyfriend, who disguised his narrow features and green eyes behind a shaggy mane of dreadlocks and his amiable nature behind a growly voice and prickly manner. He was an artesano who worked primarily with silver wire, and spent many an afternoon sitting on the sofa, pliers in hand, creating intricately beautiful pieces of jewellery and swigging on a caguama. When he got too drunk to continue working he would turn his attention to the TV, which at that time of day was usually playing '*Dora La Exploradora*' to Trico's two-year-old niece Jacky. Occasionally he would turn to her and humbly request to change the channel, but Jacky was undisputed queen of the remote control and very rarely permitted it. If Trico and Chino still hadn't come to rescue him after a couple more caguamas, he would warm to the programme and was sometimes even inspired to join in Dora's sing-along English lessons.

Exactly what Trico's father thought of it all was hard to tell. Due to his job, he was rarely in the house. He was a large, barrel-shaped man by the name of Margaro, who the other residents of the barrio referred to affectionately as Don Mago (Mr Wizard) on account of his thick white hair and beard or, less affectionately, as Don Amargo (Mr Bitter), on account of his relentlessly bad temper.

Arriving home late at night from a long journey, he would bang the front door open, slam a caguama or six-pack on the coffee table in the living room, light a cigarette, and bellow at the ceiling above which his wife lay sleeping: 'Elvira! I'm hungry!'

A moment later Elvira would appear, bleary-eyed and wrapped in a dressing gown, to prepare him a plate of eggs or *chilaquiles* (deep fried pieces of tortilla, cooked in spicy tomato and onion salsa and topped with fresh cheese), which half the time he wouldn't eat because by the time it was ready he'd be asleep on the sofa, snoring loudly.

I was always terrified of Don Margaro. There was one key reason for this: I could barely understand a word he said. I was acutely embarrassed and frustrated by it; generally my Spanish comprehension was reasonably good. But Don Margaro said everything in a gruff, half-slurred shout that not only was completely incomprehensible to me, but also convinced me that whatever he was saying, he must be extremely angry. On one occasion I still cringe to remember, I thought he was ordering me out of his house, and was halfway through stammering my apologies and promising to leave first thing the next morning when Trico intervened to explain that he was actually telling me to make myself at home there. A phrase along the lines of 'my house isn't grand but you treat it like your own' sounds very much less welcoming when spoken in a tone somewhere between a growl and a shout by a man glaring at you from under a fearsome pair of bushy grey eyebrows.

Such was the enigma of Don Margaro. He had the aura of a thoroughly unpleasant man. And in several ways he was: hard-drinking, foul-tempered, and something of a bully, particularly to his long-suffering wife. But he was also exceptionally generous to me, and to many others. His house wasn't grand, as he said, but the whole neighbourhood and most of Trico's friends did treat it as their own. (Trico swore to me that he once had 12 of his friends living in the storage room adjoining the kitchen for over two months.) Don Margaro, albeit with very bad grace, shared everything he had. I am told that he could also be very funny in a dry sort of way and told some brilliant stories, if only I could have understood them. Unfortunately, after about our third attempt at communication, in which I sat like a rabbit in the headlights trying desperately to work out whether I should be laughing or apologising, he decided that I was impossibly stupid, and ignored me from then on.

Over the long period during which Trico and I returned intermittently to San Luis, I never did manage to 'crack' Don Margaro, a failure I still regret. In retrospect, I think my mistake was never buying him the one present that might possibly have redeemed me in his eyes: a really good bottle of alcohol. This was because I was always haunted by the memory of one occasion when, in a particularly belligerent (and drunk) mood, he had glared over at me and demanded, in such emphatic tones that even I understood: 'You think I'm a drunk, don't you?' After that I was so ridden with paranoia that he would take any alcoholic gift as a confirmation of this suspicion that I stuck to 'safer' confectionery-based options, which did not interest him in the slightest.

ψ Ψ ψ

The house lay on a quiet backstreet, affectionately decorated with potted cacti and a small shrine to the Virgin of Guadalupe. It was a comfortable but not opulent neighbourhood, past the point where the stone and wrought iron of the city centre gave way to brightly painted concrete and brick, but before it faded into the greying industrial slums of the poorer suburbs. There was a relaxed, familial vibe to the area – residents left unwanted objects on trestle tables outside for others to take at will, little boys played football in the road, and fathers sent their seven-year-old children out to buy them cigarettes from the corner shop. A string of broken fairy lights dangled across the street, left as a memento of a much-enjoyed Christmas party several years before.

The whole neighbourhood was a warren of flat-roofed houses and hidden courtyards. Each house had access to at least one yard and usually two (a shared entrance way and a private area with a concrete washing station) and each yard had a flight of external steps by which the residents could access the roof. Here, they would come to hang their washing, dispose of odd pieces of scrap, or get away from the extended family which circulated constantly through their homes. By way of the roof, one had access to at least 20 different yards and 30 different houses. Often the residents of the barrio would not bother going onto the road at all, preferring to pop across the roof to pay a visit to a friend or relative.

I always felt that the neighbourhood was best appreciated from the roof. I enjoyed wandering around the barren stretch of concrete, peeking surreptitiously into the various yards, each one a snapshot of a different family life. Here, a woman bent over the wash station, scrubbing determinedly at a stain on her husband's trousers, a small child clutching at her knees. There, a group of youths sitting on the steps, passing a caguama, deep in gossip or the football scores. Even when no one was outside, stories could be imagined from the sounds and smells coming from open doors and windows: a family quarrel, a drunken singalong to a warped cassette of *norteño* classics, the impassioned speeches of a *telenovela*, tortillas starting to char after a few seconds too long on the *comal*. Overhead loomed billboards advertising toothpaste or banks, invariably featuring a model with skin at least three shades lighter than the palest local resident. Here and there, the flat expanse of roof was interrupted by a block which poked its head above the rest, where some enterprising family had procured the capital to build themselves an extra storey.

Trico's was one of these families. The extra block housed his parents' bedroom, which was accessed by the outside steps – an arrangement they only regretted when it rained which, San Luis being a desert town, it hardly ever did. The room directly beneath was where Trico and I slept. Lying on the bed with the door open, we had a view onto the house's private courtyard, the roofline of the kitchen opposite, and a small section of sky.

About ten days after our first arrival we lay there at dusk, enjoying the warm air of a balmy evening. Trico was pensive.

'Do you believe in ghosts?' he asked me suddenly.

'No. Do you?'

'Yes. I've seen one, many times. He used to appear on that rooftop when I was lying in bed.' He pointed through the open door at the section of rooftop visible from where we lay. 'Just a shadowy figure, staring at me.'

'Always the same figure?'

He nodded slowly. 'My brother.'

I remembered the shrine in the living room: a tiny shelf by the door, on it a photo of a young boy, and a red lamp in the shape of a candle. Each night, the last thing Elvira did before going to bed was to turn on the little lamp, bathing the room and the child's smiling face in a soft, red glow. It seemed such a private ritual that I had never wanted to ask who he was.

'Is that... the boy in the photo in the living room?'

'Yes. He was only twelve when he died. He was the twin of my eldest brother, Cesar.'

'What happened?'

'He was on the bus, coming home from school. The bus arrived at the stop just round the corner from the house, where he always got off. You see how careless the bus drivers are here. Unless there are lots of people waiting they barely stop, just expect people to jump on and jump off. His bag got caught in the bus door as it pulled off, and he fell and hit his head on the road. He was dragged along for a whole block before the driver realised and stopped the bus. He was taken to hospital but he died from his injuries.'

'How awful... I'm so sorry, Trico.'

He shrugged, with a very strained nonchalance.

'I was only six. I still remember him though. He was cool. He and I were the naughty ones, always playing pranks. Cesar and Marco were the good ones. Maybe that's why it was hard for my parents to see me, because I reminded them of him.'

'Why do you say that?'

'After he died they sent me to live with my grandparents for a while. I think it was hard for my mother to cope. She had to look after Cesar. He saw it happen.'

'That doesn't mean it had anything to do with you, though. I can see how much your mother loves you. I'm sure she wanted you back as soon as possible.'

'Yes. I know that now. But back then... Even after I came back, it was horrible to see her so sad for so many years... I was too little to understand...'

He gazed out at the darkening sky over the rooftop, as if he still saw the shadowy figure there, staring at him. There was a long moment of silence before he spoke again.

'It's not easy living with the ghost of your brother.'

8
The Missing Half

The avenue where most of the artesanos set up their stalls ran along the side of an attractive yellow church in the colonial centre of San Luis. The artesanos would sit in small groups on the cobbles, important pieces of string or wire protruding from their mouths, their wares arranged on coloured blankets or trestle tables in front of them. It was a convivial place, where everybody was permanently borrowing something from somebody else, conversation was regarded as more important than sales, and any passing malabarista was guaranteed to find welcoming company and an open caguama. At the end was a leafy plaza around a fountain, where street vendors sold *totopos* (deep-fried corn chips) with salsa and couples strolled hand-in-hand, gazing up at the carvings across the façade of the church. It had a pleasant, almost Mediterranean atmosphere: colourful without being gaudy, warm without being sweltering, and lively without being raucous.

Yet even here, in this most European of settings, a pre-Hispanic influence was starting to reassert itself. A couple of evenings a week, a group would gather in the courtyard behind the church to practise traditional Aztec dances, complete with rattling ankle cuffs made from dry seed pods, though not with the headdresses that were reserved for ceremonies or displays for tourists. Some days, the artesanos would swig not from a caguama, but from a plastic bottle containing a milky white liquid called pulque – an alcoholic drink made from the fermented sap of the maguey cactus, once sacred to the Aztecs but later prohibited by the Spanish and now only found in dusty shops on the outskirts of the city. In the jewellery of the artesanos, too, a pre-Hispanic inspiration was clear, both in the motifs and patterns they used in their designs and in the stretched piercings many wore in their ears and lips, imitating the adornments worn by the Mayan and Aztec warriors.

Pre-Hispanic revivalism is not a new trend in Mexico. Back in the 1930s, Frida Kahlo, with her long Tehuana skirts and braided hair, and her husband Diego Rivera were among the forerunners of the movement to celebrate the indigenous side of the Mexican heritage after centuries of it being viewed as inferior and slightly shameful. But the latest resurgence of interest is part of a movement that has grown in recent years in ex-colonies around the world, perhaps in response to the homogenising influence of a globalised mass culture and the need to recreate a distinctive cultural identity. In countries where there was never extensive integration between the indigenous and invading populations, it is often seen as something slightly ridiculous: an attempt by the descendants of conquerors to 'reclaim' a heritage they never had. But the movement has particular resonance in Mexico because, unlike most ex-colonies, the majority of the modern population is mestizo. The blood of the repressed pre-Hispanic peoples does indeed run in their veins, and shows clearly in their faces. There is a growing sense, particularly among the younger generation, of having been cheated of one half of their identities, of being left somehow incomplete. In certain circles, the quest for this missing half results in a peculiar New Age mythology of its own: a jumble of rituals and legends drawn from Mexico's ancient tribes and surviving indigenous peoples and upheld as a sort of alternative gospel. The flavour of this mythology varies across the country, depending on the culture of the indigenous people of that region. Around San Luis Potosí it is heavily influenced by the beliefs of the Huichol people, who are famous for their ritual consumption of the hallucinogenic peyote cactus which grows in the desert in the northern part of the state. As in Huichol art, the motif of the peyote plant recurred frequently throughout the work of the artesanos: a squat circular bulb (or 'head') a few centimetres in diameter, scored in radial segments and with a central tuft of whitish hairs. Echoing the words of the Huichol themselves, the artesanos and malabaristas spoke of the desert in hushed and reverent tones: a sacred place where one could find the 'medicine' that would help them to 'reconnect'.

At first I was sceptical about their borrowings from pre-Hispanic traditions, questioning the accuracy of their reinterpretations, their romanticised view of some famously bloodthirsty tribes – the Aztecs, for instance, were such brutal rulers that, when Cortez arrived, the smaller tribes of the region promptly sided with the Spanish in the hope of finally getting rid of them – and the logic of combining the legends of disparate peoples who often lived centuries apart. Then I realised the absurdity of demanding that mythology be accurate, or culture consistent. Both things are, by their nature, fluid. My only concern is that in the fetishising of indigenous culture, it is sometimes unclear whether the surviving indigenous population comes off better or worse. The Huichol are a case in point.

The Huichol (or Wixáritari, in their own language) do not live in the state of San Luis Potosí, but in an area some 500 kilometres to the west, on the conjunction of the states of Zacatecas, Nayarit, Jalisco and Durango. Here they live humbly, surviving mainly off subsistence farming, tobacco cultivation and the sale of traditional artwork made from vibrantly coloured yarn or tiny beads. Every year they embark on a pilgrimage to a patch of desert in the north of San Luis they know as Wirikuta. This is where they gather the peyote which is the cornerstone of their religious rituals and through which they contact their ancestors, gods and spirits. Unlike other groups such as the Tarahumara who have been ravaged by alcoholism, converted to Catholicism (albeit their own strange, hybrid version) and bullied and bribed into swapping their traditional crops for marijuana and opium poppies, the Huichol have remained determinedly aloof from European culture. They do not look for trouble. Nor do they look for friendship. Although their lands and pilgrimage routes are continually threatened by mining and urbanisation, they have managed to resist both assimilation and integration, and many of them continue to pursue their own traditional lifestyle in the sparsely populated regions of the north. Their culture has proved itself resilient in the face of centuries of repression. But whether it will survive many more decades of admiration remains to be seen.

Since the 1960s, when Aldous Huxley sang the praises of mescaline (the psychoactive chemical in peyote) in essays such as *The Doors of Perception* and *Heaven and Hell* and Carlos Castañeda popularised the peyote quest in *The Teachings of Don Juan*, the effect on the Huichol has been mixed. On the one hand, increased knowledge of and respect for their culture has provided them with valuable support in various campaigns to have their rights to their ancestral lands recognised and their pilgrimage routes protected. On the other hand, the peyote across the northern deserts has been decimated. The peyote is a slow-growing cactus, which takes several decades to reach maturity; it is a finite resource, at least for this generation. Once found in abundance, it has now all but disappeared from large tracts of the northern desert, much of it used to produce powdered mescaline for Western markets. While I was in San Luis, two European men were caught driving out of Wirikuta carrying 900 peyote plants.

The Huichol do not claim an exclusive right to the peyote, seeing it as a gift from the earth which is the property of all. They do, however, ask that it be treated respectfully, with sensitivity to its environment and the mystical character of the vision it confers. It is not something to be bought, sold, or used recreationally. In deference to these issues, the banda of San Luis made trips to the desert only rarely, and had a long list of rules to be observed whilst there. Trico had been talking of making such a trip ever since we arrived in San Luis, but insisted we wait until his friend Barbon arrived. Although the Huichol keep largely to themselves, a patient and understanding outsider may sometimes secure an invitation to one of their ceremonies. Barbon had recently returned from one such ceremony in the mountains of Nayarit, and carried a blessing from a shaman for our own journey.

Barbon arrived early one morning, having hitched through the night on a truck from Tepic. He was a hippie of a more old-school variety, with a monastic air of serene authority of which, I was amused to note, Trico was rather in awe. He was the only person I ever met who could silence Tricopsycho with a single disapproving look. The aura was enhanced by a thick mane of hair and beard, which gave him the appearance of an ascetic hermit, and made him look at least 10 years older than he actually was. He brought with him not only a blessing from his shaman, but also instruction in correct procedure with regards to the peyote. With the greatest solemnity, he imparted these instructions to me.

> Never pick more than you intend to consume in the desert. Waste nothing, and take nothing away with you.
>
> Do not pick the smallest heads of the cactus. Allow them a chance to grow.

Do not pick the largest heads. They are older than you are; they deserve respect.

Cut the plants just below the surface of the soil and cover the stump with earth. Leave the root, so it will re-grow.

Do not pick isolated heads. Search until you find a large number in a concentrated area, and then only take a few. Never cut a whole patch.

Leave an offering, to show your respect and gratitude to the desert.

'Do you think you can do that?'

'Of course.'

So we packed the sleeping bags, borrowed a pair of huge clay cooking pots from Elvira's kitchen, and headed north towards Matehuala, the last town of reasonable size on the edge of Wirikuta. Güera and Chino had other things to do and stayed behind but Oscar, who never seemed quite sure where he was anyway and would happily go anywhere with no luggage on a moment's notice, decided to join us. We hitched a ride in a van, where we sat in the back in total darkness along with several crates of dead chickens, falling over each other at every turn of the road.

ψ Ψ ψ

Matehuala was a hollow-feeling town where people rattled around like loose pieces in a folding chess set and everyone seemed to look lost, no matter how many decades they'd lived there. During the day it just about managed to maintain a charade of self-importance, but as night fell a cold, dry wind would pick up from the *altiplano*, blow the last stray people from the streets, and leave it bleak and abandoned.

We arrived about half an hour before sunset. The van dropped us off under one of the white and slightly pointed arches – like the divorced halves of an oversized McDonald's sign – that mark the entrances to the town. The locals say with no apparent sense of irony that God shall reach down on Judgement Day and lift the entire city up into Heaven by these arches. In the meantime it must be content where it is, in the desolate purgatory of the South Chihuahuan desert, and the arches seem to serve as the city's gesture of defiance to the wilderness outside, letting it know where its territory ends and theirs begins.

Trico could hardly contain his excitement.

'You can *feel* it,' he kept saying, bouncing up and down on the balls of his feet. 'Can't you? Can't you just *feel* it?'

We hitched a ride to a plaza, in the centre of which an understated statue celebrated the hero of some long-forgotten mining disaster. By now it was dark, and the only lights left on the square were the sickly bulbs of two taco stands, like small boats anchored in a midnight bay.

Trico was unfazed. He knew, he said, a guy who owned some cabins where we could surely stay for a night before heading into the desert the next day. The only problem was that he couldn't remember where they were. The plot of land where they were built definitely backed onto the fairground but, as a throb of noise indicated that the fair was currently in Matehuala and we had no intention of paying to enter, we would have to sneak in to look for it. We left Barbon and Oscar with the bags while we went to skirt around the edge of the fairground, looking for a way in. Eventually we found a wooden fence at the end of an alleyway where a couple of boards had rotted and broken to create a small hole. We crouched and ducked through it.

We emerged to surprise a short, dumpy man in a top hat and exceptionally dirty tailcoat who had just finished taking a piss a couple of metres along the same fence. He had the disorientated expression of a mole emerging from underground and a Dalí-esque moustache which he wore like a lucky charm, touching it occasionally as if to reassure himself it was still there. Trico asked him if he knew how to find the cabins. He touched his moustache, thought about it for a moment, and decided that he did.

'First, come with me,' he said. 'You want to smoke?'

He led us between the dark hulks of caravans and generators to a tall, square tent with vertical stripes, like a 1920s bathing tent. Lifting the flap of material at its entrance he motioned to us to duck inside, letting the flap fall behind us. The fabric was thick and heavy and blocked the light completely. The interior was pitch black.

'Sit down, sit down,' the man urged. This was difficult because we couldn't even see each other, let alone any places to sit. I fumbled around below me, came up with an upturned bucket, and sat on it. Nobody said anything for just long enough for the blackness to become suffocating and an irrational panic to start rising in my throat.

'It's very dark in here.' Trico's disembodied voice came from somewhere to my right.

The man lit a pipe and his face flared briefly orange, the shadows of his moustache curving up towards his eyes like tusks.

'Darkness is necessary for a human being,' he said. 'That's why we like to sit in this tent.'

The lighter clicked again and I jumped as a different man's face flared into view, a little to the left of where the first man's face had appeared a few seconds earlier. It looked craggy and demonic and about a hundred years old, appearing as it did unexpectedly from the void, eaten by shadows. I wondered how many more of them there were in there.

'Silence is also necessary for a human being,' the first man continued. 'I haven't heard silence in more time than I can remember. Even at night there are the generators, and the noise of the drunks shouting outside. Sometimes I wonder how much longer I can take it.'

Trico lit the pipe and it was his face's turn to become briefly the only thing in the universe, up-lit and distorted. From outside we heard shrieks and laughter, the heavy throb of machinery, a discordant symphony of piercing electronic tones. A chorus of vendors hawked peanuts and candyfloss and ice cream, their voices adopting the same automated, expressionless tunes of vendors the world over. I felt the pipe pressed into my hand and took my turn to light it. My whole sphere of vision burst briefly into light, then contracted to a glowing ball in the bowl of the pipe before turning back to darkness. I handed the pipe back to the man and he threw back the flap of the tent and led us outside.

'*Adios!*' I called to the man in the tent. There was no reply.

We walked through the shadows into the cacophony of lights and noise that had traumatised the man in the top hat so much. He shuddered theatrically. Yet even here there didn't seem to be enough people to make it feel fully alive, just neon lights and whirring rides screaming hysterically at each other like some warped electronic nightmare. I wondered how different the fairs had looked and sounded back in Doña Maria's day, and whether she would still find such joy there now.

The cabins turned out to be accessible through the back door of a bar at one side of the fairground. The bar was depressing, in the unapologetic way that Mexican bars often are. It had beige walls and minimal furniture, its only decoration a large poster for Tecate beer featuring a girl in a bikini and a cowboy hat. It was the sort of bar that should be dark and smoky, where one's sorrows can be not only drowned but hidden from the world in a dingy corner. But here a glaring bulb in the centre of the ceiling left them exposed and ugly. Three barrel-shaped men with sagging eyes and black moustaches sat hunched around a table, each with a litre of beer in a smudgy brown bottle. At first glance they appeared to be deep in conversation, but when I tried to catch what they were saying I realised that each was expounding on a topic completely unrelated to that of any of the others, not listening to any of them and only barely listening to himself. The talk, it seemed, was a tedious formality which served only to justify their continued drinking. A ropey CD player in the corner emitted an extravagant wailing, no doubt from a man who looked very similar to the men at the table.

The man in the top hat shook hands with both of us and promised us free rides on the rollercoaster later, if we could find him. 'Just ask for Honguito,' he said. (The nickname means 'little mushroom'.)

The cabins were dotted around a small field of mud and worn grass. Dirty and in varying stages of disrepair, they were mostly empty, but a few contained some musty pieces of furniture and were still wired into the electricity mains. The owner, who remembered Trico well, insisted we sleep in the least dilapidated and refused to take any money for it. He proudly pointed out that it even had a working cassette player, before adding as an afterthought: 'I hope you like Black Sabbath and José Alfredo Jiménez. They're the only ones that work.' There was a wooden shed outside partitioned into two cubicles, one of which housed a toilet and the other a rusted showerhead that belched tepid yellow water for exactly 25 minutes between 8.45 and 9.10 a.m.

It was a strange place, not open to the public but rather to a network of indigenous artesanos, freaks and itinerants who knew of it by word of mouth; a few teenage boys from the town used it as an escape from their parents' houses for purposes of smoking or sex. Apart from a couple of these boys, the only person staying there that night was a grey-skinned man of about 30 with long, fluid limbs that seemed to move with an odd, disjointed ripple, like the tentacles of an octopus. Attracted by the luxuriant tones of José Alfredo Jiménez (accompanied by a plaintive squeal from the cassette player), he turned up at our cabin just after we returned with Oscar and Barbon and graciously accepted our invitation to share a caguama. He introduced himself as Merlin. He had, he confided once his tongue had been lubricated with alcohol, previously been a small-time dealer of ecstasy and methamphetamine in the back-alleys of some north Mexican city he refused to name.

'Not worth it, man, not worth the risk, y'know? It's not that I think that you, y'know, but it's that, well, I'm trying to distance myself from that life, you understand?'

He had lived quite happily off his little business for a while, selling only to his friends and trusted acquaintances. But then he had got greedy, started to widen his circle of customers, and before long came to the attention of the police (which was bad), and the cartel men (which was worse).

'They phoned me up, demanding money. I don't know who gave them my number. I didn't have the amount they asked for. I told the guy I didn't sell that much; I didn't have that much money. But he didn't believe me. Or maybe he did, he just didn't care. He told me "You've messed with the wrong people now, *puto*," and then he hung up. I didn't wait around to see what he meant.'

He had left town and disappeared into the desert. He claimed to have stayed there for six months, taking water from small creeks or ranch houses and only returning briefly to the villages when his diet of rice and *nopales* made him ill and he was forced to go in search of other food.

'Alone, man, six months alone. In one week you start to go crazy, y'know? You start seeing faces in cacti and rock formations. In two weeks the faces become your friends; you start to talk to them, start to talk to yourself. In one month every leaf and pebble and wisp of cloud has its own personality. Eventually, you forget your own name, where you came from, where you are and why you came there in the first place. Forget that anything exists outside the desert. You lose yourself completely, and only when you lose yourself completely do you realise who you really are. Who we *all* are.'

'And who are we?'

'*Everything*, man. We are all *everything*.'

He now lived in the smallest of the furnished cabins, for which he gave 20 pesos per day when he had it, and never-fulfilled promises to do various bits of handiwork when he didn't. He talked vaguely of someday going back to the city, but it was obvious the concept held no real appeal for him. In his peculiar way, he seemed happy where he was.

Merlin, I came to realise, was not a particularly unusual character for Matehuala and the surrounding villages. Deserts have always been the last refuge of the lost and the insane, their vast stretches of emptiness promising silence and freedom from the expectations of the achievers, hurriers and demanders who populate the cities. But the desert is rarely the embracing mother they are searching for. The desert of northeast Mexico is a grumpy, belligerent creature. It has no billowing dunes or lush oases, just mile after mile of cracked fawn-coloured dirt, scrubby bushes and indignant cacti. In time all but the most hardened seekers are spat back out and end up making strange half-lives for themselves on the outskirts of towns such as Matehuala, washed up in the no man's land between dreams and reality.

9
Wirikuta

It was Hermano Sol who led us into the desert. He must have been watching us for quite some time, although nobody realised he was there until he fell on my head.

We had spent the day in Matehuala. I sat with Oscar on the plaza, jewellery spread out on a cloth in front of us, while Trico and Barbon juggled in a nearby semáforo. We sold little. Oscar would lose himself in delicate twists of wire as he sculpted a necklace or pair of earrings, and viewed customers as an annoying distraction. Whenever a couple of girls strayed towards us showing a cautious interest in his creations, he would bark '*sin miedo!*' ('without fear!' – meaning 'don't be scared!') at them but in such an irritated tone that their usual reaction was to scurry away. He never seemed sorry to see them go.

When Trico and Barbon returned, they were accompanied by a fair-haired boy with horsey teeth and wildly roving eyes. They had run into him in the semáforo and recognised him from Mexico City. The lifestyle of the malabaristas was such that, across the country, all of them either knew each other or at least had several friends in common. 'People call me Lalo,' the boy told me, on introduction. 'Short for *La Locura* [The Madness].' There was something about the tension in his figure and sudden, emphatic reactions that made me see what they meant.

In the late afternoon we hitched a ride out of Matehuala in the back of a truck that smelt of old straw, the interior of the container lit by stripes of coppery light that slanted through the gaps in its boarded sides. It let us out in one of the tiny settlements that are the last lonely outposts on the edge of the desert. The sun was falling behind the village, the streets empty and the sky crimson, night already lurking in the shadows between the buildings.

'It will be dark in half an hour,' Barbon said. 'I say we sleep under the gazebo on the plaza for the night and walk into the desert in the morning.'

The gazebo was raised a few feet above the level of the plaza, with a peaked roof over the top and a wrought-iron railing around the edge. We sat in a circle in the middle of it, preparing *tortas* from the bread rolls and fresh cheese we had brought from Matehuala market, using the lid from a can of refried beans to cut ragged slices of tomato, onion and avocado. We chewed wordlessly in order to better appreciate the rich, velvety silence of the night, broken only by the purr of a generator somewhere in the village and, very faintly, the far-off cackles of the coyotes from the wilderness beyond.

Hermano Sol must have approached stealthily, padding noiselessly on his bare feet. And Barbon and Oscar, sitting opposite me, must have been deep in meditations of their own, because when he toppled from the railing to land heavily on my shoulders I was caught completely off-guard. Trico and Barbon jumped to their feet to drag him off. He shrugged them off with grunts of irritation.

He was a leathery man of about 50, who, despite the cold of the desert night, wore nothing but a pair of jeans and a blue and white checked flannel shirt, open except for one button at the top which was fastened under his chin. With every gust of wind the sides of the shirt would flap open, revealing a gaunt, hairless chest and a belly whose sagging skin betrayed the ghost of a long-lost paunch. His feet were bare, with prominent purple veins and long, gnarled yellow toenails. He pushed himself up to kneel stiffly in the centre of the circle, bolt upright from the knees, imperious and immovable as if carved from granite, like the statue of some ancient and terrible god. The dim light of the streetlamps cast orange shadows over the hollows of his face. He looked slowly at each of us in turn without moving his head, merely swivelling his black eyes to stare piercingly into ours with an expression of such crazed authority that nobody cared to tell him that he was kneeling on the cheese. We waited for him to say something. Eventually, Barbon tentatively broke the silence.

'Aren't you cold, *amigo*? Do you want a blanket?'

The man swivelled his accusing glare onto Barbon then rigidly and emphatically shook his head. Barbon risked a small chuckle.

'And here we are all huddled up like penguins!'

There was a further pause before the man replied in a rasping voice he seemed unaccustomed to using.

'What cold, brother, what cold? We are here in the presence of our mother earth, this sacred desert, the sacred medicine peyote. We have in our hearts the vibration of all that is beautiful in the universe, as imparted by our friends the stars and our sister moon. We alone have the truth, my brothers, we alone. What cold? What cold?'

Barbon had no answer to this. Behind the man's back, Oscar rolled his eyes. But Lalo was gripped.

'Yes!' he exclaimed, rocking frenziedly backwards and forwards. '*Yes!*' Then, as if the man couldn't hear him, added excitedly to us, 'I *love* this guy!' before turning back to him and asking, 'What's your name, brother?'

'They call me Hermano Sol [Brother Sun],' the man said. He didn't say who 'they' were.

Barbon gave a small shrug, as if to say that he was perfectly capable of playing this game if we really wanted to. He rolled a cigarette from a pouch of loose tobacco he carried with him, while the man continued to talk about the various relatives he had in the surrounding landscape.

'Sacred tobacco, brother?'

Hermano Sol stared at it for a moment before accepting it and taking a deep drag. He then passed it to Lalo. Oscar was closest to him but, as Oscar was by now humming a little tune to himself and fiddling with a loose thread on his trousers as if completely unmoved by the sacredness of the moment, he had clearly decided him unworthy. We shared the sacred cigarette between us. Then, he drew himself to his feet.

'Will you follow me, brothers?'

'Where to?' Barbon asked.

'To the desert, brother, to the desert. Can you not hear it calling? Can you not *feel* it?'

Barbon glanced questioningly at us.

'Come *on*,' Lalo urged, tense and almost shaking with impatience. 'What are we *waiting* for?' Then, before any of us could reply, announced, 'I'm going with you, brother.'

We looked at each other, making 'why not?' faces. The moon was close and shining white, only a day off full. It should be bright enough to see by. We gathered our possessions and set off after Hermano Sol as he led us through the outskirts of the village and into the emptiness of the desert. He strode regally ahead of us, seeming not to notice the sharp stones and cactus spines beneath his bare feet. I was about to ask him how he did it, then thought better of it. (I imagine the answer would have been something along the lines of 'What spines, sister, what spines? We are blessed to feel the sacred prickles of our cousin cacti imparting the energy of the mother earth into our sacred feet...')

We followed him for two hours: far enough for the lights of the village to disappear over the horizon and the bickering coyotes to sound uncomfortably close as they volleyed their high-pitched *yayayayayayas* to each other across the space where we walked. The cacti struck hostile silhouettes in the moonlight. Eventually we arrived at a place where the peyote grew in great tessellated clumps under the *gobernadora* bushes, and Hermano Sol stopped walking.

'Here?'

'Here.'

As we gathered stones and wood to make a fireplace, he vanished into the night as mysteriously as he'd come.

ψ Ψ ψ

In the morning Trico and I walked out from the camp, leaving Lalo stirring the embers of the previous night's fire and Oscar and Barbon gathering dead wood from among the scrub. Unwilling to sabotage the strange geometry of the peyote forests, we were in search of smaller, lonelier plants.

By daylight, Wirikuta looks like the seabed it once was. Strange cacti make shapes like corals. Grey branchless trunks protrude from the earth with explosions of spikes like sea urchins on the end. Squat magueys splay their wide leaves out from ground level, each ending in a threatening, spear-like point. The ground is baked hard and scattered with rocks, small pebbles and dead wood. The *gobernadora* bushes that carpet it look from a distance soft and delicate, like fronds of seaweed, from closer up like fragile bundles of twigs, but when you brush against them turn out to be tenaciously tough and scratchy. Smaller cacti nestle among the stones and scrub like sea anemones, looking spongy and defenceless until you are fool enough to touch them. Once, I thoughtlessly bent to examine a round one covered in pretty yellow dots, and found my fingers carpeted in tiny hairs that itched furiously and were all but impossible to extract. The landscape is desolate and never-ending, giving a surreal perspective to a few clumps of mountains on the distant horizon which stand out from the surrounding flatness as if carelessly dropped there, their every ridge and valley highlighted by the play of sunlight and shadow.

'In Huichol legend,' Trico said, 'this land is where the sacred blue deer once ran across the earth, leaving the peyote in its footprints. On some of the plants, the shape of the segments still resembles the print of a deer's hoof.'

The peyotes tend to lie half-hidden, peeking out shyly from the roots of the *gobernadora* bushes. We crouched and with our fingers, gently brushed away the veils of dust which coated their faces and dug our nails under their plump cheeks, scraping away the dirt and small pebbles around them until they stood out ripe and bare. Under the bulbous head, they tapered to a conical root worming down into the earth. Placing a tough cotton thread along the backs of their necks, we decapitated them with a single slicing cut, leaving the root behind. The heads split easily into radial segments and could then be cleaned by prising out the tufts of hair with fingernails.

'Eat your first one raw,' Trico instructed me. 'We'll make a tea later with the ones we take back to the camp. But the first one you should taste.'

Before I ate it, I sat cross-legged among the cacti, opposite Trico, and he took my hand in the grip that has become one of the symbols of the Mexican New Age movement. You each curl the four fingers of your right hand towards the palm to make a hook with which you clasp the other person's hooked four fingers. As you both continue to curl your fingers as if making a fist, your hands roll into each other and you wrap your thumb around the outside of the other person's forefinger. Seen from above, your two hands form a spiral. This, so they say, represents the Mayan *Hunab Ku*: the centre of the galaxy, and the gateway to galaxies beyond. You then detach your index finger from the spiral, and point it outwards into the solar plexus of the other person. This represents the Mayan expression *in lak'ech*, which the Mexican philosopher Domingo Martínez Parédez translated as '*tú eres mi otro yo*', or 'you are my other I'. All of these interpretations are disputed, the exact details of the ancient Mesoamerican beliefs having long since been lost, but the sentiment is undeniably beautiful.

'*Buen viaje*, Cat,' Trico said. Good journey.

I popped the segments into my mouth. They were gritty with dirt, and so bitter I struggled to chew them. Swallowing almost made me retch. Trico laughed at the expression on my face.

'Keep chewing! Really taste it. This is one of the most precious things you will take from Mexico. Appreciate it.'

We walked onwards, the vastness of the boundless earth humming from every horizon to build into a rich and silent chord resonating into the sky. And as I kept chewing, it began to crystallise.

I can think of no other way to describe it. My perception deepened in a way that made normal vision seem two-dimensional, and any object I focussed on would become the centre of the universe, from which all surrounding matter radiated outwards in geometric mandalas of infinite complexity, like snowflakes under a microscope, but continually expanding. Every sense tingled. The spectrum of visible light extended, allowing me to see great sweeps of ultra-violet beaming through the space around me, and my ears seemed to be picking up an impossibly high-pitched symphony of minute vibrations and insect voices. My legs carried me forwards, and I heard Trico's voice clear but far away telling me of rituals in which one would walk alone for four days through the desert, eating and drinking nothing but peyote. The plant contains enough water to keep you alive, but the quantities you must eat ensure that you float constantly on a plane of reality far removed from any that you have previously known...

Hours later, back at the camp, I took a notebook and attempted to describe it. The visions had started to lessen in intensity, but were still very much present. Reading it now, it is a blend of utterly incomprehensible and surprisingly lucid. At times the writing wanders away in more senses than one, both off the lines of the page to branch out in strange and spiky directions of its own, and also out of anything recognisable as the English language. But in-between these interludes, I appear to scold myself, and force myself to return to straight lines and grammar. In those bits, this is what it says:

> I see space as an intricate web of points. Each point has a gossamer-fine thread of colour linking it to every other point. A barely touchable matrix containing illusions of other things that aren't there. Everything has itself and then another, finer self projected on a different layer of reality both behind and in front. Many, in infinite layers of regression... Too many little conscious spaces. Hard to stop moving in-between perspectives, and how the world would look if I were a fly. Or a colour. Or a thread of music... Keep losing myself. Try to follow one idea, but can't. Distract myself with another point or thread or colour and try to trap it in one second of my thought but nothing will flow under inspection. Each thread of thought breaks itself up over and over and I chase the fragments of what it was but they keep dividing and everything I catch is only a half of a half of a half of what it was... Everything is too delicate to touch with eyes. Can't speak or touch with words. Words are like hands over cacti. They brush over points which are too fine to touch...

ψ Ψ ψ

In the evening, we made a tea with the plants we had collected, sweetening the brew with segments of orange, sticks of cinnamon, and chunks carved off a cone of the hard cane sugar known in Mexico as *piloncillo*. We passed the pot between us, its base still blackened from the fire, its steam rising in thick tendrils to mingle with the wood smoke and shroud the emerging stars.

Night deepened, the darkness swelling around us, leaving our globe of amber firelight drifting in the void. We talked in murmurs, barely louder than the whispering and spitting of the flames.

As the tea soaked into my brain and the blackness became a sheet of unnamed colours, I walked away from the fire to lie spreadeagled on the earth, gazing up at the stars. Trico followed and lay down beside me. Softly, we heard Barbon's voice singing by the fire.

'...*Gran bufalo blanco*
Símbolo de mi madre tierra
Cubreme con tu manto
Cuándo yo muera...'

...Great white buffalo
Symbol of my mother earth
Cover me with your mantle
When I die...

Away from the fire, my eyes adjusted to the darkness and the stars began to multiply, breeding exponentially like bacteria in the centre of my vision, even as they rushed outwards towards the edges of the earth, and downwards to fleck my face like raindrops with tingling pinpricks of light. I struggled to find the words to share it with Trico.

'*Hunab Ku,*' I said.

He smiled.

Closer to the horizon, the moon hung full and swollen with light, encircled in a soft rainbow halo.

'Do you know the Aztec legend of the moon?' he asked.

There are many different Aztec legends of the moon, of varying degrees of bloodthirstiness. 'Tell me.'

'There were four ages of the earth before the one we are in now, but they were all destroyed because the gods were not happy with the humans they had created. For the fifth age, the Age of Movement, the plumed serpent Quetzalcoatl made new humans out of *maíz*, the staple of Mexican life. Those are the Mexican people: people of the corn. But for the new world to survive, it needed a sun to light it. To create the sun, one of the gods would have to sacrifice himself by jumping into a fire, but none of them would volunteer. Eventually, the gods chose the proud and boastful god Tecciztecatl to be the sun, and the small and humble god Nanahuatzin to be the moon.

'Both gods approached the fire. But Tecciztecatl was frightened by the flames, and would not jump. Eventually, Nanahuatzin threw himself into the fire, and so he became the sun.

'Tecciztecatl was ashamed that he had been shown to be a coward by the weakest of all the gods, so to regain his pride, he jumped into the fire after Nanahuatzin. Now there were two suns. The gods could not allow that, and would not permit Tecciztecatl to steal the glory that Nanahuatzin had won by his bravery. So to darken Tecciztecatl's glow, they threw a rabbit in his face.'

'... A *rabbit?*' I was tickled by the image. It was like something out of Monty Python, the machismo of the story suddenly collapsing into silliness – or perhaps a pleasing dash of Mexican surrealism. 'Why a rabbit?'

'Look! Can't you see it?'

He pointed up at the moon. From Mexico's angle, and with a certain degree of imagination, the craters on the moon can indeed be seen to take the shape of a rabbit.

We were silent for a moment, lost in our own thoughts. Then I began to see lights brighter than stars dancing in the sky. They would hover in one place for a short while, wavering slightly and taking on tints of red or green. Then, in a sudden movement too fast to register, they would flash across the sky to reappear in a new position, flickering and changing colour as before. At first, I thought they must be a hallucination from the tea we had just drunk, but when I glanced over at Trico I could see that he was watching them as well. These strange lights are a well-known phenomenon across the desert of north Mexico, whose cause has still not been explained.

'What do you think they are?' I asked him. His lips curled into a quixotic smile, driving the dimples into his cheeks. His eyes glittered.

'*Naves espaciales.*' Spaceships.

'If a spaceship landed here right now,' I said, 'and the aliens told you that you could go with them and travel through the stars to other planets and galaxies, but if you did then you could never come back to earth – would you go?'

Without hesitation: 'Of course.'

ψ Ψ ψ

We stayed in the desert for five days. We had dragged with us a huge bag of food we had brought from Matehuala, along with two 20-litre *garafones* of water. Until our supplies ran out, there seemed no reason to leave.

Each of us settled into our own roles in the camp. Oscar would disappear for many hours each day to wander alone through the desert. Occasionally we would spot him, far in the distance, prancing across the horizon with peculiar, awkward hops like a baby antelope. He would always return laden with great bundles of firewood tied up in the sleeves of a jumper, as gruff and prickly as ever.

Barbon and Trico took on most of the cooking duties, brewing up stews of vegetables with rice or soya in richly spiced sauces that bubbled over the sides of the clay *olla* to fizz and spit on the fire. They made soups as well, into which they carved chunks of potato and chilli, and porridge in the morning with fruit, cinnamon and piloncillo. In between meals, Barbon occupied himself principally with yoga and meditation, Trico with malabares, angling himself towards whichever horizon struck him as the most beautiful at that moment.

I would chop vegetables and wash the plates and pots, striving to use as little of the precious water as possible. In the first couple of days I spent my free time writing, walking or meditating until, on the third day, I picked up Trico's clubs and realised, with a sudden revelation, that I could juggle.

I had more or less mastered the basic juggling pattern in San Luis, but never with much finesse. I seemed unable to choose or predict where each club would fall, and would be tense and awkward as I struggled to catch them, my face contorting in concentration. But after a mug of peyote tea, the movement of the club seemed predetermined, I would see its path before it fell, and my hand would be there to meet it. I cannot explain how this works, although I imagine that the Huichol would not find it surprising. Excited, Trico started to teach me tricks. Within a few hours, I had learnt double-spins, under-arm throws, columns (two clubs in one hand), and the Mills' Mess – a pattern in which the arms are continually crossed and re-crossed – so named because when its inventor, Steve Mills, attempted to teach it to a group of proficient jugglers at the 1975 International Juggling Convention in Los Angeles, they declared in frustration: 'This is a mess!'

Trico was astonished. 'I never thought anyone could learn Mills' Mess so quickly,' he said – before adding, lest I got too cocky, 'especially someone who took weeks just to get the bloody *cascada*.'

From then on, I spent several hours a day juggling. Once I got over the thrill that I could actually do it, I found it unexpectedly meditative. Just as Indian yogis chant mantras to obliterate thought and focus the mind during meditation, I found the rhythmic and repetitive actions of juggling a kind of physical mantra, allowing the brain to transcend trivial worries or reflections and be at peace with itself.

Although Lalo was also a skilled juggler, he did not practise during our time in the desert. Nor did he walk, or do anything much at all, beyond his bit to keep the fire stoked and the camp running. He seemed to view all such things as distractions from his main purpose for being there: thinking, and eating peyote.

Lalo ate peyote with the same crazed intensity with which he did everything else. He spurned tea or sweeteners, preferring to stuff his mouth with the segments until he resembled an irate hamster, and then chew doggedly for half an hour or more while staring intently into the fire. With every swallow, he would replenish his bulging cheeks with fresh pieces. One day, after a particularly foul swallow, he suddenly gagged, and spat the full mouthful out into the fire. Barbon looked up at him, and shook his head solemnly.

'Don't disrespect, Lalo,' was all he said. During the night, Lalo rolled too close to the fire, and a stray spark fell onto his sleeping bag and set it alight. By the time the heat woke him, it had burnt a wide hole in the fabric and singed the side of his leg. Barbon was in no doubt that the two incidents were connected. Lalo refused to accept this, but I noticed that he behaved more calmly, and ate less peyote after that.

During the afternoon of the following day, he pulled from his bag a set of dog-eared books and pamphlets and, spreading them open and examining them intently, began to scribble symbols and figures in a small notebook.

'What are you doing?' I asked.

'Mayan astrology. I don't know much yet; they have several different calendars representing movements of astrological bodies and different cycles of time, so making predictions is very complicated. But I'm trying to learn.'

'What are you working out there?'

'The *kin maya* for some people I know. I suppose it's kind of like a star sign. But because the Mayan calendar is more complicated and more attuned to the movements of the stars and planets than the Western one, it's much more accurate. Tell me your date and year of birth and I can work out yours.'

I told him. Scribbling illegible pencil marks in his notebook, he converted it into a date in the Mayan calendar before performing a long series of sums. The whole process took about ten minutes. Finally, he drew five symbols on a fresh page of the notebook: one in the middle, with four more in a cross shape around it. He ripped the page out and handed it to me.

'The one at the top represents your guide: the person or energy that guides your learning and development, towards which you are progressing. The one on the right represents the energy that will complement your own in any situation. The one on the left represents the energy that opposes or obstructs you – although, as your opposite, it can also have the most to teach you. The one on the bottom represents your occult energy, which you can only discover through self-transcendence. The one in the middle is you.'

'What am I?'

'*Serpiente roja.*' Red serpent.

'What does it mean?'

'It has to do with survival, and constant self-recreation. Just as a snake changes its skin, you are always changing yourself and your life, seeking out adventure and danger in order to destroy your old structures and rebuild yourself anew.' I thought about it, immediately recognising myself in the description and wondering whether it was so vague that everyone would recognise themselves in it. Lalo paused, and I saw his eyes wander to the slender tattooed serpent coiled around my wrist.

'It's interesting you have that. Why did you make that?'

I looked at it. It was slightly crooked, done on an impulse a couple of years previously on the opposite side of the world, but its meaning had done nothing but increase for me since the day it was made. I had been staying at the time in a small community of travellers in Calcutta. The man who introduced me to the tattooist was a beefy European skinhead in his late forties with a fake passport, dozens of tattoos and a scar left by a bullet in one arm. He said he was wanted in his home country, for a crime that would probably get him at least 10 years in prison, if not life. He said he believed that he deserved to suffer for what he had done, but rather than going back and wasting all those years in jail he had fled to Calcutta, where he was doing a secular penance for his crime by spending his days wandering the streets of a city notorious for its poverty, collecting the sick and dying and carrying them to the hospices where they could get medicine and relief for their pain. Sometimes he would find people being eaten by rats or maggots while they were still alive. On those days I would find him in the evening, sobbing into his beer. I was intrigued by him. I had never before met someone who so thoroughly confounded my ideas of what constituted a good person, or an honourable life.

One day I went with him to a basement in a Calcutta back street, where he was planning to add to his vast collection of tattoos. The tattooist asked me if I wanted one as well. Seeing that he worked well and had rigorous hygiene standards, I accepted. I rejected all of the designs in the book he showed me and sketched my own on a scrap of paper. It was no great artwork, but I knew what I wanted. 'It was inspired by a myth I read in the *Ramayana* – one of the Hindu holy books. In the *Ramayana* they speak of three worlds. Earth is the realm of men. Heaven is the realm of the gods. The third world is the *naga* kingdoms, which are ruled over by serpent lords called 'naga'. But it isn't hell. It is described as an underworld more beautiful than heaven, which is used various times throughout the story as a refuge by those who, for whatever reason, cannot remain in the realms of gods or men. The demons flee there when they are exiled from the kingdom of Lanka. But so do the mystics and prophets when they face danger on the earth.'

Although my reading of the story was simplistic, I had been deeply struck by the idea: a parallel reality where both vanquished demons and misunderstood prophets sought shelter. We draw our own meanings from mythology, and in my fanciful interpretation the naga kingdoms were a symbol for 'alternative' communities around the world, with the mélange of freaks and itinerants who inhabit them. Like the naga kingdoms, these communities often feel like a refuge for all those who, for whatever reason, don't fit into 'normal' society. They contain plenty of lunatics, junkies and no-hopers. But they also contain people who seem genuinely inspired, daring to live differently and forge an alternative reality, dreaming of a better world. And many more people who walk a delicate line between the two, combining elements of both in proportions that are never quite clear.

I had always been attracted to those communities and lifestyles in which the nature of reality, and the problem of how best to live, were constantly under question. Yet I also recognised how easy it would be to lose yourself there, jumbled up among the devils and the saints, the lost and the mad and the maybe-enlightened. How do you tell which is which? Or which you are? That's why I had tattooed the snake – my own little naga. Just to remind myself that the difference between good and evil, heaven and hell, or madness and sanity, was never as obvious as we like to think. To keep questioning.

I couldn't then have found the words in Spanish to explain all of that to Lalo. But he smiled, a little dreamily, at the story of the naga kingdoms and I think, perhaps, he understood.

ψ Ψ ψ

When the last drop of water fell from the last *garafón*, we knew it was time to leave. We packed our things, gathered every scrap of our rubbish, and scattered the stones and ash from the fire. We left no sign that we had ever been there except, according to the instruction of Barbon's shaman, a small altar built of rocks, on which we placed a few pieces of quartz crystals and a handful of corn. Then we trekked back to the village, pausing on the periphery to fill bin bags with the rubbish that forms a tide-mark around most desert settlements. Many locals see the desert as a barren wasteland, good for little more than dumping rubbish. I felt honoured and grateful to have experienced it with people who loved it enough to show me its beauty.

We hitched a ride to Matehuala in the back of a pickup. Trico pointed through the dirty rear window into the cab.

'Look. Someone else coming from the desert.'

The man in the passenger seat was dressed all in white, with brightly coloured embroidery around the hems of his simple cloth shirt. I recognised it as Huichol traditional dress.

The Huichol, also hitchhiking, disembarked in another village before we arrived in Matehuala. He looked at us quizzically.

'*Peyoteros?*' he asked.

We nodded, and I felt a little uncomfortable.

'*No traen nada?*' You are not carrying anything?

We shook our heads.

'*No traemos nada,*' Barbon told him. '*Lo que crece en el desierto se queda en el desierto.*' What grows in the desert stays in the desert.

He smiled before turning away.

10
Playing the Semáforos

~~✺~~

On our return to San Luis, I made my debut performance at a semáforo. It was also the first time I ever spun fire.

I am not particularly proud of this incident. Trico and Chino were spinning fire staff in a semáforo outside a girls' school, and the crowd of lip-glossed spectators they had gathered had brought out an unfortunate side of all of our characters. Tricopsycho was in his element.

'Hey, girls, this trick is for you!' he would call out to them, provoking a flurry of urgent giggling. 'It's one I learnt in France!' (Trico had never left Mexico in his life.) Chino, who had been chatting to the girls between red lights, was too lovesick to be playing his best and Trico, realising this, was strutting around with his chest thrown out like a peacock in season, the undisputed star of the show. Occasionally he would pause to tell me that I had better watch out because, as I could see, he had many admirers.

I had been practising on the rooftop since I first arrived back in San Luis, and a few days previously Trico had helped me make my own fire poi out of dog chains, wire and tightly rolled denim, but I still hadn't played with them while lit. Sitting on a wall, watching the scene with narrowed eyes, I was making rapid calculations.

Was I very good at spinning poi? No. Was I good enough to do it for 50 seconds with fire without setting myself alight? Possibly. If I managed it, would the girls know enough about poi to realise that my standard wasn't very high? Probably not. Would a successful performance show that bunch of short-skirted teenagers that I held the cards in this semáforo? Definitely. Was this the most mature and sensible way to deal with the situation? Probably not. Was I going to do it anyway? Yes.

As Trico and Chino did the charol, I soaked my poi in gasoline and shook off the excess (an essential stage in the process if you don't want to spray everyone in the vicinity with petrol while playing). By the time they had got back and the light was turning red again, I was ready. Chino, cocking an eyebrow at Trico, gave me a light.

I wish I could say that the performance was an unqualified success, but I suspect that it more closely resembled a frantic attempt to swat away a pair of persistent flaming bees than the gracefully ethereal dance I had been aiming for. I was nervous of the fire, surprised by the roar of the burning gasoline flying past my ears, and made tense and awkward by the knowledge that everyone in the crowded street was looking at me. To compound my embarrassment, I was so preoccupied with not tangling the chains around my body or hitting myself on the head that I completely forgot to count the seconds of the semáforo and only realised my time was up when I found myself marooned in a rising tide of honking traffic and had to run back to the pavement without collecting a single peso.

Whether I succeeded in impressing the girls, I'm not too sure. But it hardly seemed to matter. Trico and Chino knew me well enough to understand what the attempt had cost me and had nothing but rapturous praise. Seeing the scepticism on my face, Chino added kindly: 'Everyone's a bit nervous on the first semáforo. Don't worry. It will get easier.'

Playing semáforos made a huge difference to my relationship with the banda. Before, I had felt that I was speaking a different language twice over. Since leaving Master in Durango I hadn't had a single conversation in English, and I was struggling with the loss of personality that is familiar to anyone who has learnt a second language at a later stage than childhood. I had never realised how dependent I was on words to communicate not only what I wanted to say, but also who I was. I became convinced that my perceived personality must reflect my conversation: slow, unconfident and limited. Attempting to solve the problem by adopting wild gestures and facial expressions in place of words had so far only succeeded in earning me the nickname '*la loquita*' – 'the little crazy girl'. Although I comforted myself with the thought that 'crazed' was at least better than 'boring', it couldn't win me the true friendship and understanding that can only be built through communication. In that, I was lagging sadly behind. I coped fairly well in one-on-one exchanges because they allowed me time to think, but in a large group conversation would flow faster than I felt able to keep up with, and I would frequently lapse into long silences. The effect was exacerbated by the fact that the most common topics of conversation were circus skills and semáforos, neither of which I had much to say about in any language. At times, it was hard not to feel that I simply didn't belong there.

As soon as I started to play semáforos, everything changed. It not only gave me some kudos within the group, but also gave me something easy to talk about. I felt my social disadvantage shrink as my experience grew.

There are more things to consider when playing the semáforos than one would imagine. The first step is to get the gasoline. This is easy enough; the only complication is that a lot of petrol stations won't sell it to you unless you have a particular kind of container, preferably one of the opaque plastic ones that usually contain engine oil. These are often to be found in the rubbish bins next to the petrol pumps, so you have to rummage through the crisp packets and food scraps in the bins until you come up with something appropriate. (This was humiliating at first, so I'd try to wait for a moment when there were no cars at the pumps and I'd have as few witnesses as possible. After the first few times I got used to it and stopped caring.) Then you have a further rummage for a plastic bottle, preferably two-litre, which you cut in half in order to fill it with petrol at the semáforo and use it to soak your wicks. I once made the mistake of trying to use a large polystyrene cup before discovering that polystyrene dissolves on contact with gasoline.

With a couple of litres of petrol and a container ready for soaking, the next step is to find a good semáforo. One with several lanes of traffic has the advantage of maximising the number of spectators with an unobstructed view. But it can also cause difficulties with the charol, as it requires a certain amount of running and weaving between cars to pass by all the windows. If you fail to time it right you find yourself stranded in the middle of the road as the lights turn green, frantically dodging traffic as you struggle back to the pavement, your shame broadcast to the street by a chorus of jeering horns. This is particularly frustrating if a coin is still being waved at you out of a window two lanes across and you are faced with the choice of either holding everyone up and making a run for it, or watching the apologetic shrug as the coin is withdrawn and your potential benefactor sails off across the intersection, leaving you in a bad mood for at least the next three red lights. If the twin glints of silver and gold indicate that it's a 10-peso coin (the most you are ever likely to get from any one car) you shout desperately, '*Avéntalo, avéntalo!*' (Throw it, throw it!), and then have to waste the first few seconds of the next red light searching for it in the gutter or between the wheels of waiting cars. If working alone, therefore, a semáforo with two lanes is generally the best option. The wider semáforos are better saved for when working in pairs or small groups.

Having found a semáforo of appropriate size and with a reasonable volume of traffic, you then stand and watch it for a couple of minutes, counting the number of seconds that the light stays red. Under 45 is no good, as you need to allow at least 10 to 15 seconds (depending on amount of traffic and width of semáforo) to collect the money, and a 30-second show is barely a show at all. A 50-second red is just about acceptable; between one minute and one minute fifteen is ideal. You then have to remember how long to allow for your performance, and count the seconds while playing. When you are distracted and dizzy with fire, fumes, adrenaline and concentration, this isn't as easy as it sounds.

For a novice, the first 10 minutes at a semáforo are frequently miserable. You are awkward and tentative, and it shows. Eyes remain averted. Windows remain closed. On the street you have no stage to validate you, no trappings of drama to hide behind. Alone in an unforgiving landscape of hostile buildings and grumbling traffic, you feel lonely and exposed.

But then slowly, a small miracle starts to happen. Sometimes it starts with the first smile, or the first satisfying heaviness of a 10-peso coin. Other times it seems that the energy of the fire itself possesses you, transports you, and suddenly your body has a mind of its own, moving in ways you'd never thought of, making shapes that are traced in flame and then gone, faster than you can register what they are. Road, cars, buildings, the whole drab reality of the intersection vanishes and all you see is whirling light, all you hear is the continuous whoosh of burning gasoline. You are dimly aware of the life of the city in constant flux around you and, in a strange role reversal, you become the one fixed point in this age of movement. And then you disappear.

This is the secret joy of the semáforos. They are the perfect arena for a shy person to become a performer. They grant you anonymity. The conveyor belt of the city traffic system shuffles your faceless audience past in conveniently timed batches, allowing you to reinvent yourself with each red light. Mistakes of previous semáforos are unimportant. The next 50 seconds are all that matter. You think you are not a natural performer? Who are 'you'? 'You' no longer exist; 'you' are as fluid as your audience. 'You' will be gone in a minute's time. In the semáforo, you not only transcend the mundane ugliness of your environment, you transcend yourself.

And it shows. At least, I assume it does. Because suddenly, windows open. You see the faces you pass as a blur of white teeth and warm eyes. Children squeal and bounce in their seats. Total strangers press coins into your hands and – most bewildering and thrilling of all – thank you. And you grin dazedly as the cars move away, shouting '*gracias!*' aimlessly as your unknown benefactors slip off into the night.

After a couple of hours of breathing clouds of exhaust and gasoline fumes your eyes water, your chest aches, and a furtive probing of the gunk building up in your nose reveals it to be black and the consistency of dried glue. But by then you don't care because you're high on the buzz of fire and endorphins (or is it the gasoline?), your bag is heavy with coins you barely remember collecting, and in your mind you're already savouring the cold beer you'll buy at the first shop you walk past. And invariably that beer is the best you ever tasted – so good you need another one, just to relive the joy of it, and another and another until the bulging sack of coins is no longer so heavy and you solemnly count the remainder of it and set it aside for breakfast the next morning.

It was only once I started playing semáforos that I became fully sympathetic to the heavy drinking of the malabaristas. Alcohol is the only thing that takes away the taste of gasoline, and you have to keep playing semáforos to procure the money for more alcohol. It is a vicious circle, but not an unpleasant one, and after a while it becomes increasingly inconceivable to think of doing anything else.

ψ ψ ψ

The other semáforo performers were a mixed bunch. In general, they would claim semáforos on a first-come-first-served basis. There was a certain etiquette though, and to hog a prime location during peak hours for several days in a row was considered bad form. There were only a few exceptions to this rule, and these were for people whose priority right to a particular semáforo was already firmly established and clearly justifiable.

There was, for instance, a semáforo not far from the city centre that was the undisputed territory of a wizened cripple who made his living as a fire breather. Seated in a rickety wheelchair with a bottle of gasoline between his knees and a homemade fire torch in his hand, he would wheel himself onto the semáforo at each red light, take a swig of gasoline, and blow a long plume of flame across the street. The whole act took about ten seconds, which was fortunate because his lack of functioning legs put him at quite a disadvantage when it came to the charol. Everyone who regularly passed his semáforo must have seen him a thousand times, but still they continued to donate. There seemed to exist an unspoken consensus that, in recognition of his initiative and resilience in the face of terrible circumstances, contributions to him were a moral obligation. This was an attitude I became familiar with in Mexico. The elderly and the infirm were generally looked after by their families, and there was little state protection for those who weren't. Many were dependent on donations. In supermarkets, for instance, there would be a person packing the shopping at every till. The vast majority of these people were over 70. They were unpaid, and took home only what people gave in tips. With fumbling fingers, they usually packed shopping more slowly than the customer could have done it on their own. Yet I never saw anyone reject the service, or fail to tip.

I would have loved to know how the crippled fire-breather had ended up working the semáforo, but unfortunately his teeth and throat had been so eroded by years of swilling petrol around them that it was impossible to understand a word he said. He always seemed in good spirits though, and would wave cheerily at us any time we walked past, baring his blackened gums in a friendly smile of greeting.

'Can you breathe fire?' I asked Trico once.

He snorted. 'Of course I can. It's just spitting. I don't, though.'

'Why not?'

'It's really bad for you to do it with gasoline. Destroys your throat and lungs. Besides, gasoline is a volatile fuel; there's a risk it can back-burn down your throat. There are fuels that you can use more safely, but they're too expensive to use in the semáforos.'

It was for this reason that the malabaristas tended to look down on the *tragafuegos* (fire-breathers). It was seen as an inferior type of performance, only done by those who didn't have the skill to do anything else or the dedication to learn. Apart from the cripple (who had an obvious excuse), the *tragafuegos* were seen as little better than the kids who would stand on the semáforo throwing a single ball from hand to hand: mere beggars and junkies, asking for charity. The malabaristas, by contrast, had a strict work ethic and were perfectionists when it came to the quality of their performances. They would spend several hours a day practising and many of them would refuse to do a charol if they felt a particular semáforo performance had been substandard. I'm not sure whether the difference was fully appreciated by the spectators, but the hierarchy was keenly felt in semáforo society.

There were other types of performers as well: clowns, living statues, acrobats and magicians. There was a pair I used to see around San Luis who did a peculiar act involving a ball, a hoop, a bag, a whistle and a step-ladder that I could never quite see the point of. As far as I could tell, the main talking point was that one was very fat and one was very thin, and both were bald, half-naked and painted silver. Trico didn't approve of that one either.

'The paint they use makes you sick if you leave it on too long,' he told me. 'It's alright as long as you remove it every night, but you need a special cleanser to get it off which is quite expensive, so generally they don't.'

I imagined their domestic life: shopping, eating dinner and sleeping with their girlfriends, all while silver and hairless like sci-fi aliens, and (if Trico was to be believed) slowly poisoning themselves with toxic paint.

ψ Ψ ψ

Sometimes, the most talented of the malabaristas would be spotted in the semáforos and invited to do a private performance. Back in Durango, some of the banda had done a show for the opening of the Faculty of Law in Durango University. In San Luis, they did a full cabaret, complete with outrageous harlequin costumes, for the engagement party of the son of one of the richest local families. These sorts of invitations always caused great excitement. Firstly, because they gave an opportunity for creative expression which was severely limited by the short time slots of the semáforos. Secondly, because the pay was good, allowing a riotous drinking bout afterwards. (Money was never saved for longer than 24 hours or so, except for a very specific purpose such as the purchase of new juggling clubs. None of the malabaristas I knew had a bank account, and saving money just for the sake of it struck them as both selfish and illogical.) Thirdly, I think, because it was a confirmation of what they always believed: that their art really did have value.

One day, Trico was spotted in the semáforo by a professor from the University of San Luis Potosí and invited to give a juggling class to a group of students. To his elation, he was paid a fee of 1,000 pesos. It was the largest amount of money I'd ever known him to have at any one time.

'A thousand pesos! That's a lot of caguamas, Trico,' I told him. He gave me a disapproving look. Trico had never quite got his head around the British style of teasing.

'Don't be silly,' he told me sternly. 'I wouldn't waste a thousand pesos on caguamas.'

I had never heard Trico describe any amount of expenditure on caguamas as a waste before. I was intrigued.

'What are you going to spend it on?'

'Something I've been wanting for a very long time. At least three years.' His eyes gleamed with excitement. '*Una jirafa.*'

I wasn't sure I'd heard him right.

'A giraffe?'

'Yes.'

I ran quickly through a mental list of possible questions, trying to decide which sounded the least ignorant. It wasn't much of a choice.

'What do you want a giraffe for?'

He gave me the impatient look that he reserved for when I'd said something particularly stupid.

'To ride it, of course. What else would I do with it?'

'Um, OK.'

I was silent for a moment, apprehensive that whatever I said next would be met with equal scorn. Eventually, my curiosity got the better of me.

'Where are you going to get a giraffe from?'

'That's what I've been trying to work out. You can't buy them in Mexico.'

'I didn't think so.'

'You can order them over the internet, but they take weeks to arrive. Besides, you need a bank account. And I'm pretty sure it would cost more than a thousand pesos.'

'I imagine it would.'

'But I'm thinking I could probably *make* one.' Seeing the look on my face, he added hastily: 'It wouldn't be a *real* one of course. But it would do for now. A thousand pesos should be enough for the materials. And I can get Rustico to help me with the welding.'

I opened my mouth, and then closed it again. I would find out soon enough.

Rustico was Trico's uncle. He owned a small workshop just down the street, and spent about 20 per cent of the time working and 80 per cent of the time drinking, along with most of the other men under 50 in the barrio. A cheerful bunch, they were usually to be found gathered in a storage room off the street, seated on crates or upturned buckets amidst a clutter of brooms and broken machinery. As they were usually drunk and all seemed to be related in some way, I had come to think of them as the San Luis drunk uncles. They were, however, a distinctly higher calibre of drunk uncle than the one in Chihuahua. Not only did they have jobs (at which they must secretly have worked pretty hard to be able to afford all that alcohol) and the ability to form coherent sentences, but they practised their alcoholism with a flair that raised it practically to the level of an art form. Using a board balanced on crates as a table, they would put in the extra time and effort to turn their tequilas into *vampiros* and their beers into *micheladas* – a sort of beer cocktail made with tomato and clam juice, lime, salt, *salsa valentina* and soy sauce which is much, much more pleasant than it sounds. If truly inspired, they would even frost the rims of their plastic cups with lime juice and salt. They were also fiercely loyal to the other residents of the barrio, and could be relied on to help in any situation.

Early the next morning Trico disappeared into Rustico's workshop and didn't emerge for the rest of the day, except to run over the road every half hour or so to fetch another caguama. With each trip, he got progressively more excited.

'It's looking incredible!' he would tell me. 'Even better than I hoped! Just wait until you see it!'

At five o'clock he finally emerged: sweaty, dirty, but beaming from ear to ear. He was wheeling before him a unicycle several inches taller than he was. Its pedals were at chest height, connected to the wheel by a bike chain. He had painted it pillar box red, with silver splodges. It had a few tumescent lumps where the pieces had been welded together, but other than that looked remarkably professional.

'Isn't she *beautiful?*' he cooed. I noticed that, like a ship, 'it' had become a 'she'. 'My very own giraffe unicycle!'

He tenderly stroked the unicycle's silver-blotched body.

'Loquita,' he said, without taking his eyes off it. 'Let me introduce you to... *La Flaca.*'

'Flaca' means 'skinny girl'.

I could already see that Flaca and I were going to have problems.

11
La Migra

I still maintain that if it hadn't been for Flaca, Hele and I would never have ended up in jail.

Flaca was only a couple of weeks old when Hele swept onto the scene, heartbroken but defiant, having finally accepted that the renovation job required to turn Jorge into the man of her dreams was too grand a task even for her. Despite arriving with very little luggage and six months' worth of grievances, she still managed to convey the impression that this was all part of the plan. 'I have plenty of better things to be doing than looking after some useless man,' she declared, accepting the caguama Trico passed her and taking an elegant sip. 'Besides, Chihuahua is a dump. San Luis has culture, charm. It's really where I wanted to be all along.'

Hele had a fascinating ability to make all of life feel like a telenovela to which only she had the script. She blazed from one drama to another with indomitable zeal, punctuated by theatrical flares of emotion which would scorch all around her with their intensity whilst leaving her undiminished. She was the sort of person who could weep stormily for half an hour without a single blotch or trace of puffiness marring her alabaster face. After a few days in San Luis, she seemed more at home in Trico's house than I felt after many weeks and was rapidly attracting a phalanx of devoted admirers.

One Saturday evening not long after her arrival, we were preparing to go to a trance party which Trico had been looking forward to for weeks. He was determined that we should play at least three hours of semáforos before going in order to have enough money to enjoy it in style. At dusk, the three of us trooped down to a big intersection where we knew the takings would be good. Trico and I had played several times before at this semáforo, but never since the arrival of La Flaca.

By then Trico was quite comfortable riding Flaca, but still hadn't got the hang of mounting her from the ground. Doing so involved steadying her with one hand, placing one foot on the top of the wheel, then pushing off the wheel to reach the nearer pedal with the second foot and using the continuing momentum to push off the pedal and land on the seat. Despite many hours practising out in the yard, Trico still tended to jump too far and sail over the top of the seat to land heavily on the ground on the other side. The alternative was a complicated and time-consuming procedure requiring a high wall and at least one assistant. As this was impractical to repeat for every semáforo, he had to stay mounted between red lights, either pedalling backwards and forwards to maintain equilibrium or clinging to a lamp post for balance while he rested his legs and I did the charol. Unable to reach the gasoline container, he would pass his fire clubs to me to soak and relight for each performance. The effect was spectacular: a slender figure bobbing two metres in the air in the middle of a busy road, illuminated by dancing flames. I would accompany him by spinning fire poi on the ground below, and Hele heightened the drama by beating a syncopated tribal rhythm on her djembe. We were attracting quite a lot of attention. As it turned out, rather too much attention.

We had played only three semáforos and collected 21 pesos when the men arrived. They were dressed in dark trousers and jackets, with no official markings but an unmistakably official look. One of them tapped Hele on the shoulder just as I came back from doing the charol.

'Passports?'

'Sorry?'

'We are from the immigration police of San Luis Potosí. Your passports, please.'

We looked at each other nervously.

'We don't have them with us. We left them at our friend's house.'

'You are supposed to have them with you at all times.'

'We're very sorry. We can go and get them if you like.'

They conferred quickly in whispers.

'Come with us please.'

By now Trico had hopped down from his unicycle and come over.

'What's going on?'

'You are the friend of these girls?'

'Yes.'

'You are Mexican?'

'Of course.' Few people looked more Mexican than Trico.

The man turned back to us.

'Is this the friend who has your passports?'

'In his house, yes.'

'Go and bring them,' he told Trico.

'Where are you taking my friends?'

'To the immigration centre of San Luis Potosí. You know where it is?'

Trico gulped. 'Yes.'

'Is there a problem?' Hele asked.

'No,' the man told her, unconvincingly. 'Just a routine check.' We glanced at Trico for guidance.

'You better go with them,' he told us, adding under his breath: 'Be polite. *La migra* have more power than the police round here.' Then, out loud: 'I'll bring your passports.'

The immigration centre was within walking distance. There was a white bus parked outside, with bars across the windows. It did little to calm our nerves. We were led through a gate into a courtyard, and up a shallow flight of steps. Now that we weren't keeping warm with exercise, the night air prickled our bare arms with cold. We sat on the steps, hugging our knees.

A while later Trico was back. He wasn't allowed to enter the courtyard or talk to us, merely ordered to hand our passports through the gate. It didn't seem like a good sign. Two more men came out of the building, joining the first two to examine our passports.

'You have here tourist visas.'

'Yes.'

'Not work visas.'

'Do we need work visas?'

'You were working, weren't you?'

'Not really. We were in the semáforo.'

'You were taking money?'

My alarm mounted. I knew they had seen me going round the cars.

'I was collecting money, yes. My friend was on his unicycle; he couldn't reach down to the windows. I was helping him.'

'You know it is illegal for a foreigner to earn money in Mexico without a work visa?'

'We knew it was illegal to have a job in Mexico, but we didn't realise that it was illegal to do street performance. People only make donations if they want to, and we're not taking employment from Mexicans.'

I thought of all the foreigners working cash-in-hand in bars and language schools across the country, taking jobs that could easily have been done by local people. I had never heard of anyone getting in trouble for it. I had a strong suspicion that our current predicament had less to do with visa regulations than it did with the instinctive mistrust that exists between authorities and itinerants across the globe.

The men conferred in whispers again.

'Come inside.' The two men who had come outside turned and walked back in, taking our passports with them. The two remaining men indicated to us to follow them.

'Excuse me?' Hele asked one of them, with careful politeness. 'Can you tell us how long we will have to stay here?'

The man shrugged.

'A few days, maybe.'

'A few *days*?'

'Or a week. *Quién sabe?*'

I felt panicked tears prick the corners of my eyes, and struggled to hold them back.

'Can I – can I say goodbye to my boyfriend, please?'

He looked at me, a little oddly.

'Is that man with the very large bicycle your boyfriend?'

I resisted the urge, drilled into me by Trico, to explain the difference between a bicycle and a unicycle.

'Yes.'

A nasty smile curled the corners of his mouth.

'Don't worry,' he told me. 'I'm sure you'll find another one in the next country.'

ψ Ψ ψ

The bureaucratic procedure in the centre seemed to go on for hours. Our details were recorded by a toad-like man wedged uncomfortably behind a white table. He filled in the relevant forms with the meticulous but shaky capitals of a child just learning to write. Squinting at the code strip along the bottom of the photo page of my passport, he carefully recorded my surname as 'G B R R A I N S F O R D'. I was about to point out that 'GBR' stood for 'Great Britain' when Hele nudged me sharply under the table. I saw her point. If I was going to be arrested, it probably wasn't a bad thing for it to be under the wrong name.

We were both biting our tongues, trying to follow Trico's instruction and remain polite. The effort lasted until they started to ask us 'medical' questions.

'When did you last have sex?'

'Neither of us could be pregnant, if that's what you're asking.'

'I am asking when you last had sex. Was it last week? Last month? Yesterday?'

'That,' Hele spat, 'is absolutely none of your business.'

He smirked across the table at her, apparently taking the response as an admission.

'I would like to call my embassy,' Hele told him icily.

He thought about it.

'Do you know their number?'

This caught her off-guard. 'Not from memory, no.'

He looked smug.

'Then how do you propose to call them?'

After an explosion of indignation from both of us, he eventually promised that we could call them on Monday morning. Finally, our pockets were emptied out, our jewellery and shoelaces removed, and we were led through a heavy door into a cramped antechamber. The guard locked the first door behind us before opening the second and ordering us through.

The space we entered had a concrete floor and walls, and an iron spiral staircase like a fire escape that led up to a concrete balcony. It was partially open to the sky, but with a heavy iron grille over the opening. One bathroom and four cell-like rooms faced onto this space: three onto the bottom level and one onto the balcony. During the night, inmates were locked into these rooms, where they slept on blue mats on the floor, but during the day the doors were opened and they were allowed to mingle. There were about 25 people in there: mostly men, but also a handful of women and two small children. Hele and I were instructed to go up the stairs to the room on the second level, where the women and children slept. Two young women were sitting on the mats, talking quietly. They looked up as we entered. There was a pause.

'Hi,' one of them said, with a small smile that managed to convey just the right balance of welcome and commiseration. 'Is it your first time?'

'Sorry?'

'It's my second time. I'm not going to give up, though. I'm going to keep trying until I make it!'

We blinked at her stupidly, too distracted with worry to work out what she was talking about.

'Where are you from?' she asked.

'England and Estonia.'

She looked confused.

'Isn't that in the United States?'

'No, Europe.'

'You mean near Spain?'

'Sort of.'

'Oh. But don't they give you visas to the States?'

'Yes, usually.'

Her confusion deepened.

'Why are you here then?'

We explained what had happened. She started to chuckle, unbelievingly.

'So you're not trying to get to the States?'

'No.'

'You want to stay in *Mexico*?'

The two women were Hondurans. They had been caught on the highway to Monterrey when their bus had been stopped in one of the random searches conducted by the immigration police to catch illegal immigrants from Central and South America on their way to the US border. Like most of the other inmates they were disappointed but resigned to their failure, and already planning strategies for the next attempt.

'Fucking typical,' said Hele bitterly, as we sat glumly out on the balcony, watching the men milling around the cells below. 'I've spent tens of thousands of pesos in this country, maxed out a credit card, and they're gonna deport me for earning seven fucking pesos in the semáforo.'

'They won't really deport us, will they?' My tone pleaded with her to agree.

'Of course they're gonna fucking deport us.'

'Why are you being so negative?'

'Why are you refusing to face facts?'

'Because they're not fucking well facts yet, that's why,' I snapped.

'Why are you getting angry?'

'You were the one getting angry! I was trying to be positive before you started being all gloomy!'

'Oh, grow up.'

And we were off, bickering hysterically about nothing in particular, until we were interrupted by a guard telling us it was time to get into our cells for the night. I balked at being locked into the claustrophobic, windowless cell, and begged to be allowed to sleep on the balcony. The guard said he would have to ask his superiors. When he returned, to our surprise he told us to follow him. He led us out of the cell block and back through the building, to an empty room separated from the offices by a glass wall. Two mats had been placed on the floor.

'You can stay here for the weekend, while no one is in the offices,' he said.

I'm not sure what precipitated the sudden change in attitude towards us. Possibly it was simply that our situation was unusual, and the different officials were not in agreement about how to deal with it. But perhaps their hearts had been softened by a good word on our behalf.

'A woman was here, asking after you,' the guard told us. 'She asked if we could give you these.'

He handed us a bundle of clean clothes, including several thick, warm jumpers. Exhausted, distressed and overwhelmed, I felt myself choking up with gratitude. Trico's mother knew enough about semáforos to know that the clothes we were wearing would be stinking of car exhaust, sweat and gasoline. And, having seen us leave the house in thin trousers and T-shirts, she knew we would be cold.

'Be grateful you're not the two Argentinean boys who were caught being living statues in the plaza a couple of months ago,' the guard told us, not unkindly. 'They were painted silver for two weeks.'

ψ Ψ ψ

Sunday was a long day. The room we were in was an extension with a glass ceiling, so we were woken at dawn by the sunlight on our faces. Breakfast was substantial, but tasted of cardboard. We complained a bit to occupy the time, and when that got boring we argued instead. This seemed self-defeating, so we decided to go Zen, and did half an hour of yoga. Then we realised that an audience had gathered in the adjoining office to snigger at our upturned bottoms in 'downward dog' pose, so we went back to complaining. Lunch was pieces of gristle in a sauce with the consistency of snot. I knocked on the door and asked for a pencil and paper and, to my surprise, was brought some. A drawing that started with an aimless spiral evolved into a man in a suit crying as he shared a picnic with a peacock and a fish, while a worm ate into his brain to emerge from his right ear and vomit small objects into his tea. I was adding some shading to the worm's teeth and wondering what Freud would make of it when my pencil was confiscated (apparently I might use it as a weapon) and replaced with a magazine containing various articles about the importance of choosing the right make-up for my skin tone, and how to tone my *pompis* (buttocks). I read. Hele brooded. By dinnertime, I had strong and well-informed opinions about the difference between peach and magnolia, and Hele was starting to wonder why she had ever left Chihuahua. Had life with Jorge really been so bad? At least in Chihuahua, she pointed out, she didn't have to ask for permission to go to the toilet.

I have never been so glad to see the sky fade to black.

ψ Ψ ψ

By the time a guard arrived at eight o'clock on Monday morning we were already standing by the door, glaring through the glass with as much dignified outrage as we could muster, bursting with the tirade that had been building up since Saturday. The second he opened the door, we were off.

'Now can we call our embassies?'

'Not now.'

'But we were promised we could call them on Monday morning!'

He shrugged.

'Later. Maybe. Come with me.'

'Where are we going?'

'In an hour, people will come in to start work. You must go back to the cell block.'

He ignored us completely as he escorted us through the offices, back into the cell block, and slammed the door behind us. Deprived of a recipient for the tirade, we redirected it at each other. The other inmates looked on, with expressions ranging from sympathetic amusement to outright scorn. Finally, when we stopped to draw breath, one of them cut in.

'Don't get angry,' he advised us, in English.

We bristled in righteous indignation and launched into identical rants enumerating all our extremely good *reasons* for being Angry and that treating us like this was simply *unacceptable* and how our Human Rights had been *infringed* and as soon as we got out of there we would make *sure* there were Consequences for what they had Done, and so on and so forth. He waited until we had finished, then sighed deeply.

'Still,' he counselled, 'better you don't get angry.' He said it with the weariness of one speaking from bitter experience.

'Where are you from?' Hele asked him. He didn't look or sound Latin American. 'Why are you here?'

'I am from South Korea,' he told us. 'I am in Mexico just for holiday, just to travel. I am travelling all over South America now for three years. I arrive in Mexico and they give me visa stamp in my passport, 180 days in Mexico. But they stamp it bad, so the 1 in 180 is on a line in my passport, so you don't see it. In San Luis Potosí they check my passport and they tell me, "You have only visa for 80 days, and already you stay more than 80 days. You are here illegal."'

'But that's ridiculous. They never give 80-day visas, always 180. Surely they must know that.'

'Yes. They know that.'

'So why don't they give you a new stamp and let you go?'

'I get angry. Now I am here already five days.' He leant closer and spoke in a low whisper. 'These sons-of-bitches, they are not caring about justice, they are not caring about people. They are only caring about money, and about ego. You treat them like big man, you are out soon. You get angry, you stay here as long as they want. You want cigarette?'

'We're allowed to smoke cigarettes here?'

'No. But everybody do it and the guards they say nothing. I think they know that some of these people, without cigarettes probably they kill them. Juan has some *mota* [marijuana] as well, if you want smoke later. It helps with not to get angry.'

He led us up the stairs, where we shared a cigarette under the iron grille across the roof. I had always insisted (with varying degrees of truthfulness) that I didn't smoke, but right then seemed like a good moment to start. Gradually, we calmed down enough to start getting to know some of the other inmates.

Juan was a cocaine trafficker from Colombia. Or at least, so he claimed. To hear him talk one would have thought him to be the heir to Pablo Escobar, in which case you had to wonder what the hell he was doing in immigration jail in San Luis Potosí. He was toned and good looking and wore a wife-beater and a perpetual smirk. His every movement was accompanied by a nonchalant flexing of his muscles, followed by a furtive glance around to check that everyone had noticed and was suitably impressed.

'It was my twenty-third birthday last week,' he told us. 'Fucking shit, stuck in here with just these *pendejos* for company. Last year I was coked up to my eyeballs in a private club in Bogotá being lap-danced by two Brazilian prostitutes. Fucking hot. Tits bigger than your head.'

He caught one of the children staring at him with wide eyes and a perturbed furrow on her brow and held out his two hands, cupped inwards, about a foot from his chest to make sure she was clear on what he meant.

'Bigger than your *head*,' he repeated.

One of the other men, a Salvadoran named Miguel, rolled his eyes.

'Shut up, Colombia. Nobody gives a fuck.'

The men never used their real names, preferring to address each other by the name of their country of origin. Thus, even the most banal conversation took on the tone of a pressing international debate, like some degenerate United Nations.

'El Salvador's a *maricón* [faggot],' Juan snorted.

'You guys are lucky,' Miguel told us in English. 'We're gonna be stuck with that asshole in a fucking bus six hours to DF. Maybe even further if they take him down to the border. Hopefully they'll just shove him on a plane to Colombia and be done with it.'

'You don't think they'll take us to DF as well?'

He chuckled. 'Nah, man. They take us to the central detention centre in DF to await deportation. They're not gonna deport you. You guys are from Europe. They're just leaving you in here for a while to get you so scared and desperate you'll pay whatever amount of money they ask you for to get out.'

'We don't really have a lot of money at the moment.'

'Oh. You're pretty fucked then.'

'And how long's "a while"?'

'Well, legally they're supposed to deal with all cases within ninety days.'

'Ninety days?!'

'But then legally they're supposed to do a lot of things. Doesn't mean they actually do it. All of us Central Americans just have to wait until they have enough people to fill a bus back to where we're from.' His eyes lit up as an idea struck him that he apparently found amusing. 'Maybe you'll have to wait until they have enough people to fill a plane back to where you're from!'

'I'm from Estonia,' Hele told him. 'I doubt there's a plane-load of Estonian citizens *in* Mexico, let alone being deported from Mexico for immigration offences.'

'Could take a while then.'

'I wouldn't be out in this lifetime, that's for sure.' She turned to me.

'You're lucky. You're British. At least you have drunken yobs and football hooligans to be deported with.'

'How do you speak such good English?' I asked Miguel.

He sighed.

'I've lived in the States for most of my life. I arrived there with my mother when I was still very young. She left El Salvador just after the civil war and managed to get with me all the way to Los Angeles. She had family there who'd emigrated a few years earlier. They say it was easier to cross the border back then. I grew up in LA. I never had official papers, but there are loads of people like that. You can still have a normal life. But two years ago, I got a felony conviction and was deported back to El Salvador.' He shrugged helplessly. 'Fucking stupid, I know. What am I supposed to do in El Salvador? I barely remember living there. I still have family there so I went to live with them, but there are so few opportunities for me there. In LA I had friends, a girlfriend, a job working with my uncle... my whole life was there. I've been trying to get back ever since. I got all the way to Juárez last time, but I was caught trying to cross the border.' He shook his head. 'You guys should be glad you're here and not in Juárez. This place is fucking *luxury* compared to there.'

The only person we spoke to who was not trying to get to the US was Paco. He was a cheering presence in the detention centre, as he was also the only person who was there by choice. A gaunt and rather simple man in his mid-forties, he was also originally from El Salvador, but had come to Mexico three years previously. He had managed to find work and send enough money back to sustain his struggling family, but after three years he was desperate to see them again. Unwilling to waste any of his hard-earned money on travelling back, he had come to the immigration centre and reported himself as an illegal immigrant. He was now cheerfully awaiting deportation, passing the time by daydreaming about the presents he would buy for his wife and two little daughters when he got home. Wise to his game, the immigration officials had already kept him there for three weeks but, as he told us philosophically, three weeks wasn't much when he'd been away from his family for three years. Besides, in the detention centre he got three meals a day and a television, which was considerably more luxury than he was used to.

The television was on a wooden shelf high in the corner where the ceiling met the wall, over the hollow of the stairwell. All the time we were there, it played grainy *Pink Panther* clips on continuous repeat. The two children, a boy and a girl of about five and seven, sat cross-legged on the balcony, watching it enraptured, along with several of the men.

The children's mother was a stocky, gentle Guatemalan woman of about 35 with huge, round eyes like polished obsidian. She spent most of her time washing – herself, her clothes, her children – and when there was nothing left to wash a tiny furrow of distress would crinkle her brow and she'd sit, awkward and quivering slightly, until enough time had passed that she felt justified in washing one of them again. She was one of those women so accustomed to domestic drudgery that it had become her life raft, something to cling to or to repeat like a prayer in troubled times, her own silent, dutiful communion with God. Watching her, I felt sure that the most tragic stories in the jail were the ones that weren't being told.

Around mid-morning, the door was opened and a young couple ordered inside. Both looked about 19. The girl's eyes were red and puffy from crying. The boy looked terrified.

'Where are you from, brother?' Miguel asked him.

'Ecuador,' he answered, in a tiny voice. The girl let out a sob. I imagined all the miles of gruelling and dangerous journey, all the hours of suffering and hope it must have taken them only to end up here, in a grey concrete cell block: the end of the line.

12
Deportation

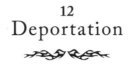

It may have been Flaca's fault we got arrested, but it was definitely my fault we got a deportation order.

It happened like this.

Just after lunch, we had a visit from a representative of a human rights organisation. He listened with resigned patience to the complaints of the Central Americans who had been there for several weeks already, but showed much more interest in me, Hele and the Korean. Perhaps words were then had with the officials, because soon after he left I was summoned from the cell block. Hele and I were not summoned together, which was the first thing to make me suspicious.

Trico was waiting in the front office. I ran to him and hugged him.

'Are you OK, Loquita?'

'I'm OK. What's going to happen though – are they going to deport us?'

'No. I'm pretty sure they'll just give you a fine. All the banda is outside in the semáforo, working. They should have the money together in the next few hours.'

My fine turned out to be just under 600 pesos (about £30). I paid it from my overdraft, hearing my father's voice in my ears. *Freedom is having enough money to tell all of them to fuck off...* A sheaf of papers was then produced.

'Sign.'

'Wait... let me read them first.'

The woman behind the desk clicked her pen impatiently as I struggled through the text. It was virtually impenetrable: a dense Spanish legalese that I could just about follow, but without appreciating the nuances. I felt increasingly nervous the further down I got. At the end of the final page were spaces for four signatures: one from an official, one from me, one from a witness, and one from a translator. The space for '*Traductor*' already had a signature scrawled across it.

'Before you sign it,' the woman instructed me, 'you must write a declaration at the bottom confirming that we have given you food and fair treatment.'

She started to dictate the declaration, which I slowly and uncertainly copied down until we reached the bit about 'fair treatment'. Then my pen paused, hovering over the paper.

'Why is there a signature for a translator here when we have never had a translator?' I asked.

'Why do you need a translator?' she demanded. 'You speak Spanish.'

'I speak reasonable conversational Spanish. That doesn't mean I can fully understand a legal document.' I waved the sheaf of papers. 'You must understand that I am unwilling to sign a document in a foreign language that says I had a translator when I didn't.'

'It's just a statement of events leading to your arrest,' she said. 'Just write the declaration, sign it, then you can leave.'

I could feel Trico's tension beside me.

'Just sign it, Cat,' he urged me. I could feel myself panicking and was powerless to stop it. What was this thing I was signing? Who knew what clever clauses could be thrown in that I would struggle to understand in English, let alone in Spanish? What if I was inadvertently confessing to something? By declaring I'd received 'fair treatment', would I be signing away my only chance to contest it?

'I'll sign it if I can put a note in the declaration saying I never had a translator. Or at least cross out this signature of some mystery translator I never met,' I said at last.

The woman's expression had gone very cold.

'You had better discuss it with the chief of the centre,' she said. She led me across the office to where a pot-bellied blonde man sat working. He had a face like a pug and a thuggish demeanour.

'She doesn't want to sign,' she told him.

'Just *sign it*, Cat,' Trico pleaded one last time. I vaguely remembered his last warning before we were arrested. *Be polite.* La migra *have more power than the police round here.* I should have listened. But I had fallen prey to a mounting hysteria and was not about to back down.

'I will sign it; I just don't want to put this thing about "fair treatment". It says here I had a translator, and I didn't. How is it "fair treatment" to make me sign a document stating something that we both know isn't true?'

The man glared at me.

'You won't make the declaration?'

Last chance.

'No.'

He glared at me a moment longer and then made a sudden movement, as if he were about to hit me. I flinched. But instead, he seized the sheaf of papers, tore them in half, and then in half again. The pieces fluttered to the floor.

'Fine. Have it your way. Deportation.' He turned to the guards. 'Take her back inside.'

'*No mames*, Cat,' Trico shouted. (Literally meaning 'don't suck', *no mames* is used colloquially to express outrage or disbelief.) 'I can't do anything now. That's it. They're deporting you. You fucked it.'

Stunned and disoriented, I was hustled back inside. Hele stared at my white face.

'What happened?'

'I fucked it.'

We were left there another couple of hours, by which time I was in tears and begging any guard or official who poked their nose round the door to let me sign anything they cared to produce. It was bad enough that I'd messed things up for myself, but they had decided that Hele and I came as a unit, and my punishment should also be her punishment. She was admirably calm about the whole thing.

'It's alright. There's nothing we can do now. Just be really polite and try to get the best deal we can. You have to remember, this isn't Europe. You can't expect them to follow the law just because it's the law. That's not how it works here. Surely you've noticed that by now.'

I nodded glumly. I had.

The next time they summoned me, there was a girl sitting next to the woman. She had prominent teeth and hair in a ponytail and looked about 18.

The woman indicated her.

'Your translator.'

The girl started to read through the sheet in painfully slow, hesitant English, slashing some sentences in half and skipping some altogether when the words were too obscure or the syntax too complicated. Listening to her, I understood less than I had when I read it myself. I interrupted only once.

'Look... can I just sign it please?'

The woman gloated.

'No, you asked for a translator. Now you have one. You have to listen to the whole thing.'

At last the girl finished and I signed. I wrote the declaration affirming that I had received fair treatment. I was given a piece of paper stating that I had been issued a deportation order and had 15 days to leave the country. Then I sat and watched as Hele was summoned and the whole process was gone through all over again. Then, finally, we were returned our confiscated possessions and allowed to leave.

As we walked out the door, we heard the girl turn to the woman and ask excitedly: 'Did I do OK?'

ψ Ψ ψ

With 15 days to leave the country, there was only one thing to decide: north or south? I put in a strong bid for south.

'Guatemala is beautiful. You guys would love it. Or we could go to Belize! Come on, why the hell would we go to some godforsaken shithole on the US border when we could be on a Caribbean beach?

Hele, however, wasn't so sure.

'That's all very well, but what would we do if they don't let us back into Mexico?' This was a very real concern. The woman in the centre had been vague about how long we would have to wait before we were allowed back into the country. Several days of phone calls to various officials and embassies had left us none the wiser. Guesses had ranged from one hour to five years.

'I'd rather be stuck in Belize than stuck in Texas. Especially in the middle of December.'

Hele's reasoning was along different lines. 'I'd rather be stuck somewhere that I know something about and where I have an embassy that can help me. There is no Estonian embassy in Guatemala or Belize. Besides, if the worst comes to the worst and we have to sneak back across the border, it's much easier heading south than heading north. Trust me. The Juárez–El Paso Bridge may be like entering a fortress going in one direction, but you can pretty much stroll across it in the other. When I came back to Juárez after renewing my visa in the States I actually had trouble finding the immigration office. There's not much of a problem with illegal immigration *into* Juárez.'

'Would we do that?'

'I like to keep my options open.'

'Are you suggesting we go to *Juárez*?'

Trico chipped in.

'Marco – you know my brother the truck driver – he always drives the same route: between San Luis and Nuevo Laredo. He's sure to be heading that way in the next few days. He can give us a ride straight to the border and pick us up again a few days later, if all goes well.'

'Sounds perfect,' said Hele.

Reluctantly, I resigned myself to going to the United States. It was an irony that I'm sure would not have been lost on Miguel, the Honduran girls, the Ecuadoran couple, or indeed any of the inmates in the detention centre.

It was three days before Marco was assigned his next trip to Nuevo Laredo, a city on the Rio Grande in the eastern border state of Tamaulipas. While waiting to leave, we had several visitors to the house, all nobly volunteering to resolve the problem by marrying Hele. Chino offered. So did one of the drunk uncles. Güera called round to apologise for being unable to propose herself, but as same-sex marriage was illegal in San Luis Potosí she would be equally happy for Hele to marry Oscar. Hele graciously declined all offers, thanking everyone for their kindness but informing them that unfortunately, no foreigner would be granted residency on the basis of marrying a Mexican, unless the Mexican owned property and could prove he was able to support both himself and her. The next morning Oscar's father, a wiry little man with a head that looked like an egg in glasses, turned up on the doorstep twanging poignantly on an out-of-tune banjo and assuring anyone who would listen that his house was his own.

Marco was leaving shortly before midnight, and that evening we gathered in a flat where several of the artesanos were living, to drink increasingly emotional toasts to each others' health in the three days to five years it would be before we saw each other again. When Marco honked his horn outside, several came downstairs to see us off. Oscar, who had been toasting with even more emotion than the rest and was now cross-eyed and stumbling (though still clutching a caguama), clambered into the cab mumbling something unintelligible about helping, and promptly passed out on the bed behind the driver's seat.

'What's he doing here?' Marco demanded.

Trico shrugged, lifting the mat of dreadlocks to peer underneath. 'Dribbling, by the looks of it.'

'Nobody said anything about there being four of you.'

Trico shrugged. 'He didn't say anything about coming until five minutes ago. I did try to talk him out of it.'

Marco sighed and turned the key. 'Well, I can't wait around here for bloody ages. I have to be in Nuevo Laredo by nine.' The truck grumbled into life, vibrating hard as we pulled out into the street. Oscar slept peacefully on.

Hele and I dozed fitfully through the drive, squashed up at the end of the bed with Oscar's feet. Trico sat in the passenger seat and talked to Marco between brief naps. We pulled into Nuevo Laredo in a listless grey light that felt like dawn, though it must have been a couple of hours afterwards. Hele and I dragged ourselves upright. Trico leant round and poked Oscar with relish until he finally lifted his head. His bloodshot eyes squinted blearily into the cold light.

'Where the fuck am I?'

'Nuevo Laredo,' Trico informed him. 'You decided to come with us last night, remember?'

Oscar stared at him. For a moment his eyes read blank confusion before being filled with the horror of recollection. Turning his back on us with a deep groan, he buried his head under the pillow.

Trico crowed with laughter.

'I did tell him he'd regret this in the morning. But no, no, as always the *pinche borracho* [bloody drunk] thought he knew best.'

A muffled voice emanated from under the pillow.

'*Hijo de su puta madre!* Of all places to wake up with a fucking hangover – Nuevo fucking Laredo.'

13
Borderlands

~~~≈≈≈~~~

Although at that time, in late 2009, Juárez still held the unofficial crown for 'City one would least like to visit in Mexico', Nuevo Laredo was already a close runner-up. Some commentators confer on the city the dubious distinction of being the true site of the beginning of the cartel wars. Most accounts trace the beginning of the wars to 2006, at the time of Calderón's election and subsequent clampdown on the drug lords, but as far back as 2003 Nuevo Laredo had already witnessed a vicious public shootout between police and alleged drug-traffickers that raged for 40 minutes and was said to have turned the city into a battleground. The cause of the violence was the same in all but details as that in Juárez: two rival cartels fighting for control of the lucrative trafficking routes into the US. In the case of Nuevo Laredo, the struggle was between Chapo's megalomaniac Sinaloa Cartel and the Gulf Cartel. After the leadership crisis following the arrest of the Gulf Cartel leader Osiel Cárdenas Guillen in 2003 had plunged that group into disarray, Chapo had attempted to expand his territory into the state of Tamaulipas, flouting the *pax mafiosa* that had previously existed between rival gangs and explicitly stating his intention to gain hegemony over the Mexican drugs trade. The violence has continued in Nuevo Laredo ever since.

In retrospect, we were lucky not to have been there a couple of years later. By 2012, the headlines flashing around the world from Nuevo Laredo would tell of bomb blasts strong enough to be felt in Texas, 14 dismembered men found in the back of an abandoned car, nine bloodstained corpses (five men and four women) hanging from an overpass over a busy semáforo, to list just a few incidents. The semi-literate message printed on a banner which was left hanging over the bridge alongside the hanging cadavers would read:

Fucking whores, this is how I'm going to finish off all the fuckers you send to heat up the territory. I'm gonna put you in your place, you have to fuck up sometime, and that's when we are going to fuck up El Gringo, who keeps setting off car bombs, and Juanito Carrizales all fucked up because I killed that fucker El Tubi, who was crying and crying like a little bitch, and Metro 4, there you were begging for mercy from Comandante Lazcano when he was beating the shit out of you, R1 in Reynosa, now you're getting mixed up in other people's business, that's OK, here are your guys, the others got away, but I'll get them. Sooner or later. See you around fuckers.

The victims referred to are Gulf Cartel members but the message was not from Chapo, who fancies himself as the Godfather of the Mexican drugs trade, writes with cold authority (sometimes signing off with the words 'sincerely: your father') and would scorn a message so laden with expletives, colloquialisms and bad syntax. By 2012, Chapo had joined forces with his old enemies to combat the rising power in Nuevo Laredo.

It didn't feel like it at the time, but late 2009 turned out to be the calm before the storm. A new horror was already brewing for the northeastern states of Mexico.

ψ Ψ ψ

The outskirts of Nuevo Laredo were bleak and lifeless, and every second vehicle we passed was a police truck. Oscar strode ahead in search of a caguama to cure his hangover. He had refused to return to San Luis with Marco. Behind his charade of grouchiness, Oscar was fiercely loyal.

Yet even a caguama seemed hard to come by. Every shop we passed was closed, with corrugated iron shutters drawn down over the doors and windows. Oscar's mood worsened.

'I fucking hate the vibe in these border towns. I feel I can hardly breathe here. And you know what? Every time I come to the border it gets worse.'

I've read that on warmer days, in better times, Nuevo Laredo was full of

Texans popping over the border for a day of cheap shopping. But there was no sign of them as we approached the plaza nearest to the border crossing on a grey December morning. There were trees in the plaza and a small gazebo, and a few boot-blacks and artesanos who struggled valiantly to keep up an appearance of the vitality that gives most Mexican towns their character and charm. But it was a weak, half-hearted vitality, because nobody lingered around the plaza just to pass the time of day. Nobody laughed. No couples held hands. This sullen and subdued Mexico was not the country I had grown to love.

'Before we do anything else,' Oscar insisted, 'we need to find a bar and have a beer together. Just in case – well, just in case we don't see you again as soon as we hope.'

We could find only one bar near the border crossing that was open at that time of day. It had a dingy interior and wooden swing doors like a saloon in an old Western movie. There was a television over the bar and a larger one on the opposite wall, both of them showing the same DVD of hardcore pornography. A morose prostitute with mousey blonde hair sat at the bar eating peanuts from a bowl. As soon as we walked through the door, she plastered herself over Trico and Oscar and glared at me and Hele as if we were trying to move in on her territory.

'Do we really want to stay here?' I asked, once they had extricated themselves.

'I really want a beer,' Oscar declared emphatically. 'I don't give a fuck about anything else right now.'

We ordered four beers and tried to have a conversation, but it was hard to concentrate when the person you were speaking to was framed by a backdrop of penises and buttocks thrusting determinedly above their head. Eventually we gave up and watched the film. It had the unprepossessing title of *Booty Clapping 2* and was aimed squarely at the section of the market with a penchant for voluminous arses and the way the fat on them wobbled when they were moved vigorously up and down. (The Mexicans have a great appreciation for large behinds, so the audience for this sort of thing is wider than you might imagine.) Before each sex scene the woman would stand with her back to the camera and bounce repeatedly up and down for a minute or two, until her bottom was juddering and quivering like a giant blancmange. With the viewer's appetite thus whetted they would proceed to the sex scene, the camera still fixed doggedly on the woman's flapping buttocks. It was oddly hypnotic. We laughed and made jokes for the first few minutes but then gradually fell silent, staring expressionlessly at the screen.

At the end of the film the barman made to start it from the beginning again and we shook ourselves hurriedly into action. We walked down to the border crossing, where Hele and I hugged Trico and Oscar and promised that we would see them soon. If all went well, we would meet them back in the bar in a couple of hours. We were refusing to contemplate any other possibility.

We joined the queue in the border control office. Upon reaching the front, we handed our passports and deportation orders to the official behind the glass window. He studied them carefully, but without comment. He turned the papers over several times.

'Where is your receipt?' he asked at last.

'What receipt?'

'It says here you were given a fine. Where is the receipt to prove you paid it?'

'We, um, we don't know. We weren't told anything about a receipt. Just that we should show this paper on the border when we left the country.'

The official raised an eyebrow.

'So you didn't pay the fine?'

'No! No I mean yes, yes we did pay the fine. They wouldn't have let us go if we hadn't. But the deportation order was the only document they gave us. We don't have a receipt.'

The official yawned and held out our deportation orders.

'You cannot leave the country without the receipt.'

We stared at him.

'But we have to leave the country. We have a deportation order.'

'That may be. But you cannot leave the country without the receipt.'

'But we don't have the receipt. We weren't given a receipt. So what you're telling us is that we can't stay in the country, but we can't leave the country either?'

'I am telling you,' he repeated, 'that you cannot leave the country without the receipt.'

We stared at each other, momentarily lost for words.

'What should we do then?'

'I don't know,' he replied in a bored tone. 'It's not my problem.'

We walked in silence back to the bar. *Booty Clapping 2* was still playing. The morose prostitute was still eating peanuts. Trico and Oscar were nowhere to be seen.

'Excuse me?' Hele asked the prostitute. 'Have you seen the two boys we were with earlier?'

The prostitute glanced round at us, with utter lack of interest.

'They your boyfriends?'

'One of them is.'

She turned back to the peanuts.

'Gone off with another woman,' she said with her mouth full.

'What? Did you see them with a woman?' I asked.

'All men are the same,' she informed us laconically. I wasn't sure how to respond to this.

'But we've only been gone twenty minutes.'

She shrugged, as if to tell me that if I was foolish enough to put my faith in the treacherous hearts of men, that was my funeral. We left her with her peanuts and went to look for Trico and Oscar.

We eventually found them wandering back onto the plaza. They had been to the semáforo, but had been ordered to move on by police and threatened with arrest, though luckily allowed to keep the money they had collected. We told them what the official had said. Trico sighed.

'We better call the centre.'

We went to an internet café, found the number, and called the detention centre in San Luis. They were very sorry (they didn't sound very sorry) but it was the weekend, and nothing could be done over the weekend. We would have to wait until Monday. The day was Saturday. Marco would return on Monday morning, and leave for San Luis again that evening.

We went back to the bar.

'I'm not watching *Booty Clapping 2* again.'

'What do you suggest we do? Go on a scenic walking tour of Nuevo Laredo?'

We had another beer and watched *Booty Clapping 2* again.

ψ Ψ ψ

I was woken at about three in the morning by Trico's voice calling me from outside, with the choked urgency of one desperate to be heard, but by one person only. I went onto the outside landing, which overlooked the street.

'Trico! Where the hell have you been? Where's Oscar?'

Trico's face was haggard with worry.

'I lost him. There was a man with a gun... he said he was going to kill us. We ran. I don't know where Oscar went.'

My head was pounding with sleep and confusion, which vented itself in fury.

'What the fuck were you doing out at this time? We were so worried when you didn't come back. I even went looking for you, wandering around bloody Nuevo Laredo on my own in the middle of the night. Where the fuck were you?'

'We came here, but they wouldn't let us in. We tried to go back to the bar, but it was closed. We went to sleep in a car park, but then the man with the gun came... Cat, we have to find Oscar.'

I swore at him, and went into the room for my shoes. On hearing of our predicament during the long wait through the day, the barman had offered to let us stay in the bar for the night. Halfway through our fourth viewing of *Booty Clapping 2*, however, Hele had put her foot down. She had managed to regain the use of her maxed-out credit card with a few calls back in San Luis and, she declared, if there was ever a time to use it, this was it. We checked into a hotel room, the first any of us had slept in for months. Oscar, however, was uncomfortable. He had come along thinking he could help, and this turn of events was a blow to his pride. Having spent all his money, been prevented from working, and had the hospitality offer he'd won from the barman rejected, he felt not only useless, but a burden. He and Trico had paced the room awkwardly like caged animals while Hele and I wallowed down in the fluffy white bedspreads to discuss the situation and read. Eventually, they announced that they were going back to the bar. They had not returned.

I hadn't realised before the extent to which access to a bank account, even one with negative money, could create a division between us and the banda. I had thought of the world of cash machines and credit cards as the 'real world', and the world of hand-to-mouth travel as a strange and thrilling fantasy. Now, suddenly, I saw it through Oscar's eyes. To him money had weight, came with contact of hands and eyes, and was counted by stacking it in piles and lining them up on the pavement. Barring that, favours were earned through exchanges or friendship. That was the 'real world'. He understood theoretically, of course, the workings of a bank account. But he had never had one himself, and a world of plastic cards, codes, imaginary wealth and hypothetical values made him suspicious and uneasy. On returning from the bar and being refused entry to the hotel because of his gutter accent and dishevelled appearance, his pride had not allowed him to shout to us for help. He preferred to sleep in a car park. And Trico preferred to stay with him – until the man with the gun appeared.

Trico and I wandered into the darkened streets, flinching at movements in the shadows, calling Oscar's name but not daring to call it too loudly. Eventually, Trico suggested checking the car park where they had been sleeping before. And there we found him, curled up in foetal position behind a shed, bad-tempered and shaking with cold. The man with the gun had gone, he told us gruffly. He was fine.

'He could come back, Oscar,' Trico said. 'We can't stay here.'

Oscar just grunted.

'Oscar, come with us,' I pleaded. 'I'm sure they'll let you in this time. I'm not leaving you here.'

He refused to budge.

'You go back, Cat,' Trico told me. 'I'll stay with him.'

Something inside me snapped.

'*No mames!* I'm fed up with this! As if things weren't bad enough without you two pulling this macho bollocks! Do you really think I could sleep knowing you were out here in the cold with some lunatic with a gun looking for you? I'm not moving until both of you come with me.'

I looked at Oscar. Trico looked at me. Oscar looked at Trico. Nobody moved. Exasperated to the point of hysteria, I decided that drastic measures were necessary. I removed my shoes, socks, jumper and jeans, and stood before them in nothing but a light cotton dress. The temperature was close to zero, and I immediately felt goose-pimples sweep across my flesh.

'You better come quickly, Oscar, or I'm going to freeze.'

A minute passed. Oscar glared at me, but didn't move. I put my hands to the hem of my dress.

'Don't make me do it, Oscar.'

'*No mames*, Cat!' Trico shouted.

I don't think I would actually have done it. But the bluff paid off. Oscar got to his feet, muttering furiously, and I hurriedly pulled my clothes back on. At the hotel, nobody challenged us, and we went up to the room.

'I'll get in with Hele,' I said. 'You two share the other bed.'

But Oscar had already curled up angrily on the floor, in the corner by the door, like a dog.

ψ Ψ ψ

On Monday morning, we called the detention centre again. Could they fax the receipt to the border officials in Nuevo Laredo? No, they couldn't. It had to be collected in person. We called Elvira. Could she go to the centre, pick it up, and fax it to the internet café where we were? Of course. Anything she could do to help. We called back an hour later. They had refused to give it to her. It could only be given to the people to whom it had been issued.

'The way I see it,' Trico said, 'you have two options. We could go back to San Luis with Marco tonight, pick up the receipt from the detention centre, and come back to Nuevo Laredo with him on his next journey.'

We groaned in despair. Another 10-hour journey each way, then – assuming we got back into Mexico – hitching all the way back to San Luis or waiting another three to four days in the hellhole of Nuevo Laredo for Oscar's next trip.

'Anything but that! What's the second option?'

'You could pay the fine again.'

We stared at him.

'We can do that?'

He looked surprised.

'Of course you can. That's what they want. I thought you just didn't want to let the *culeros* get away with it.'

'Why the fuck didn't they say that?'

He laughed, shook his head and rolled his eyes, all at the same time.

'You still don't know *anything* about Mexico, do you?'

Freedom is having enough money to tell all of them to fuck off. Thank heaven for the dreaded plastic, after all. We couldn't get to the border crossing fast enough.

Laredo International Bridge is an immense concrete monstrosity spanning the grim brown waters of the Rio Grande. It has a pedestrian walkway down each side and four traffic lanes in the middle. The two lanes going north are divided from the two lanes going south by a line of plastic barriers. The northbound two are jammed with traffic; the southbound two are all but empty. You wonder what it would take for someone to face facts and move the barriers across a lane.

Hele and I joined a throng of coffee-skinned pedestrians shuffling along the northbound walkway. With plastic and European passports in hand, the crossing seemed unfairly easy. We emerged on the other side in Texas.

I don't know what I expected. Maybe rodeos, green baseball pitches and ruddy-faced people in cowboy hats saying, 'Howdy, y'all!' Or at least prices in dollars and people speaking English. Instead prices were in pesos, everyone spoke Spanish, and the only signs we had crossed the bridge at all were that the buildings were greyer, there were no plazas, and everything was twice as expensive. It felt like a lobotomised version of the town we had just left. To be fair, we never strayed far from the border. But I imagined all those Latinos, after however many months of bureaucracy it took to be permitted to cross the bridge, taking their first steps into the fabled Land of Plenty and thinking – *God, is this it?*

The one thing I had hungered to find was a bookshop – preferably several storeys high, with armchairs in cosy recesses, where shelves rolled away from me like waves, rippled with the spines of countless books in my own language. After months of watching my index finger make achingly slow progress across lines of text which yielded their treasures to me only with great reluctance, the thought nearly brought tears to my eyes. But no such place appeared, and something about the atmosphere made it feel ridiculous to even ask. Instead, we ate soggy nachos with a rubbery cheese sauce the colour of egg yolks and wandered limply around shops full of clothes that we couldn't afford and didn't suit us. Then Hele said: 'Let's go home.'

We sailed down the southbound walkway without looking back, and the new shift of immigration officials barely glanced at our passports before stamping them and welcoming us to Mexico. Back in the bar there were hugs, laughter and free beers, and even *Booty Clapping 2* struck me as a touching celebration of the fuller female figure. We had a brief scare on our way to meet Marco, when Trico and Oscar rashly attempted to play a couple of semáforos and a police pickup swept out of nowhere to bundle us into the back along with several bullish youths in body armour with rifles at their hips. But they seemed more playful than malicious and after interrogating us on the nature of our relationships, demanding to watch Trico juggle and relieving us of our coins, they let us go.

Rumbling south, plastered in smiles, Oscar turned to me and Hele.

'You girls be *careful* from now on, OK? Because I never, *ever* want to go back there again.'

14
Saint Death and the Ball Game
~~~

We were careful – at least to the extent that we avoided semáforos that were anywhere near the San Luis immigration centre. Hele even left San Luis altogether, taking a trip with some of the banda up to the old mining village of Real de Catorce, and then to a circus school in a squatted building in the northern city of Torreón. But we didn't stop playing semáforos.

How could I stop? To stop would mean leaving. Leaving would mean losing Mexico, losing Trico, losing the intoxicating freedom that meant I could go anywhere, at any time, with only a couple of chains and a pair of scissors, and know I would survive – not to mention losing the freedom from my natural shyness that I had discovered in those glorious blazing seconds under the red traffic lights.

But of course, however little I wanted to admit it, in challenging my right to accept money in Mexico the officials in the immigration centre did have one valid point. Both of these newly found freedoms were, essentially, being funded by the generosity of others, often from backgrounds that offered them much less opportunity than my own.

This is the moral dilemma of hand-to-mouth travel. It throws you into intimate contact with a country and its people, giving you an accelerated crash course in language and culture. It makes you vulnerable, and in doing so opens worlds and stories and hearts that would otherwise be inaccessible. At least superficially, it breaks down the barriers created by money and privilege, and allows you to share in a common humanity. But the equality is illusory. Even if your lifestyle is the same in every aspect as those you share it with, the fundamental difference is that you are there by choice and they often are not. What right did I have to be surviving off donations from local people, rather than going home, getting a job, and coming back with foreign money to inject into the Mexican economy?

I found myself wrestling with this dilemma every time I went to the semáforo, judging myself more or less harshly depending on my mood. Between charoles, I compiled myself a mental list of justifications for what I was doing, here presented in descending order of disingenuousness:

One: I needed the money. My bank account was empty and I needed what I earned in the semáforos to buy food and make contributions to Elvira's household just as the others did.

This, I was well aware, was a weak excuse. I may not have had any 'actual' money, but I did have an overdraft which was available to draw on in emergencies. Clearly, it would not have lasted forever, but it was enough to buy a plane ticket back to the UK. And even if I hadn't had this resource, I had loving and supportive parents who would have helped me to get home if I had found myself in real trouble. So, although I needed to play semáforos in order to remain long in Mexico, there was no denying I was doing it by choice.

Two: I wasn't taking very much, and every peso I did take was going straight back into the pockets of Mexicans in the shops and street stalls I spent them in. The impact was negligible in comparison to, for instance, the many foreign mining concessions around northern Mexico which took the country's resources, marred the landscape and polluted the water, then siphoned the profits straight into bank accounts in North America, Europe, and various assorted tax havens.

This was true, but one can hardly justify an action on the basis that someone else is doing something worse. Besides, the mining companies, unlike me, could (and did) at least claim to be creating employment.

Three: I was providing a genuine service. I could see from people's smiles that it really did brighten their day to have a dose of colour and drama injected into a normally monotonous journey. The service came with no price tag, but that didn't mean that it had no value. Those who did not wish to give money were perfectly welcome to enjoy it for free or ignore it. In fact, some of my favourite moments in the semáforos were when a window was rolled down, and someone told me: 'I'm so sorry, I have no change, but I really enjoyed that. Thank you.' The vitality that street performance adds to a city is something that is unquantifiable, but very real.

I do believe this; I wouldn't have continued to play semáforos if I didn't. I did not see the donations I received as charity, but as payment for a service, in accordance with what that service was worth in the eyes of each spectator. But this did not change the fact that the service I was providing could be (and was being) provided equally well (and frequently better) by Mexicans. Street performance is subject to the laws of supply and demand just like anything else, and the more malabaristas there are in an area, the less each one is likely to earn.

Of course, the real reason I was playing semáforos was simple: I loved Mexico, and I wanted to stay there. I loved the malabaristas and their lifestyle, and I wanted to live it with them and be accepted by them.

Funnily enough, more than all my justifications, that was the one reason to which people were invariably sympathetic. Mexicans tend to be both fiercely proud of their country and hopeless believers in love. Quite often in the semáforos people would ask me where I was from, and I would tell them. Frequently, the next question was: 'And why are you here, so far from home, playing in the semáforos?' Most Mexicans see any form of semáforo work as dirty and unpleasant, and find it hard to conceive that anyone would prefer it to being in England, a land of untold comfort and riches. I would answer, honestly: 'Because I love it, I love Mexico, I love the friends and boyfriend I have here, and I don't want to leave.' The response, invariably, was a wide smile, and often a larger tip than usual. 'How *good* that you like Mexico so much, güera!' they would say. 'Good luck! Take care!'

As my standard of performance got better, Trico and I started to hitch out from San Luis to play in surrounding towns where malabaristas were less common and donations correspondingly more generous. We slept on plazas, in shop doorways or even, after a good day, in paying guest houses. Both of us were high earners by malabarista standards: Trico for being exceptionally talented, me for being female and fair-skinned. We found that both of these characteristics were better appreciated in daylight, so we played fire less and less. Instead, Trico would juggle neon-coloured clubs atop Flaca and I would tie bunches of long coloured ribbons to my poi, whose satiny sheen reflected the sunlight as they swirled around my body. When my juggling got good enough we would sometimes play passes together (in which six or more clubs are juggled between two people, passing them between each other in different rhythms) with Trico on the unicycle and me on the ground.

Trico was a hard taskmaster. Not only was he unforgiving to imperfect throws of mine (*'No mames*, Cat, I'm on a two-metre tall unicycle! How do you expect me to catch that? Concentrate, please!') but he refused to take it easier on me because I was inexperienced ('How are you going to improve if you don't want to be challenged?'). He would alternate simple underarm throws with unexpected tomahawks, helicopters and straights, and shout in exasperation if I failed to catch them. ('Tomahawks' are thrown in an over-arm downward spin, 'helicopters' high with a horizontal spin, and 'straights' directly across, with no spin. These throws tend to arrive very fast or at strange angles and can be fiendishly difficult to catch.) Occasionally my own patience would run out also, and the performance would end ignominiously with us swearing at each other in the street.

When we applied ourselves and kept our tempers, the lifestyle was far from one of poverty. Playing in separate semáforos we could make at least 100 pesos an hour each – which, considering that minimum wage in Mexico is 50 pesos a day, is a respectable income. Even working three hours a day was sufficient to stay in a small but comfortable guest house (around 100 pesos a night in the smaller towns), eat in restaurants (about 60 pesos each would buy us our favourite *caldo de camarón* – a rich and spicy prawn soup we ate with avocado, crunchy tostadas, *salsa valentina* and generous amounts of lime), give some away to other performers or beggars (what goes around, comes around), finish the day pleasantly drunk and still have enough for breakfast the next morning. The hours in the semáforo were hot and thirsty ones of sunburnt skin and fume-burnt throats but still, there are definitely worse ways to earn a living than playing in the sun.

Of course, there were also bad times. Days when we couldn't keep smiling through our aching heads and blistered hands and feet and the drivers, sensing our lack of enthusiasm, would give nothing. Nights when we found ourselves stranded in cold and inhospitable places, with nothing to do but wrap ourselves in our one tattered sleeping bag and wait it out until morning.

But these bad times were promptly forgotten with the next caguama or *caldo de camarón*.

In this way we explored many of the regions of San Luis Potosí and surrounding states. Sometimes we went alone, sometimes with other malabaristas or artesanos from the banda of San Luis. Often we would run into other itinerants from the vast network around the country, travel and perform with them for a few days or weeks, and then go our separate ways. Oscar was our most consistent companion, particularly when we headed west into the plains of Jalisco, where a concentrated Spanish presence over the colonial era had brought wealth, sumptuous architecture and (I suspect of greater interest to Oscar) some of the most classically beautiful women in Mexico.

I was astonished and humbled by the kindness we received. Not only when asked for, in the semáforos or on the highways, but entirely unbidden, with no thought of any return. Henri, for example, who never let us pay more than half price for one of his tostadas with *ceviche* (raw fish salad with chilli and lime), and insisted we sleep under the porch of his restaurant in case it rained. Or the woman who ushered me in off the street after an argument with Trico to ply me with food, promise to get me a steady job in the local Soriana (a Mexican supermarket chain) and offer to introduce me to the eligible males of the neighbourhood.

Almost as fascinating as the people we met were the places we passed through: Guanajuato, reminiscent of Zacatecas with its alleyways, cobbles, unexpected flights of steps and tiny balconies, with the added intrigue of damp tunnels where the maze continued beneath the earth; Lagos de Moreno and San Juan de los Lagos, with their rococo churches and pretty plazas; Tampico, on the east coast, where families holidayed with resolute cheerfulness against a backdrop of grey sea stretching out to the oil rigs that patrol the Gulf of Mexico...

But it was La Huasteca Potosina, the beautiful southern hinterland of the state of San Luis Potosí, that most captivated me. Here, the mountains and high-altitude desert that cover the north of the state give way to verdant subtropical forest sprinkled with grottos and waterfalls as the land plunges down towards the sea. Out in these rural areas indigenous culture resurfaces, folk music is gayer and brighter, garments are coarser and more colourful.

We journeyed there with Hele and her new boyfriend Alvaro, a reflective, classically good-looking *malabarista* with whom she was now living in a small rented house on the outskirts of the city of San Luis. Having found herself research work she could do via the internet, she had solved her financial problems and was no longer reliant on playing *semáforos*, but still had a taste for travel and adventure. We were both eager to see Xilitla, a village in the lush hills of La Huasteca which, in the mid 20th century, had become a magnet for the more eccentric breed of English expat. The poet Edward James had built his own surrealist castle in the forest nearby where he had hung out with artists such as the painter Leonora Carrington.

The castle both embraces and is embraced by the jungle. Trees and waterfalls run through as well as around it, their forms sculpted to imitate the structures of the castle, just as the structures of the castle are sculpted to imitate nature. There are strange curved recesses like snail shells, columns in the shape of snakes, freestanding staircases spiralling towards the sky, only to spiral down to earth again without leading anywhere. I lay – only slightly uncomfortably – on a flat rock carved with an imprint in the exact shape of Edward James and gazed up, as he must once have done, at the sunlight filtering green through the trees.

'*Pinches ingleses,*' Trico announced admiringly. '*Bien pinches locos.*'

Bloody English people. Really bloody crazy.

There were no *semáforos* in Xilitla, so we had to be a little more creative in order to eat and drink. Sometimes we would trek down the hill to the petrol station on the outskirts of the village to juggle and spin poi on the forecourt for the cars at the pumps. Or we would brave the crush of the huge indoor market to perform in between pyramids of fruit, slabs of bleeding meat, clouds of flies and great hessian sacks of dried chillies, and walk away with bags full of the vegetables, rolls of bread and chunks of cheese which the laughing stall-holders threw to us.

Flaca was an enormous help on these missions. Often we wouldn't even have to try to earn money. Merely strolling through the market or past the plaza, we would be greeted by cries of: '*Oye, chavo, que onda con la biciclota?*

A poco sí te subes? ('Hey, kid, what's with the big bicycle? Do you really ride it?'), to which Trico would answer, quick as a flash: '*A poco no!* What will you give me if I show you?' Any donation was accepted, however small or strange. Often, though, they were generous. Trico was now adept at mounting from the ground, and the feat was undeniably impressive. We got some good meals that way.

Trico was fiercely protective of Flaca. Once in Xilitla we left our camp unattended to go and buy pulque, and came back to find that our brand new tent and all our bags had been stolen. Trico thanked God that we had taken Flaca and all the circus toys with us. That night, sleeping under the gazebo on the plaza, I woke up shivering with cold. Trico had his back to me. Propping myself up on my elbow I saw that he was sound asleep, Flaca cradled in his arms. Tired and grumpy, I shook him awake.

'Trico, I'm cold.'

He squinted at me in irritation. 'What do you want me to do about it?'

'I want you to hug me and not Flaca.'

'But Cat, what if someone runs off with her?'

'Who would have any use for a two-metre tall unicycle, apart from you? What if someone runs off with *me?*'

My voice was getting more high-pitched. I was genuinely upset. He chuckled disbelievingly.

'What's the matter with you, Loquita? You're acting really strange.'

'It's just,' I stammered, feeling suddenly foolish, 'it's just that sometimes it feels like you love Flaca more than me.'

Even as I said them, I realised how ridiculous the words sounded. Trico, however, did not try to deny it.

'One day you will abandon me, Cat,' he said. 'Flaca is always here. She never complains or argues; she carries me and she helps me earn my food. She is the one girl who will never leave me.'

'I'm not going to leave you,' I said.

'Yes,' he insisted. 'You will.'

But he turned round and hugged me after that.

The next day, we moved on through La Huasteca. We passed through Tamasopo, where multiple waterfalls shower from a towering cliff, splitting and rejoining as they hit rocks in their path, and finally dropping into a wide turquoise pool with pebble beaches, ideal for swimming. At El Ojo de Dios (The Eye of God), we swam through an underwater tunnel towards a blaze of cobalt light, emerging in a spectacular natural colosseum of rock with waterfalls thundering on all sides.

In Ciudad Valles, Hele and I were offered 1,600 pesos to dress up in denim mini-shorts and clingy white vests and wave coyly to the audience at a motocross show whilst holding up signs displaying the riders' names. This was quite a boost to our egos, until we emerged from the changing rooms in our skimpy outfits and saw our new employer stare in horror at our unshaven, bruised and mosquito-bitten legs.

'I didn't know you were that sort of girl,' he groaned.

'If he's going to pick up girls with dreadlocks in the semáforos,' Hele reflected later as we shared the excellent mescal we'd bought with the 600 pesos he'd given us for wasting our time, 'I don't know what he expects.'

Further west, where the jungles open onto arid plains, we came to the ancient city of Tamtoc. Until relatively recently, most archaeologists believed that ancient cities were only to be discovered towards the south of Mexico and that with very few exceptions, the peoples of the north were nomadic hunter-gatherers who left little lasting trace of their presence. In the last decade this theory has been overturned, with a rash of discoveries of pre-Hispanic sites in the states north of Mexico City. When we were there, Tamtoc was one of the most recent of these finds, and still largely unknown.

The site was enormous, sprawled across a plain of sun-dried grass. There were no fences, no 'keep off' signs, and almost no other visitors. Nor were there any information boards, and we wandered around the ruined foundations with a rich sense of mystery, feeling the presence of the unknown inhabitants resonating from every weathered stone. After a few hours, Hele and Alvaro managed to tag onto the back of one straggly guided tour, and afterwards came to where Trico and I were juggling on a hill overlooking the site to share with us what they had learnt.

'Near to where we are now was a temple to the sun god. From this hill, the priests could see the sun rise red every morning, and believed that it was red because it had been fighting through the night with the forces of darkness beneath the earth and would surface in the morning still stained with the blood of the battle. Over there,' Hele waved a hand towards an empty field, 'was where the ball game was played, but the site of the court is threatened because it is not yet officially protected and the man who owns the land wants to build there. They think that the game was one of the ways in which the people supported the sun in its struggle against darkness.'

The ball game was a sport with ritual associations played across much of Mesoamerica. While its exact rules and significance varied between regions, it features in both Aztec and Mayan mythology, was powerfully symbolic when played as part of religious ceremonies, and in some places (though probably not in Tamtoc) ended with the sacrifice of the losing team.

Alvaro was pensive. Staring out across the baked grass and piles of stone, he said: 'Funny, isn't it? Faced with great and terrible forces with ultimate power over their lives and deaths, what did they do? They played a game.'

Trico gave a barking laugh.

'Our ancestors, eh, Alvaro? Their blood runs in our veins.'

We gathered the clubs and walked back towards the entrance, the sun already reddening as it sank towards the horizon, preparing to re-enter its eternal battle with the forces of darkness.

ψ Ψ ψ

That constant whisper of the pre-Hispanic past was part of what made life in Mexico so intoxicating. Mexican poet and essayist Octavio Paz put it best in his acceptance speech when he was awarded the Nobel Prize in 1990.

> The temples and gods of pre-Columbian Mexico are a pile of ruins, but the spirit that breathed life into that world has not disappeared; it speaks to us in the hermetic language of myth, legend, forms of social coexistence, popular art, customs. Being a Mexican writer means listening to the voice of that present, that presence.

I had already been struck by the way the banda incorporated pre-Hispanic influences into their own subculture, but this was far from unique to them.

The legacy was everywhere: not only in the vibrantly coloured garments of the indigenous women preparing quesadillas over rustic hotplates on the edges of the markets, or in the Mayan and Nahuatl words that still crept into the language, but also where you would least expect it. Many people we met on our travels around the country seemed unremarkable until a chance turn in the conversation revealed their dedication to some unfamiliar pre-Christian belief or practice. An accountant who picked us up while we were hitchhiking through La Huasteca, for instance, turned out to have a second identity as a self-mutilating moon-dancer at the pyramids of Teotihuacán.

Often, pre-Hispanic ideas were blended into the more 'respectable' Christian ones. According to legend, the Basilica of Guadalupe, the most visited Catholic shrine in Mexico, was built after a vision of the Virgin Mary appeared to an indigenous peasant walking on the hill of Tepeyac, and requested that a church be built on that spot in her honour. A temple to the Aztec mother-goddess Tonantzín had previously occupied the site but it had been destroyed by the Spanish shortly after the conquest of Mexico. The dark-skinned Virgin of Guadalupe is thought to be a syncretism of these two holy mothers: a unifying figure that fuses indigenous with Christian belief.

But she and San Judas de Tadeo, patron saint of lost causes, are not the only revered figures in Mexico who sit a little uneasily beside the standard Catholic pantheon. First prize in that respect must surely go to La Santa Muerte: Saint Death. Usually portrayed as a skeletal figure in a long robe holding a scythe, La Santa Muerte is thought to be Mictecacihuatl, the Aztec goddess of death, under the guise of the Virgin so beloved in Catholic iconography. She is still revered by many, particularly among the working classes, and believed to be able to grant favours beyond the power of other saints. Her worship has long been condemned by the Mexican Catholic Church and most shrines to her are clandestine and well hidden, although there are a growing number of more public ones. I was once startled, on rounding a corner in the Tlatelolco district of Mexico City, to stumble into an almost life-size statue of her, seated in a high-backed Gothic armchair with an owl on one shoulder and a snarling jackal-like creature on the other.

The fixation with death in Mexican culture is something that strikes many travellers, but I think I felt it more keenly than most, for an entirely coincidental reason. I pronounce my full name (Catriona) with the emphasis on the 'i' and a subtle slide past the third syllable: Cat-*ree*-a-na . The subtleslide was so subtle, however, that the third syllable was invariably lost on people who heard it. '*Catrina!*' they would exclaim, eyes widening. '*Como la muerta!*'

Yes, I would admit. Like the dead woman.

Catrinas in Mexico are model skeletons with eerily fixed grins, which are dressed up in elaborate costumes and shown going about their daily lives – in a dead sort of way. In artisan markets it is not uncommon to find whole stalls dedicated to them: skeleton cooks preparing a meal, skeleton lovers locked in a bony embrace, skeleton mariachi bands playing a silent tune. The most well-known *catrina* is a woman in an elegant floor-length dress trimmed in fur, with a wide-brimmed hat and jewels at her wrists and neck. The message, it seems, is that death is our shadow at all times; its certainty accompanies us through every action of our lives. It is the one sure fate which awaits us – rich and poor alike.

The mere mention of my name would often lead into a long conversation about death: ghost stories, the loss of loved ones, several detailed accounts by people who had been 'touched by death', which is how the Mexicans describe it when you wake up and are conscious but cannot move, stricken by terror but cannot scream. These conversations were never melancholy, but conducted in tones of breathless excitement. To the Mexicans, the contemplation of death is as thrilling as it is frightening.

In the Mexican mind, the dead are never truly gone or far removed from Earth. Although, as Catholics, most profess to believe in Heaven, one gets the impression that in the secret depths of their subconscious, the dead are much closer, much more *alive* than that. Ghost stories are common, and widely believed. On the Day of the Dead, 2nd November, offerings of food and drink are left out for departed loved ones, and some families even sit in the cemetery through the night to share it with them.

Objects that had belonged to the deceased may acquire mysterious properties, as if inhabited by the souls of their previous owners. The example that lingers in my mind is a story that I heard from my friend Xochitl at Mexico City University, in the south of the city, generally referred to as UNAM (Universidad Nacional Autónoma de México).

Having been addicted to travel ever since leaving school, I had not so far been to university myself. I loved the buzz of UNAM, the earnest debates of the students as they hurried between lectures or sat out on the lawns, the spectacular octagonal library through whose glass ceiling the light fell in shining prisms into the central hall, overlooked by four floors of reading rooms. I had become acquainted with the site well enough to know where my kindred spirits could be found: hanging around the excellent student-run vegetarian *comedor*, outside of which a few artesanos set up their stalls and youths with multiple facial piercings shoved copies of the student anarchist newspaper into my hands. It was here that I had arranged to meet Xochitl.

Xochitl (the name means 'flower' in Nahuatl) was one of those calmly radiant people who make the world feel brighter just by being in it. She was a friend of Trico's who spun fire, made jewellery, and studied movement therapy. The last time I had seen Xochitl, her shoulder-length dreadlocks and round, cheerful face gave her the appearance of a rag-doll. But when I greeted her now, her head had been completely shaved. She looked beautiful, powerful, as regally feminine in her baldness as a Masai queen.

I hugged her and ran a palm across the soft contour of her scalp.

'You look amazing, Xochitl. Like an African *guerrera* [female warrior] What made you decide to cut off your dreads?'

Her smile wavered. But eventually, after we sat down, she told me the story.

'Throughout my childhood, I had one very close friend. We grew up together, went to school together, knew each other's families. Not long ago, she met a boy. He had a strange vibe, slightly dark, but she was intrigued by him. He invited her to go to the desert to eat peyote with him.

'For years she had had beautiful long dark dreadlocks. A few days before she went to the desert she cut all of them off, leaving only a couple of centimetres of hair behind. She said it was part of the cleansing that would culminate in the desert – a transition to a new phase of her life.' Xochitl took a deep, shuddering breath. 'He killed her, there in the desert. Nobody knows why. I think he just went crazy. When you eat peyote you go very deep into your spirit, and if there is darkness there it will come out. If you go with a shaman, they have the knowledge to channel that darkness away from you, to free you from it. But alone... alone it can destroy you. Maybe in his trip he thought she was a monster, or a demon. Who knows? When they found her body, her skull had been broken with a large stone. He had disappeared.

'When I found out, I didn't leave the house for several days. But finally I thought of her mother, who I had also known for many years, and knew I should go to tell her how sorry I was for the loss of her daughter. I went to see her, and we cried together. She had found the dreadlocks that my friend had cut off, and was treasuring them as the last piece she had left of her. But she knew how much we had meant to each other, so she gave me two of them, as a memento. I used thread and a crochet hook to attach them to the ends of two of my own locks.

'That night, I had a terrible nightmare, so vivid it was indistinguishable from reality. I was there, in the desert. The heat haze was so thick it distorted my vision, but slowly it cleared enough for me to make out a river, and I walked towards it. I stood on the bank and looked across.

'There was my friend, on the other side of the river. She was all alone, crying, and she looked so tiny standing there in the middle of all that emptiness. I called out to her but she showed no sign of having heard. I looked at the river, but it was a furious torrent of brown water, churned to froth as it raged over hidden rocks. I knew I could never cross. I couldn't reach her. I woke up crying, and I couldn't get back to sleep.

'The next night, I had the same dream. And the next, and the next. Every time I closed my eyes, I saw her. Sometimes I would even see her with my eyes open, her face imprinted across my vision like a watermark.

'Finally, I couldn't stand it any longer. I needed to free myself... to purify myself, as she had tried to. It wasn't enough just to cut off the locks that had been hers. That would be like throwing her away. I had to cut all of them – to start again. I made sure there wasn't a single piece of hair left on my scalp.

'Since then, I can sleep.'

15
La Chaparrita

During those months, I not only learnt to love Mexico with intensity, but to love with the intensity of a Mexican. With typical British reserve, my first instinct was to be cautious with my emotions. A simple 'I love you' was not something I surrendered easily, and I had been grateful for the two levels of love that are expressible in Spanish: '*te quiero*' for sincere affection, and '*te amo*' for full-blown passion.

Trico and I, however, had whipped through the *te quiero*'s and *te amo*'s at what felt like breakneck speed (though I suspect it was rather restrained by Mexican standards) and were already obliged to find more imaginative ways to express our feelings.

'You are my sun, my light,' we would coo to each other, between tender kisses. 'When you look at me I feel myself at the centre of a universe of radiant colours. When I hear your voice my heart soars through the stars on a comet of joy.'

Such proclamations are really the minimum required to sustain a Mexican relationship; anything less would sound cold and heartless. At first, as a cynical Brit hearing the words in translation in my head, I had found it difficult to say them with the necessary seriousness and conviction.

But Mexico has a way of stripping your defences. Each moment demands to be seized *now*, whole and shining, free from reasons or consequences, or lost forever. It was this spirit, this lust for the sharpest tangs of joy, anger and sorrow that had captivated me in Trico, and it was this spirit to which I became addicted. I think we even got a little competitive with the drama of our declarations. Sometimes we would be moved to tears by the depth of our adoration and cry with happiness in each other's arms, feeling our souls fly away on the wings of a golden eagle above the clouds and into the heavens...

Shortly after we would have a screaming fight over a missing sock and break up *forever*, packing our things and writing each other histrionic letters of farewell. I would then sob bitterly and write long elegies of despair while Trico drowned his sorrows with caguamas, until he would sidle back a couple of hours later and take my hand in the now-familiar spiral grip of the *Hunab Ku*. We would then uncurl the index fingers to point into the solar plexus of the other. *In lak'ech. Tú eres mi otro yo. You are my other I.* The whole cycle – ecstasy, fury, misery and reconciliation – would then start again.

The real problem was not the fighting but the one thing we didn't fight about – the elephant in the room, hidden behind all the broken juggling clubs and lost jumpers and unshared bottles of mescal. In successful relationships, partners work together, balancing each other, taking turns to give and receive attention. We were both the sort of people who make better friends than partners.

Trico was a showman, not only by occupation but by nature. He had a compulsive need for attention and a charisma that put all around him in shadow. The people in his life were the audience for his show. He loved them, respected them, and tried to do right by them, but deep down he had no doubt whose show it was.

I had my own sort of egoism: a compulsive need to collect stories, to study people like specimens, to slot them all into some imagined grand structure. The people around me were characters in my story. I loved them, respected them, and tried to do right by them, but deep down I had no doubt whose story it was.

Ironically, I think the inherent instability of our relationship was reflected in the gesture we had adopted as the symbol of our love. First: *Hunab Ku*. The spiralled hands, the union of souls. Then: *in lak'ech*. The detached fingers, the switch of focus from the union to the individual. *Tú eres mi otro yo.* There is a subtle yet vast difference between telling someone 'you are my other I' and telling them 'you are my other half'. In each other we saw a beautiful, exotic, mysterious projection of ourselves. But neither of us was looking for completing.

The union was always going to fly apart.

ψ Ψ ψ

It was during Phase Three of one of these cycles that a small boy knocked on the door of the house where we were staying with Oscar in Lagos de Moreno to inform us that our crazy friend with the very large bicycle had been arrested for being '*ebrio y escandaloso*' – drunk and scandalous.

'Interesting,' Oscar mused. 'I've seen him arrested for being drunk many times, but never for being scandalous. I wonder what on earth he did.'

'I suppose we should go to the police station,' I sighed. 'See if we can persuade them to let him out.'

Oscar looked at me sternly.

'Cat, we both know that he has been a *pendejo* all day. I think a night to calm down and think about it would do him good. Besides, I am drunk, you are drunk, and the last thing we need is to all end up in jail. You could even be deported again, and I've already explained to you my feelings about Nuevo Laredo.'

'What should we do then?'

'Have another caguama. And think about it in the morning.'

We had another caguama, and late the next morning went down to the police station. Usually public drunkenness in Mexico earns an automatic 36-hour internment and the only way to get out early is for somebody to pay a fine, whose amount varies across the country. None of us had enough money to pay it, but the policemen seemed amused by the whole episode and agreed to let Trico go, as long as we kept a closer watch on him in future.

'Listen, Cat,' Oscar said, as we waited for him to emerge. 'We must tell him that we have been working *all morning* to pay his fine, otherwise you can imagine how angry he'll be.'

It was good advice. Trico was hungover, in a foul mood, and it was only his grudging appreciation for our loyalty that prevented him from venting his fury on us. He was evasive when we quizzed him on exactly what he had been doing that was so scandalous. It had all been a huge misunderstanding, he insisted. He had been doing a show for some children and they had liked it very much and they had been laughing and *absolutely not* screaming. We never discovered the truth of the story.

We calmed him down with a caguama and some particularly good tostadas at a street stall we knew of, and gradually he emerged from his sulk enough to inform me that next week, we were going to walk 200 kilometres in five days, from San Luis Potosí to the cathedral town of San Juan de los Lagos.

'Um, really? Why are we going to do that?'

He explained, a little sheepishly, that during the long night in the cells when he realised that Oscar and I were not going to come for him, he had had an unexpected reversion to Catholicism. Knowing that if nobody came to pay his fine he would be forced to spend another night in jail, he had made a desperate prayer to La Chaparrita, the much-revered icon of San Juan de los Lagos, promising that if she allowed him to get out the next day, he would accompany his family on their annual pilgrimage in her honour.

I thought about it. I was tempted to protest that, as Oscar and I had been working *all morning* to pay the fine to get him out, it was a bit unreasonable to expect me to walk 200 kilometres to express my gratitude to an icon I'd never heard of from a religion I didn't believe in. But as that had been a lie in the first place, it seemed churlish not to let La Chaparrita take the credit on this one.

There was nothing for it but to walk 200 kilometres to San Juan de los Lagos.

ψ Ψ ψ

The shrine to La Chaparrita is one of the most venerated in Mexico. During the four pilgrimages a year, up to 250,000 pilgrims walk there from their home towns across the central belt of the country. The biggest of the pilgrimages, the one we were to participate in, is that of Semana Santa, or Easter.

La Chaparrita – literally 'The Little Short Girl' – is a statue of the Virgin brought to the cathedral of San Juan de los Lagos in 1542 and believed to have miraculous healing powers. She is represented by a voluminous triangle of blue dress, with a small round head like a bobble on top. The first time I saw her, I thought she was a hat. I did not share this information with any of the throng of devotees who had gathered for the beginning of the pilgrimage.

No, actually, I have to confess that we didn't quite make it to the beginning of the pilgrimage. We made a minor calendarial error and, arriving in San Luis a day late, had to hitch a ride to a village about 40 kilometres along the route, where the pilgrims were already settling down for the night.

On first glance, one could have mistaken the outskirts of the village for a refugee camp, until one picked up on the buzz of excited chatter, the snatches of song, and the potpourri of rich cooking smells wafting from all directions. The tiny hamlet was swamped with people and dusty trucks, crammed into every street and spilling out into the surrounding fields like a swarm of bees. Although they appeared at first to be one solid mass, on picking our way through them I saw that they were bunched into groups of extended families, usually congregated around one or more vehicles, a portable stove and a couple of trestle tables, while two or three unflappable matriarchs doled out paper plates of food with the efficiency of a production line.

The most unflappable of the unflappable matriarchs at Trico's family's camp was, of course, Elvira. She stood at a doorway in the side of an enormous yellow truck, from whose roof a tarpaulin stretched across to the top of an adjacent wall. Brothers, sisters, uncles, aunts, cousins, nieces and nephews were clustered under the tarpaulin, cross-legged on the pavement, plates on laps, elbows in each other's beans. Trico and I fought our way in and surrendered ourselves meekly to hugs, kisses, teasing and scolding from what felt like everyone simultaneously.

'A whole day late, eh? I wonder what the Chaparrita will think of that!'

'Young people these days! No sense of priority!'

'But it's so good to see you here, darling! We've missed you these last few years!'

'So you're going to walk with us, eh, Cat? Do you think you can handle it? Do they make pilgrimages where you're from?'

Then, whispered: 'Where is she from again?'

Don Margaro growled something incomprehensible and utterly terrifying. Elvira shoved plates of *enchiladas potosinas* and refried beans into our hands.

Trico's eldest brother Cesar was leaning against the wall, both hands on his leg, clearly in some pain.

'Are you OK?' I asked him.

'I'll be alright. It's not as bad as it was last year. I have a metal implant in my leg, you see, from an operation after a car accident. Walking these long distances is incredibly painful.'

'But you still do the whole pilgrimage? I'm sure the Chaparrita would understand if you walked a little less than the others, with your bad leg.'

'Oh no. It's because of my leg that I must do the whole pilgrimage, every year. I was so badly injured after the accident the doctors thought I might never be able to walk again. My parents almost had to sell the house in order to pay for my operations. I promised the Chaparrita then that if she allowed me to recover the use of my leg, I would do the whole pilgrimage every year for ten years in her honour. She healed me. Now I must fulfil my promise.'

As the sun set the clamour died away, pans were washed and beds arranged. After their long day's walk the pilgrims settled down early, and by 10 p.m. there was barely a murmur across the camps. We slept in the yellow truck, the whole family packed in like cigarettes across a floor padded with foam mats, our possessions heaped in the corners.

We were woken at 4 a.m. I couldn't remember the last time I had seen 4 a.m. from this side of the day, and took the mug of black coffee Elvira handed me in stunned silence.

The air was cool at that hour and families huddled together and hugged their arms over their chests as we tramped blearily out of the village. Some were already eating sweet bread or *tamales* (cylinders of soft corn dough stuffed with meat or vegetables and steamed in corn leaves) for breakfast; most merely warmed their hands around mugs of coffee, planning to eat at the next rest stop along the route. Trico called out greetings to acquaintances or distant family from San Luis.

There was no spectacular sunrise, only a tentative emerging of a weak sun behind a veil of cloud. But as the sky brightened, the spirit of the walkers lifted, and the silent dawn trudge broke into gossip and laughter.

I was intrigued by the variety in the ages and attitudes of the pilgrims and started mentally dividing them into categories. There were the Grim Plodders: the middle-aged men and women who took the whole thing with the utmost seriousness and walked straight-backed in dignified silence, often carrying small statues or placards depicting the Virgin. The Gay Chatterers: generally those in their thirties or forties, who seemed to view the pilgrimage more as a family bonding experience than anything particularly holy, and merrily seized the opportunity to catch up on the news from relations they rarely got the chance to spend such concentrated time with. The Sly Smokers: groups of boys in their late teens or early twenties who we would pass semi-concealed in bushes at the side of the path, from where suspicious smells (and occasionally, to us, hissed invitations) emanated. The Sprightly Skippers: children or adolescents, so eager to prove themselves they practically bounded down the road, only to turn into the Tired Whingers a couple of hours later. And already we were starting to overtake the odd pair of Devout Hobblers, although we would pass many more a couple of days further on. Old and stooped, they shuffled along on raw and bleeding bare feet.

Trico shook his head.

'Bloody crazy, these old people. They usually leave days or even weeks early to do it like that. Imagine how much it must hurt! Some of them even get down on hands and knees at the edge of San Juan and crawl the last couple of kilometres to the cathedral.'

The landscape here was dry but still cultivated – undulating hills in faded shades of greenish brown. Already, though, it was showing telltale signs of desert. When we arrived at the midday rest stop in a weathered field worn to dust by tyres, I saw several groups of women with long knives gathered around a thicket of *nopal* cacti and several more with smaller knives seated on the ground nearby, stripping the spines from the ovals of cactus flesh before passing them to the unflappable matriarchs to prepare for lunch.

The trucks would wait until the pilgrims departed and then drive the longer route round the highways to the next rest stop, in order to be there in time to set up marquees and prepare food before the walkers arrived. The unflappable matriarchs did not walk, as feeding their increasingly weary families was a full-time job in itself. Nor did the venerable patriarchs, as they were needed to drive the trucks and set up the marquees. This job clearly could also be very tiring, as by the time we arrived at each rest stop Don Margaro was usually fast asleep in the shade, one hand rested on the dome of his belly, a couple of empty caguamas at his side.

At the end of the day I felt fine, even invigorated by the walk, and congratulated myself that I was clearly in optimal physical condition. At four the next morning, I wasn't so sure. My feet ached, and I wanted nothing more than to pull the sleeping bag back over my head and tell anyone who dared to disturb me that I wasn't a Catholic, I didn't believe the Chaparrita had any miraculous powers and besides, she looked like a hat. Fortunately, a cup of coffee was placed in my hands before I had time to put this plan into action.

Over that day and the next the landscape got more arid and the fields died away into craggy semi-desert. Hills got steeper, both in reality and in our perception of them, as our bodies started to tire. Views could be majestic, across tawny plains to a backdrop of purple mountains, but as time went on we looked at the road more and more and our surroundings less and less. We became increasingly grateful for the small marquees erected at intervals of a couple of kilometres along the route, handing out cups of water, slices of watermelon, and strips of aspirin tablets. These would be shoved into our hands as we walked past without stopping, having learnt that feet are numbed by the repetitive impact of steps and it's once you stop that the pain really kicks in. When we had to stop for meals one of Trico's uncles would massage each of the family's feet in turn, kneading the knots out of the muscles with practised fingers.

As we passed through the suburbs of Lagos de Moreno, people cheered and gave us blessings. And then finally, sometime in the middle of the fourth day (everyone else's fifth), the clutter of buildings that was San Juan became visible far on the horizon. And I looked before and behind us at the river of humanity plodding, chattering, smoking, whinging (no longer skipping) and hobbling its way over the hills, aching and exhausted but together, and resolute in their faith that the Chaparrita (not to mention the unflappable matriarchs and the venerable patriarchs) would never abandon them.

ψ Ψ ψ

On the outskirts of San Juan, pilgrims were arriving not only from San Luis but from the other towns of Jalisco, León, Guanajuato, and even further afield. Trucks blocked the roads. People slept on sheets of cardboard in shop doorways, between parked cars, behind market stalls. As we trooped downhill into the town centre on the morning of Easter Sunday, the streets were a riot of colour and noise. Progress was obstructed not only by other pilgrims, but by weasel-faced men draped in trinkets shoving rosaries, crucifixes and Virgins of all shapes and sizes under our noses. Others proffered hats (I swear they were hats), gaudy necklaces or fake Rolexes. Behind them, the more permanent stalls displayed towers of the sweets for which San Juan is also famous: multicoloured spiral lollipops as big as plates, blocks of fudge and pink-and-white *cocada* (a sweet made from grated coconut). Wide-hipped women floundered through the crowd waving wooden sticks with a sample blob of *cajeta* – sweetened caramelised goat's milk, used as a spread or sauce – that frequently ended up smeared on someone's clothes, face or Virgin. Food-sellers sweated, shouted and despaired, no doubt sustaining themselves only with the knowledge that they made more money during these days of pilgrimage than in the rest of the year put together. Trico's family, ever devout, fought their way to the cathedral to attend mass. Trico and I, tired of having our feet trodden on and our stomachs elbowed and by this time thoroughly cured of Catholicism, went to the pub.

ψ Ψ ψ

The family returned to San Luis after the service, but Trico and I stayed on. San Juan had always been one of our favourite places to earn money when we wanted it fast. The constant arrival of fresh worshippers extended our novelty value pretty much indefinitely, and it helped that they were all eager to get on God's good side. It wasn't uncommon for us to receive notes of 20 pesos in the semáforos, and occasionally even 50 or 100 (perhaps from those coming out of particularly tricky confessions). Aluminium flowers would sell before we'd even finished making them. We had spent so much time there we were on pet-name terms with the elderly owners of an always empty guest house where we had two floors, two kitchens, two bathrooms, a balcony and a roof terrace at our sole disposal for 80 pesos a night, half-price-food terms with several of the street vendors, and let-me-buy-you-a-drink terms (both ways) with the residents of the poorer barrios on the hill above our regular semáforo. We determined to stay until we'd raised 2,000 pesos and then make a triumphant trip down to DF to buy all the circus toys we had always wanted, but could never afford.

It was all going so well. After a week we were already nearing our goal – and that had been while living the good life of guest houses, mescal and *caldos de camarón*. On a blazingly hot afternoon after the bulk of the pilgrims had left and San Juan was returning to its usual tranquillity, we were playing in a semáforo just up the hill from the one we usually frequented. It was a wide intersection, and the red light for the opposite lane was already occupied by a ball-juggler sweating in full clown costume and a tiny boy whose glum face looked even more pitiful under its beaming clown make-up and whose little hands could barely reach the windows as he did the charol for his father. Trico and I had already established that the glare of the sun was too bright for us to play passes without arguments, so we were taking turns doing solo performances at the one available traffic light. It was my turn. The light turned amber, and then red. There were no cars waiting.

'*Uno por la alegría!*' Trico called. One for the joy. I laughed and skipped out into the road, poi in hands.

It came from nowhere. Or rather, it came screamingly fast from the bottom of the hill, which was hidden from view by a curve in the road. I remember seeing the great metal box of the bonnet – a pickup, clearly, too big for a car – and the reflections of the clouds off the windscreen, only a few metres away from me. No time to move. I remember the crunching impact with my knees and chest. I remember being thrown through the air, landing crumpled on the tarmac above five metres away. And then I remember nothing.

ψ Ψ ψ

The sun was so bright it hurt my eyes, until suddenly it was eclipsed by a looming shadow. A smaller shadow appeared next to it from the opposite side. As my eyes adjusted to the gloom they cast, I saw that both of the shadows had enormous white grins stretching almost to their temples, red noses, painted eyelashes, and stars around their eyes.

Either this is God's warped idea of malabarista heaven, I thought, *or I'm hallucinating.*

'She's conscious!' shouted the larger shadow, abruptly removing itself from my vision. I squealed as the sun fell in my eyes. Someone put a towel over my face. I felt someone grasp my hand and heard a voice I recognised as Trico's.

'Loquita! Loquita, how do you feel? Can you hear me? Are you alright?'

I groaned from under my towel.

'Loquita, talk to me!'

'I... I'm OK... that *pendejo* didn't stop at the red light.'

Trico exhaled a silent laugh of relief.

'You sound pretty normal to me. Thank God! When I saw, I thought... my brother, you know? Both my brothers... But you're OK. Thank God you're OK!'

I heard whispered voices from behind him, in which the word 'Chaparrita' was clearly audible. I turned my head and squinted out from under the towel. I was surrounded by a dense ring of people, all staring eagerly at me. There was a murmur of excitement at my movement.

'My leg hurts,' it suddenly occurred to me. 'My knee. My right knee.' I felt a pang of dread. I had a metal pin in that knee, from an accident two years earlier in the Indian Himalayas – an accident that had earned me a month in hospital, a flight home and four months on crutches. *Not again... Don't make me leave here...* I started to cry.

'It's alright, Loquita,' Trico assured me. 'You'll be alright. An ambulance is coming. They'll take you to hospital, give you X-rays. It's all going to be OK.'

He stayed by my side through the wait for the ambulance, as I was lifted onto a stretcher and carried inside, and through the drive to the hospital. I gripped his hand with white knuckles, convinced that it was all over: Trico, malabares, and Mexico.

ψ Ψ ψ

At the hospital, my legs, hips and chest were all X-rayed and I was put in a wheelchair. After a short wait, a nurse wheeled me into a private office, where a doctor was waiting to talk to me. She held up an X-ray of my right leg. She pointed to a fine dark line across the kneecap.

'This is the only injury that comes up on the X-rays. A hairline fracture to the right kneecap. We'll put it in a splint and it should heal within a few weeks.'

'It won't interfere with the metal pin?'

'No, it shouldn't. Not deep enough. I'd say you've been very lucky to be so lightly injured, after being hit hard enough to throw you across the road. Almost miraculously lucky! Your boyfriend says you arrived in the pilgrimage... and you were playing in the semáforo; is that right? You never know... after all, the Chaparrita has a soft spot for circus performers.'

'Sorry?'

'Don't you know the story? It was one of the first miracles the Chaparrita ever performed – this was back in, oh, 1600-and-something. A family of acrobats had come to the town. They performed a trapeze act, but to make it more impressive they erected a forest of spears underneath. During the act one of the acrobats – a little girl of only seven years old – slipped and fell. She was impaled on the spears and died instantly. The women of the town brought the statue of the Chaparrita from the cathedral to where the body of the girl had been laid out and prayed over her for many hours. Miraculously, she was restored to life. It was that miracle that made the Chaparrita famous all over Mexico.'

She put the splint on my leg, prescribed me a bewildering cocktail of painkillers, and sent me out to a bed in a clean and near-empty ward.

'Just a precaution,' she assured me. 'We prefer to keep people in for a short while after a blow to the head, just in case they develop signs of concussion. If you feel fine in a couple of hours you can leave.'

Trico sat at my bedside and talked to me as I waited. After about an hour, a door opened at the far end of the ward and an elegantly groomed woman entered. She walked over to us, her high heels clacking on the linoleum flooring.

'Is she OK?' she asked Trico.

'She has a fractured knee,' Trico told her coldly. 'Other than that she seems to be OK.'

'Oh good, good,' said the woman, although she didn't look at me and didn't seem particularly concerned. 'Everything's alright then. So now – my *son...*'

Trico flared at her angrily.

'We don't *care* about your son, OK? We're waiting here to check she doesn't develop signs of concussion. Then we'll think about your son. Until then, you can wait for us outside.'

The woman pursed her lips and clacked her way out again.

'What was all that about?' I asked Trico.

'She's the mother of the boy who hit you. He's only seventeen, didn't have a licence. He stopped immediately when it happened. He was nearly hysterical, couldn't stop crying. They arrested him. He has to wait in the cells until you negotiate compensation.'

My brain swam. This was too much for me to make sense of with a head full of painkillers.

'What do you mean, until I negotiate compensation?'

He looked confused, as if wondering which part of this concept could possibly be alien to me.

'Well, obviously he or his mother has to pay compensation for injuring you, right? His mother already paid your medical bills here. But they won't let him out of jail until you sign a document saying you're happy with the amount they've given you. That's why she's so desperate for us to go now.'

'So basically... I can ask for as much compensation as I think I can get out of them? And I hold all the power, because they won't let him out of jail until I sign the document?'

'Well, not exactly. The police can say if they think you're being unreasonable. But basically, yes.'

I shook my head in disbelief. I was baffled by the system, and really not looking forward to going to a police station to negotiate compensation in Spanish with a distressed and irate mother whilst doped up on painkillers and with a pounding head, countless bruises and a fractured knee.

The mother drove us to the police station. By the time we got there all the pain had welled up again and I felt dizzy and nauseous. I wondered whether I might have concussion after all, and whether it had really been a good idea to leave the hospital so early. I took a couple more tablets. I had not been given any crutches, and Trico practically had to carry me into the police station and sit me down on the chair indicated. Two policemen stared across a wooden desk at me, while the mother stared from one side.

'So – how much are you asking for?'

I looked in desperation at Trico. How much was I asking for? I had no idea what was appropriate. The amount I could have earned in the time I would be incapacitated? The amount it would cost to support myself during that time? Did I add on any extra for pain and suffering endured? The policemen saw me looking.

'Compensation must be negotiated only with the victim,' they told Trico. 'Perhaps it's better if you leave the room.'

With a helpless shrug, Trico went out.

I put my head in my hands and struggled to think. I had been told that I couldn't put weight on the leg for 10 days and couldn't walk normally for three weeks. That meant three weeks that I couldn't work. Was it unreasonable to ask for 100 pesos for each of those days? I could certainly have earned much more than that. Plus bus fares for Trico and me to return to San Luis, as we obviously couldn't hitchhike with me in this state...

'Three thousand pesos?' I asked tentatively.

The policemen looked at the woman.

'I think that's a bit excessive,' she said. 'The doctors say she will only be incapacitated for ten days.'

They looked back at me. I felt like crying. Was I being greedy? Ten times 100, plus the bus fares...

'One thousand five hundred?'

They looked at the woman. She looked at me.

'Mine is only a humble family,' she said. 'I have seven children. We are very poor. You come from a rich country.'

I wanted to tell her that I had nothing if I couldn't work... but I was in front of policemen. Could I admit to being reliant on semáforos? Was it right for me to be reliant on semáforos anyway? As the woman said, I came from a rich country. Through a fog of pain I started imagining the seven children, seeing them with despondent hungry faces like the poor little clown child in the semáforo... Fifty pesos a day was enough to eat...

'A thousand?' I pleaded. 'I need fifty pesos a day for food, at least for the days I can't walk. And the bus fares for my boyfriend and me to get back to San Luis.'

'I don't think it's reasonable to expect me to pay *his* bus fare,' said the woman. 'After all, *he* isn't injured.'

'Seven hundred and fifty then?' said one of the policemen. The woman nodded judiciously.

'Sign here,' they told me, thrusting a sheaf of papers across the desk. What was this? Had I agreed? I thought of the hungry children. I signed.

The woman stood up, opened a stylish black leather handbag, took out her wallet, peeled three notes off the wad she had inside, and handed them to me. Then she snapped her bag shut, turned on her heel, and clacked out towards her shining silver car, pausing at the doorway to settle a pair of designer sunglasses on her nose.

'*Ay*, Loquita,' Trico said to me, as we rolled back towards San Luis on a bus that had already cost us two-thirds of my compensation, 'wasn't it obvious she wasn't poor? With those clothes, that car? San Juan is one of the richest towns in this region, with all the money that comes in from the pilgrims. And by the look of her, she was one of the richest women in it. You probably could have got five thousand out of her. Maybe more.'

'I know, I know...' I was feeling extremely foolish. 'I was an idiot. I wasn't thinking straight.'

'At least you're OK. How lucky we have nearly two thousand pesos saved, eh? But even if we didn't, you know my family would always look after you.'

I did know that. In the three weeks of my recuperation at Trico's parents' house in San Luis, Elvira did indeed look after me like a mother. If she felt I was a burden, she never showed it, and at least the money we had saved enabled us to contribute to the household.

By the time I could walk again, our nearly 2,000 pesos were almost gone.

16
Topes

The fateful trip to Chihuahua came about one afternoon as Hele and I shared a caguama at the house where she lived with Alvaro and I complained interminably about Trico. Although he had been devotedly loving and attentive in the immediate aftermath of my accident, as I recovered he had relapsed into a protracted period of Tricopsycho and we had been spending more and more time in Phases Two to Three of the love cycle.

'What you need,' Hele declared, 'is a break.'

'That's exactly what I need,' I said. 'Being with someone 24/7 would put a strain on any relationship. And it's worst in San Luis. Sometimes I feel like a tourist in his world, you know what I mean? I like the banda here, of course, but they were all his friends first. I can hardly confide in them about him, can I?'

Hele topped up her glass and looked thoughtful.

'I have a suggestion for you,' she said. She gestured vaguely around her and Alvaro's living room. 'I'm very happy here now. But I'm worried about all the stuff I left in Chihuahua. I wouldn't put it past Jorge to sell it. Some of those gowns are of great sentimental value to me. And now that I'm a bit more settled, I would really like my books back. I've been thinking of going to collect them for a while, but I'd rather not hitchhike alone and if I go with Alvaro... well, you know what Mexican men are like. It might not be a good idea to turn up at Jorge's house with a new boyfriend.'

I nodded my agreement.

'So what I suggest,' she went on, 'is that we make a trip to Chihuahua together. Just the two of us. We could stay in Torreón for a couple of days on the way – there's a banda there who've set up a marvellous circus school in a squatted building; it's well worth a visit. And I'm sure we could stay with my friend Pepe in Chihuahua and visit the banda there. You know Javi's girlfriend is pregnant? The baby must be due any day now. I would love to see them again. We'll only be gone for a week or so, but I can get my stuff back, and you can get your break. What do you think?'

'It sounds tempting... it's a lot of heavy boxes though. Could we hitchhike back with all of that? We couldn't even carry it, could we?'

'No,' she conceded. 'After all, I have all the contents of my old Mexico City apartment there, as well as my dresses and my books. But I don't see why it should be a problem. I didn't have much furniture. It should all fit in the sleeping area of a truck. We just have to make sure we always get dropped off at petrol stations. Then we don't have to carry it anywhere, just unload it from one ride and reload it into another.'

She'd thought of everything. 'I'm up for it,' I said.

'Good,' said Hele, with the air of brisk efficiency that schemes of this nature always inspired in her. 'I suggest we leave as soon as possible then. Of course, we will have to take Mjá.'

I looked at the sleek grey kitten winding itself around her feet. Like a benevolent witch and her familiar, Hele and Mjá were rarely out of physical contact. Mjá (which, purportedly, is how cats say 'meow' in Estonian) had been a skeletal stray until Hele had picked him up in Torreón on her previous visit and nursed him into glossy, complacent health. He had been her pride and joy ever since, as was obvious from being shown her post-Torreón photo albums, which largely consisted of various historical monuments and cultural sights partially obscured by Mjá's whiskered face. ('This is Mjá in the ruined village above Real de Catorce... this is Mjá with a market seller in Gómez Palacio...') She was fond of telling me that he was a more reliable and affectionate companion than any man she had thus far found. I was less convinced. I have never been much of a cat person.

'Can't we leave Mjá here?' I asked.

'Of course we can't,' she retorted. 'Alvaro has always been deeply jealous of Mjá. I couldn't risk leaving them alone together.' She sighed. 'It's one of the few things I don't like about him. Don't worry though. Mjá will be my responsibility. You won't have to do a thing.'

So we poured another glass of beer each and toasted to our resolution to hitchhike 1,000 kilometres across northern Mexico with the contents of an apartment and a cat.

On hearing of this plan Trico, demonstrating his flair for melodrama at its finest, threw a spectacular tantrum, threatened that he might be gone by the time I got back, informed his parents that I was leaving him in search of greater luxury ('*Ay, mi hija,*' Elvira said soothingly when I went to her to tearfully deny this, 'you don't think I actually *listen* to him, do you?') and then, when I was still resolute on leaving, cried bitterly and presented me with his entire collection of lucky things so that I wouldn't forget him over the impending week's separation. Consequently, along with the contents of Hele's apartment and a cat, we would also be carrying a bag of jewellery, crystals, arrowheads, feathers, and several particularly attractive rocks.

Thus prepared, we set out for Chihuahua.

We had arranged everything the night before so we could head off at 8 a.m.; we actually woke up at 10 a.m., rescheduled departure for noon, and left at 2 p.m. We town-hopped in private cars and vans for a few hours, until we were picked up by a truck driver heading for Torreón.

He was a heavy-set man with sag lines on his cheeks, as if his moustache was somehow weighing his face down, and he was singing along to a tape of particularly lugubrious *ranchera* music: lots of protracted wailing about women, and how they treat you bad, and how they can't be trusted, and how they'll leave you lonely, *ay-ay-ay-ayyy*. Between wails, he treated us to a lurid description of cock-fighting in his home village, somewhere in the highlands of Durango, focussing on the metal spikes attached to the birds' legs, the blood, the squawking and the broken necks.

'When you put them in the ring they won't fight at first... you have to hold them and clash their beaks together, something about that makes them crazy... If one won't fight or tries to run away you take it out and wring its neck... no use for a cock that won't fight... good cock's worth thousands of pesos... had a cock once that would rip a bird apart even after it was dead...'

Apparently such enormous sums were bet on these fights that it was not unheard of for a man to bankrupt his entire family in a single evening. Their womenfolk were not allowed to watch. We asked why. He snorted contemptuously.

'Women don't understand these things.'

For once, I had to agree. Pulling my jumper over my ears to block out the wailing, I settled down in the bed and went to sleep.

Hele shook me awake somewhere in the small hours of the morning. We had arrived at a fuel station on the outskirts of Torreón. I crawled out of the cab bleary-eyed and bad-tempered. The truck rumbled off, leaving us blinking on the empty forecourt.

'We should find the squat,' Hele said. 'Get some sleep. We'll never find another lift from here, not in the middle of the night.'

'Do you know the way?'

'We can ask them.' Three men were standing on the edge of the forecourt, staring at us as if we had just dropped from the sky. They stared even harder when we asked them for directions, and shook their heads disbelievingly.

'You can't walk from here. It's very dangerous.'

'Can we get a taxi then?'

'Taxis won't go there.'

'Why not?'

'Here we're in Gómez Palacio.'

Hele's eyes widened in comprehension. I was bewildered. Torreón and Gómez Palacio are the same town in all but name. Along with the smaller municipality of Ciudad Lerdo, they form part of a single metropolis called Comarca Lagunera – or La Laguna for short. The Rio Nazas which marks the border between the states of Durango and Coahuila splits the city into two nominally distinct entities, but on the ground the dividing line is barely noticeable. You merely cross a bridge from one lot of shabby sprawling streets to another lot of shabby sprawling streets. I couldn't see what the problem was. I looked questioningly at Hele.

'Because of the cartel situation?' she asked the men. They nodded.

'Here we're in Chapo's territory,' one explained. 'Torreón is the Zetas'. Taxis won't go to the other side. Not at night.'

'It was like this when I was last here,' Hele sighed. 'I hoped it would have settled down by now.'

Those early months of 2010 must have been a confusing time to be a Mexican gang member. The ex-paramilitary group Los Zetas, who had been working as the brutal enforcement wing for the Gulf Cartel since their founding members deserted the Mexican army in 1999, had declared their independence in February and viciously turned on their former masters. The established territories along the east coast of Mexico were plunged into bloody disarray as the Gulf Cartel struggled to hold their ground against the monster they had created. In desperation, they turned to the only people who might possibly be able to help: Chapo's Sinaloa Cartel, with whom they had been locked in bitter warfare for years. (One can only imagine how that conversation might have gone. Surely there can be no easy way of saying, 'Sorry to bother you, but the people we've been paying to kill you are now trying to kill us... so we were wondering if you would stop killing us and help us kill them instead?') Recognising that the Zetas, although better trained and better armed than the Gulf Cartel, were still more rabidly untrustworthy, Chapo promptly forged the alliance. Practically overnight, the Gulf Cartel and the Zetas went from being partners to being mortal enemies, and the Gulf Cartel and the Sinaloa Cartel went from being mortal enemies to being partners. You could understand them being confused.

Nowhere was this confusion more evident than La Laguna. Unsure of who was supposed to be killing whom, everybody seemed to be killing everybody. As usual, the hapless civilian population was caught in the middle. During the two days we stayed in the squat, the papers reported 28 violent deaths in the previous week. At least, Hele remarked, this was an improvement on when she had last been there a few months before, when they had reported 50 in the previous weekend.

What we would have done without the three men at the garage, I have no idea. They made some phone calls and managed to find us a taxi which would take us to the bridge, where we would transfer to another taxi for the second leg of the journey. They apologised that it wouldn't be cheap but I thought the price was pretty reasonable, given the circumstances.

ψ Ψ ψ

One travels with the intention of discovering the 'real' country, whatever that's supposed to mean, but I think of the roads between Torreón and Chihuahua as too Mexican to be truly believable, as if you had been lulled to sleep by the purr of wheels across tarmac and had a clumsy dream of Mexico, cobbled together from stereotypes and images in Western movies.

The landscape is parched and never-ending, trailing off into a heat-smudged horizon under a stubble of coarse scrub and cacti. An occasional surly village squats by the road with an air of contained menace, like a spider guarding its web. Its buildings are flat-roofed and colourless, only brightened by painted ads for Tecate beer or Coca-Cola. Every second one has swing doors: these are the bars. There are almost no women on the street, only heavy-faced men with black moustaches and Stetson hats staring sullenly into the middle distance. Rust-coloured horses are tethered to lamp posts, next to the clapped-out pickups. As you pass, the men and the horses gaze at you with identical expressions, listless but uncompromising, as if to say, 'I would kick you so hard you'd vomit out your kidneys, if only I had the motivation.'

In my head it has a name, this archetypal north Mexican village: it is called Topes. This is because each one you pass through is announced by a sign saying 'TOPES' on its perimeter. This had both Hele and me completely baffled on our earlier journeys through northern Mexico, before we learnt the Spanish for 'speed bumps'.

Somewhere in the vacuum north of Torreón we visited a particularly tragic Topes some way off the highway, without even a flow of cross-country traffic to disrupt its stagnation. We were in a ride with a weary, grizzled schoolteacher, one of those silent saints propping up this earth whose tasks are as thankless as they are endless. He took a detour off the highway to drop off a box of materials at the primary school where he taught – a tired bunker in a grubby patch of dust. He invited us to take a sip from the water tap outside and shook his head sadly when we spat it straight back out again onto the thirsty earth. It was unbearably salty.

'Do the children drink this?'

'There is nothing else to drink. All the water here is like that. Their families are very poor. Most can't afford bottled water.'

'Doesn't it make them ill?'

'They're used to it.'

'Won't they get diseases when they get older? High blood pressure? Heart attacks? Strokes?'

'*Quién sabe?*'

Chihuahua has many curses, but one of the worst is water scarcity. As population grows in the industrial north of Mexico, the aquifers of this arid semi-desert region are put under increasing strain. Climate change may be exacerbating the problem. Meagre reservoirs are drained to supply the houses and factories of the swelling cities, and forgotten rural communities are left to wither. With irrigation channels dried to a trickle, agriculture is largely gone. Even ranching is under threat as cattle starve in the parched desert. One curse feeds another. Some months later, I was to feel a stab of recognition when, in the brilliant and blackly comic 2010 film *El Infierno*, Joaquín Cosio's narco character stares out across the wasteland surrounding a village identical to all those discarded little Topes, sighs deeply, and tells his partner, 'I am in this business because there is no other.'

At a lonely fuel station, we were picked up by three men in a yellow car with heavy black fittings, giving it the look of an engorged wasp. It was suspiciously shiny and rust-free for these parts. The men were in high spirits, and told us – improbably – that they were returning from a carnival in the south to their home in Ciudad Juárez, where they would drop the wasp car off and head south again a few days later in a different car. (They told us this when we mentioned that we would be returning south in a few days. They offered us a ride back. We demurred.) They chatted gaily all the way to Chihuahua, pausing only when we passed a police car – more numerous the further north you go – when one of them would pull a gleaming mobile phone out of a shirt pocket and make a brief, curt phone call. The call was always the same.

'*Federales* [federal police],' followed by the name of our location. '*Sí. Sí.*' Then they'd hang up.

At the time, I chose to believe that they were among the lowly men hired by the narcos for the sole purpose of driving up and down these highways, alerting them to police and army positions. Looking back, I am unsure whether such a low-risk job would be so well-paid. But whoever they were, they treated us with the utmost courtesy; in fact, most disturbingly, I had to remind myself not to like them.

There is a certain type of narco who fancies himself as something of a Robin Hood figure, and enjoys indulging this fantasy with displays of generosity to harmless nobodies. One of the most recounted stories about Chapo is the time he is said to have stormed into a crowded restaurant with a gang of heavily armed henchmen, barred the doors, confiscated the mobile phones of the clientele, and then insisted on paying for everyone's lunch. Presumably such ostentatious displays are merely another way of flaunting their power and wealth. But some take it further and do put some of their bloodstained money into schools, churches and small businesses in their home towns and villages. It is a sad fact that in some parts of the country they are hailed as folk heroes for being the only people seen to be making any investment in godforsaken rural communities at all.

Monsters may be terrifying, but at least they are straightforward. They become more disconcerting when they reveal a human face.

17
Welcome to Chihuahua

Pepe welcomed us with the slightly dazed enthusiasm of a proud resident of a city where weed can be bought for around 1,000 pesos a kilo. (I was often surprised at the willingness of many people to put their money into the trade that was devastating their country. I suppose one can become desensitised to anything after a while. Or perhaps the logic is simply that, as the power of the cartels looks likely to continue as long as there are massive profits to be made in the export trade, they would rather be killed for their own habit than for someone else's.)

'Come *in*, man, come *in*. Have some, y'know, *food* or something. Good to *see* you.'

He spoke to us in English, being one of Chihuahua's sizable population of Mexican-Americans whose outstanding felonies prevent them from taking full advantage of their passports. Not that Pepe seemed bothered by it. Here he had a legitimate job which he enjoyed, rent was cheap and weed was cheaper. Why would he want to be anywhere else? He had a squashed nose, curly dark hair, and an irresistibly goofy grin which reminded me of Wallace from *Wallace and Gromit*. He gave us a spare key to the house and urged us to treat it like our own.

Rescuing Hele's possessions turned out to be a much less fraught process than we had feared. Jorge was not in town.

'He left about a month ago,' his formidable younger sister Laura told us. 'Who knows where he went. We've kept all your stuff safe for you though. Are you really not coming back, Hele?'

Hele sighed. 'You know I'll miss you all, Laura. I'll even miss Jorge. I did care about him very much... but *no mames*...'

Laura nodded sympathetically. '*Sí.* The guy's really lazy, it's true.'

As we loaded the boxes into a taxi, Elena came onto the pavement and patted Hele vaguely on the shoulder before shuffling back inside.

With our main mission accomplished, we decided to give ourselves three days in the city to wander around and catch up with friends. In the mornings we would go to the semáforos and I would spin poi while Hele played her djembe. Two güeras in one semáforo! We always left with our bags heavy with coins. Not to mention the more imaginative donations which are part of the fun of playing semáforos. Ice creams, lettuces, loaves of bread, cans of beer, fliers for parties or religious orders, phone numbers of would-be admirers...

One afternoon, while Hele got reacquainted with her beloved trunks of books, Pepe took me sightseeing around the city. We wandered around the town centre and I made appropriate noises at statues, fountains and Baroque churches. I have always been more interested in people than buildings.

'On that hill there,' Pepe pointed towards the domed brown hill which rose from the city sprawl like a whale surfacing for air, 'is a cage with a leopard in it. It was confiscated from a narco's private zoo when the army stormed his compound.'

He took me to the Government Palace of Chihuahua, an elegantly imposing building that looks from a distance like a coffin with windows. Perhaps this is appropriate, as it is the site of the death of Miguel Hidalgo, one of the great heroes of the Mexican War of Independence, whose name innumerable towns, districts, buildings and bus stops across the country still bear in his honour. He started his career as a lowly priest in the town of Dolores, before being radicalised by the poverty and exploitation of the indigenous farmers in his parish and eventually leading an army of nearly 90,000 Mexican peasants in an unsuccessful but ultimately inspirational rebellion against Spanish rule. In the wake of his failed revolution, he was captured and taken to the Government Palace of Chihuahua, where he was executed by firing squad shortly after dawn on 7 July 1811. His final known actions were to write a letter to his gaolers thanking them for their humane treatment of him, and to refuse a blindfold as he was led out to face the Spanish rifles.

A shrine is erected on the spot where the man now hailed as the 'Father of the Nation' drew his last breath, and next to it is a mural by the Mexican painter Aarón Piña Mora depicting his final moments. In it he stares resolutely at the viewer, looking haggard but unflinching, with one hand over his heart and a ring of rifles and bayonets poking into his chest.

The murals of Aarón Piña Mora continue outside the small room which contains the shrine to Hidalgo and cover the walls of the grand internal courtyard with vivid, energetic scenes from Mexican legends and history. Although he must have seen them many times before, Pepe responded to the murals with a more lively interest than I had ever seen from him.

'Aren't they *incredible*?' he enthused. 'Look at the brushwork on them! Me, I like them better than Diego Rivera's. They have so much *vigour*, don't you think?'

He continued to talk excitedly about the murals, giving a considered commentary about the style and placing it in context of the evolution of Mexican art.

'You seem to know a lot about art,' I said.

'Ah,' he said, a little wistfully. 'I was just finishing my master's degree in fine arts when I got my felony.'

Not far from the Government Palace was a grimly striking monument: a vertical pink and blue panel with a central rugged cross of dark wood driven through with rows of heavy iron nails, each bearing its own red ribbon and label with a name on it. At the base of the cross was the armless torso of a dressmaker's dummy. The label at the top of the cross read: '*NI UNA MÁS*'. Not one more.

'The monument to *las muertas de Juárez*,' Pepe explained. 'You've heard of them, right?'

'Of course,' I said, 'although I can hardly bear to think about it. What do you think the motives for the killings are? Do you think the gangs really use them as an initiation test?'

'Nah,' he said. 'It's just sport.'

'Sport?'

'Yeah. Like some people enjoy hunting, y'know? Only in Juárez they hunt women. Seriously. If you're some sick son-of-a-bitch like that and you know the right people in Juárez, you can pay them a few hundred pesos and off you go. I know a couple of guys who've had it offered to them like it's a fucking tour or something. You cruise around until you see one you like, and *bam*. She's yours to do what you like with. They dispose of the body.'

'Everything I hear about Juárez makes me want to cry,' I said. 'It barely seems possible that one city can be made to suffer so much.'

'It's not all bad,' he said. 'You only ever hear the dark stuff about Juárez. People forget that it's also just a normal city where people work, eat, laugh, fuck, fall in love and live their lives.'

'But isn't that the saddest thing of all? I wouldn't give a shit if it was just a town full of narcos killing each other. It's the normal people just trying to live their lives that are the tragedy. I know a couple from Juárez with a two-year-old son who hitchhike and sleep rough with him around the country and say they feel he's safer that way than he would be there.'

'Yeah, well, it's got a dirty vibe, that's for sure. Some good parties though. But you gotta carry a knife.'

'I don't think I'd enjoy a party where I needed to carry a knife.'

'Yeah, but you're a nice person,' he told me, in a slightly patronising tone, before adding as an afterthought: 'I'm not nice.'

'You seem nice to me.'

'I'm nice to you because I like you. And the guys that come round the house, they're my people. I'm nice to them. But with a lotta people round here... you can't afford to be nice.' The goofy grin broke out in all its glory. 'Then I have my knife!'

I steered the conversation back to Mexican muralists.

ψ Ψ ψ

The day before we planned to leave for San Luis, we went to a bar with Jorge's more industrious friends Javi and Lupita to celebrate Javi's birthday. Lupita, her due date in two weeks' time, was enormous, her tiny frame so overwhelmed by the size of her belly that she appeared almost spherical. Javi was glowing with pride.

I had always been slightly in love with Javi. Tall and square-jawed, with thick black hair and unusually white teeth for a Chihuahuan, he combined the best of both Spanish and indigenous features. He was good-natured, a talented performer, impressively dedicated to his work, and devoted to his girlfriend. I was also slightly in love with Lupita. A few years older than Javi, she was short-haired and pithy and stuck her tongue out when she laughed. She had worked as a language teacher up until the final month of her pregnancy. Above all, I was in love with them as a couple, their easy comradeship a defiant contradiction of the macho/mariana stereotype of Mexican relationships.

The bar was packed with Javi's and Lupita's friends, live bands were playing, and drinks were being spilled almost as fast as they were being drunk. When last orders were called sometime around midnight, Lupita came up to where Javi was talking to us at the bar and put a hand on the small of his back.

'I'm going to head home now,' she said. 'Will you stay out?'

'Some of the banda are going on to a club,' Javi replied. 'It would be good to go for a dance for a couple of hours. But I'll take you home first, of course.'

'I'll be fine,' Lupita smiled.

'I'll go with her, Javi,' Hele offered, before he could object. 'I'm quite tired anyway, and I should get some sleep if we're going to leave for San Luis tomorrow.' Lupita nodded at him reassuringly.

'Well, if you're sure you'll be OK,' he said. 'What about you, Cat? Do you need to sleep as well? Or will you come dancing with us?'

I didn't feel anywhere near sleep. I was loving the music, loving the atmosphere, and loving having a night out un-partnered for the first time in months.

'I'll go with you,' I said.

On the pavement outside the bar Javi kissed Lupita goodnight and she and Hele left in a taxi. The ten or so of us who would be going on to the club gathered together, formulating a plan of action.

'Doesn't Pancho have a car? Are you alright to drive, Pancho?'

'More or less. Will we all fit though?'

'Pfff. We'll make ourselves fit!' Mexican law enforcement is pretty lax on this sort of thing. Maximum vehicle capacity is basically considered to be however many you can fit in and still be able to breathe.

We arrived at the club and tumbled onto the pavement, still laughing. Inside, music was throbbing and the darkened room was heaving with people.

'Come on, Javi,' I said. 'It's your birthday and I still haven't bought you a drink.'

We pushed our way to the bar and I ordered two beers. The lights were dim and blue, laced with UV, and above a chest glowing in a white T-shirt, Javi's teeth and eyes stood out very bright in the dark skin of his face.

Shots of tequila with salt and lime followed the beers. I was starting to feel the effects of the night's succession of celebratory drinks. The music sounded distorted, and people's faces swam under the blue lights. At the bar, people pressed in on us from all sides, pushing us closer together until our chests were almost touching. I looked up into Javi's face as he laughed at whatever rubbish it was I was talking about. We were laughing at anything by that stage. His teeth were so white... I was starting to feel a little fuzzy, seeing him laugh in slow motion, like a sequence from a movie. Handsome Javi. It was a warm, dreamy fantasy, never to be drenched in the cold water of reality. He would never cheat on Lupita and I would never cheat on Trico, but that knowledge only flavoured the crush with a sweet poignancy. Javi and I existed only in that perfect floating hinterland of *what if...?*

There was jostling in the crowd and I was squashed against the bar, leaving me momentarily winded. When I looked up Javi's laughing face had gone, and a narrow gap had been cleaved through the mass of people. Javi was on the floor. I laughed, and stuck out a hand to help him up. But something was wrong, and in my clouded state I struggled to work out what it was. Javi looked different. Before he had had a dark face and a white T-shirt, but now he had a pale face and a black-stained T-shirt. He didn't take my hand.

I was still standing there, hand pointlessly extended, when I was shoved roughly out of the way. Two boys I recognised from the drive to the club were bending over and lifting Javi up between them. Some people were shouting, but I could barely hear them over the music. The crowd parted as the boys staggered towards the entrance. I followed them, stunned.

Javi's new dark-coloured T-shirt left a trail of black stains across the floor, brightening to red as we came out from under the blue lights towards the white lights of the entrance.

ψ Ψ ψ

'Ambulance! Give me a phone and I'll call an ambulance!'

'Ambulance? Don't be ridiculous, it's Saturday night. Where the hell is Pancho? *Ay*, he'll be too drunk by now, won't he? HECTOR! Stop a taxi!'

'I dunno, man, he's bleeding a lot. Do you think they'll take him like that?'

'We can wrap him in my jacket. It's quite thick. Go!'

The music kept playing; people kept dancing and shouting orders for beer and tequila at the bar as if nothing had happened. Only in our corner near the door, where Javi lay bleeding on a bench with his eyes rolling back in his head, did anyone seem shocked or frightened. I fluttered around him, desperate to help but afraid and powerless. My one attempt to do something useful had been impatiently brushed aside. An ambulance? For a mere stabbing? On a Saturday night in Chihuahua? Ridiculous.

The other boys, though shaken, were dealing with the situation with brusque efficiency, as if familiar with the procedure.

'Did you see who did it, Cat?'

'I... no... there were so many people... it happened so fast...' As I said them, I hated the lameness of the words, hated my uselessness. I fell silent.

'I bet it was that kid!'

'What kid?'

'The kid Javi wouldn't let into the other bar that time because he was underage, remember? He left with a face like murder. I bet it was him.'

'I don't even remember what he looked like... I didn't recognise him.'

'Nor me... he was dressed like a proper little *naco* though. Those are always the crazy ones...' (Not to be confused with '*narco*', *naco* means something equivalent to 'white trash' or 'chav'.)

The boy called Hector ran back in.

'I found a taxi! Driver seems *buena onda*. Says don't let him bleed on the seats though.'

Two of the boys lifted Javi up, tenderly wrapping a jacket around the ever-expanding stain on his T-shirt, now so saturated it seemed to have gone past red and started darkening towards black again. They carried him outside and heaved him into the taxi, clambering in behind him. It sped off leaving the rest of us behind.

'Come on, Cat,' one of them said. 'We'll take another taxi to the hospital.'

'Lupita...' I said. 'Who's going to tell Lupita?'

'Nobody's going to tell Lupita. Not now, anyway. With her in the state she's in? Think what a shock like that could do to her! Javi can come home and she can see he's alright, then he can tell her himself. Until then she can't know a thing, you understand?'

It couldn't have been a more different journey to our previous one. Even with three fewer people, it was still a squash. But whereas the first trip had been in laughter, this one was in grim silence.

At the hospital, I remember the crowded waiting room, the harsh glare of the fluorescent lights. I must have made some garbled attempt to get information about Javi's condition from a passing nurse, because I remember her telling one of the boys *'está loca, la güerita'* ('she's crazy, the little white girl'). The boy led me gently to the far side of the room, where we sat on the floor and he put an arm around me until I calmed down. One of the boys who had gone with Javi appeared and told us that he was conscious and they were stitching him up, and he was going to be OK, but there might be some long-term nerve damage. I was breathing very deeply, still in shock, and struggling not to cry. And then finally Javi emerged, his face grey and contorted with pain, leaning heavily on the two boys who were propping him up on either side. Everyone ran to him at once, and I lost sight of him amidst his friends. I turned around, walked alone out of the hospital, and hailed the first taxi I saw. I had seen him conscious and walking. That was all I needed. He was surrounded by people who had already proved they could handle the situation much better than I could. The sky was just starting to lighten, and I suddenly felt desperately tired.

I came in to find Pepe watching skate videos in his boxers, hissing appreciatively at successful jumps and wincing with relish at the most spectacular falls.

'Good party?' he asked, without looking up.

'Not really.' My voice sounded strange and squeaky, like a pubescent boy.

I cleared my throat and tried again. 'Well, it was at first. It...' What was I doing going through these niceties? Why didn't I just say it? 'Javi got stabbed.'

'Ooooh!' breathed Pepe, with a grimace of pained glee. It seemed a strange reaction, until I realised that he was responding to a skateboarder who had just fallen straddling a metal railing. 'What was that?'

'Javi got stabbed. Right in front of me. I was talking to him when it happened.'

'Shit,' he said offhandedly, still fixated on the video. 'They didn't hit an organ, did they?'

'No, I don't think so. He lost a lot of blood, though. And there could be some long-term nerve damage.'

Pepe chuckled. '*Pinche Javi.* Sounds like a good party then.'

I was robbed of words. Wasn't he shocked? Didn't he care? Javi was, after all, an acquaintance of his. I was tempted to grab him and shake him, in the hope of jerking some response from him that would feel like an answer for my own emotions. Perhaps sensing this, he finally glanced up at where I stood, ashen-faced in the doorway. He chuckled again, more gently this time.

'Welcome to Chihuahua.'

18
The Silent Zone

The last warmth of colour had faded from the sky, but lingered in the earth like the embers of a fire, bringing out its red tones and turning the cacti and *gobernadora* bushes into barbed silhouettes. The wheels of the truck purred south into the dusk. There was not another vehicle in sight.

We had left Chihuahua in the mid-afternoon. I was still feeling numb. But even Hele hadn't been as shocked as I expected by the events of the previous night.

'Yes, it is dreadful,' she said. 'But these things happen. I'm sure Javi will be OK. They're tough, these Chihuahuans. I don't see the point of us staying any longer. What can we do?'

So far, the journey had been surprisingly easy. A friend with a car had driven us with the boxes and furniture to a truck stop on the outskirts of the city, and since then it had all gone much as Hele had predicted. We made sure always to get dropped off at petrol stations, and simply unloaded the stuff from one ride and reloaded it into another. It all fitted in the sleeping compartment of a truck. Just about. Drivers didn't even seem particularly surprised to find two European girls hitchhiking 1,000 kilometres across northern Mexico with the contents of an apartment and a cat. These things happen.

Our real stroke of luck came a few hours south of Chihuahua, when we were picked up by Eduardo, who was going all the way to San Luis Potosí. He wore a white vest top and had an amateur-looking tattoo on one bicep, its bluish ink blurring into the mahogany skin of his arm. He was friendly, but suspicious. He had seen the likes of us before.

'They always come at night,' he sighed, leaning back in his seat and stretching his sinewy arms against the wheel with an air of resignation. 'About this time, about this place. Bloody desert's full of ghosts. I've picked up loads of them.' He paused before conceding: 'They don't usually have furniture, though. Or cats.'

Mjá was curled up in the crook of Hele's arm with an expression of insouciant innocence. He had done a poo in her hand halfway through the previous ride and was currently trying to charm himself back into her favour.

'What are they like?' I asked Eduardo. 'The ghosts, I mean.'

He looked surprised at the question.

'Friendly, usually, good company. Sometimes I talk with them all night. But at the first glimpse of sunrise they disappear. I can be in the middle of a conversation, watching the road. Then I glance round at the passenger seat and they're gone.'

'What do they talk to you about?'

'Oh, the usual stuff. The thing is, they don't even know they're dead. They're people who died out here in the desert, and every night they're trying to get back to their homes. I'm happy to help them out. Gives me someone to talk to. I get tired of driving this same road alone through the desert, over and over again. Can make you go a little funny after a while.'

'Do they ever scare you? Try to hurt you?'

'The hitchhiking ghosts, no. The dangerous ones are the ones you can't see. Sometimes I'm driving along this road late at night, when suddenly some force grabs the steering wheel from my hands and I veer across the road. And then there's the aliens.'

'Aliens?'

'Of course. Didn't you know? There are more aliens in this desert than anywhere else on earth. They've been landing here for years. Haven't you heard about the silent zone?'

'I heard stories that there are metal deposits under the earth there that distort radio signals,' Hele said.

Eduardo snorted at such gullibility.

'Maybe that's the story they tell people. The government are trying to cover it up. But it doesn't explain the mutant animals. Or the abductions. I know a driver who woke up once in his truck in the middle of the desert, many kilometres from the road. He didn't remember anything except a very bright light. That was the aliens.' He shook his head grimly. 'They've never abducted me though. Not yet.'

The silent zone was still a fair way southeast of where we were. That is, if it existed at all. But the cloud of rumour and superstition that surrounded it had spread steadily in all directions, to the point where pretty much the whole northern desert was tainted with its extra-terrestrial associations.

On 11 July 1970, a blaze of light was seen falling to earth in the desolate stretches of desert near the Mapimí river basin, somewhere to the north of Gómez Palacio. Local ranchers scratched their heads and speculated that perhaps an angel had descended. A short while later, the trucks arrived. Their coming was never announced and their presence was never explained but there they were, rumbling back and forth across the desert, searching. They were manned by the United States military. Approaching the operation in their own inimitable style, they did not see fit to ask the ranchers where the blaze of light had fallen, but instead hired residents of Gómez Palacio to assist with the search, without ever telling them exactly what they were looking for. There was no comment from Washington.

Whatever it was, after three weeks of exhaustive scouring of sand dunes, they appeared to have found it. An extension was built from the nearest railway to a point in the heart of the Mapimí Biosphere Reserve – an area that had long been of interest to biologists for its unique flora and fauna – where a small airstrip was constructed. A few wagonloads of sand were removed. And then the army personnel moved out, dismantling the railway tracks behind them. The airstrip was abandoned to fall into disrepair.

Perhaps unsurprisingly given the mystery with which the operation had been conducted, gossip spread like infection. What was it that had fallen? Why was it of such importance to the US government that they had to send secret army convoys to look for it? What had they taken away? Did it have anything to do with the unusually large animal species in that particular area of desert, or the purple tinge on the *nopales*? The rumours multiplied. It was said that magnetic anomalies in the atmosphere distorted radio signals in that location and caused compass needles to spin aimlessly. Perhaps these rogue magnetic fields were strong enough to create a vortex of energy that made things fall from the sky? What could cause such a thing? Clearly, there was only one logical explanation. It must be aliens. An alternative explanation did later emerge, which was that an Athena test missile fired in Utah had gone astray and fallen several hundred kilometres south of its intended destination, carrying a small quantity of radioactive isotope. Embarrassed by the blunder, the US military had sent convoys to retrieve the missile and remove any contaminated topsoil, and done their best to hush it up. But this story has never gained much currency across northern Mexico. It would, after all, be profoundly un-Mexican to accept such a boring explanation when a paranormal one can be found which fits just as well. La Zona de Silencio has been a Mecca for conspiracy theorists and UFO curio hunters ever since, much to the exasperation of scientists working to study and protect the unique ecosystem of the Mapimí Reserve. Particularly irritating is the habit of some of the more devout *zoneros* of stealing scientific equipment and kidnapping the reserve's endangered tortoises.

An hour down the road, the remnants of sunset had drained from the land and the desert was steeped in darkness. Eduardo pulled over in a truck stop.

'Time for a coffee, I think,' he said. 'Do you girls want one?'

Hele, who had been dozing fitfully amidst the boxes, shook her head blearily.

'I'd love one,' I said. 'Thanks.'

We jumped down from the cab and walked together to the café. A few truck drivers glanced up at us when we entered before hunching back over their own coffees. We ordered at the counter and Eduardo made a barely perceptible signal to the waitress, a sort of tiny nod, and then said: '*Tres*'. Three. She reached under the counter and handed him something too small for me to see.

There are no frills in these places, no difficult choices between lattes and cappuccinos. We sat down at a table and the waitress plonked two mugs of boiling water in front of us, along with a jar of Nescafe, a tub of sugar, and another tub of milk powder. As we stirred the sludge into our mugs, Eduardo asked me if I wanted anything to eat.

'I'm alright, thanks. Are you going to have anything?'

'No. I don't usually eat when I'm working.'

This was something I had noticed before when hitching with truck drivers in Mexico. I'd done journeys of 15 hours or more with a single driver, during which time they hadn't eaten, slept, or even stopped for longer than about 20 minutes.

'You Mexican truck drivers are incredible,' I said. 'You're like machines. How do you manage to drive for so many hours without rest or food?'

'We have no choice. We have to get there on time. Say my company gives me a journey from DF to Chihuahua. That's at least twenty hours of straight driving in a heavy truck like mine. I load at 11 a.m. They tell me: "You must make the delivery in Chihuahua at 9 a.m. tomorrow morning." I know that if I am late too many times, I will lose my job. How can I find time to rest or eat a meal?'

'That's terrible. That would be illegal in my country. How do you keep going?'

'These,' he said, pulling a strip of three pills from his pocket, and placing it on the table. 'They kill your appetite as well as your tiredness.' He jerked his head to indicate the other truck drivers in the room. 'I would bet you that every man in this room has taken, or will take, at least two of these tonight. You can't do this job without them.'

'What are they?' I asked. He shrugged.

'Do you want to try one? I would normally save one for later, but if I have someone to talk to and keep me awake then I should be alright without it. That's partly why I always pick up hitchhikers. Even the ghost ones.'

He reached over and put a small capsule of white powder on my palm. Intrigued to know what these truck drivers were taking in between picking up phantom hitchhikers and being abducted by aliens, not to mention thundering along at maximum speed hauling extremely heavy and sometimes hazardous loads, I took it, swigging it down with the dregs of my coffee. I expected it to have some mild stimulant effect, perhaps the equivalent of downing a can of energy drink. Eduardo took the other two. He paid, and we got back on the road.

About 20 minutes later I found myself rigid and quivering, my pulse racing and my eyes popping. Hands like claws on the dashboard, I started mindlessly scraping the plastic with my fingernails, inhaling great awkward gulps of air and craning forward to stare manically at the semicircle of lit highway ahead of us, wondering why the hell we weren't going FASTER? Glancing round at my swollen irises and clenched jaw, Eduardo chuckled.

'They hit you pretty hard the first time, right?'

'*Yes* man, I mean like, *no mames*, I can't *believe* you took two!' I was speaking in a sort of urgent gasp, breathing some words with trembling emphasis and practically squeaking others. '*Hijo de su puta madre...* how the fuck can you drive like this?'

He made a wry face.

'You get a tolerance to them pretty fast. These aren't even the good ones. There are a few different types. The best ones come from Guatemala, but I think there have been tighter controls or something recently, because we haven't been getting many of them. With those ones I can still be OK with two, but with these ones I'd usually take at least three on a journey like this.' He sighed. 'It's a fucking pain, because they're really expensive. Varies a bit depending on where you are, but often you have to pay eighty pesos for a pill. So if you're taking three... that's a lot of your pay, you know? And of course, you can't claim it from the company, even though they know most people can't do the journeys without them.'

'*No mames! Pinches culeros!*' I was outraged, feeling the injustice like a burn in my chest. I was ready to go out and strangle them with my bare hands. Whoever 'they' were. I had forgotten.

'*Así es,*' he answered philosophically. That's how it is.

'But isn't it dangerous?'

'Not really, once you're used to them. Less dangerous than falling asleep at the wheel.'

I wasn't sure if I believed that. I certainly felt wide awake, but also taut and twitchy, as if I could spasm uncontrollably at any minute. I could see how a truck could veer across the road under my hands. Even the story of the truck driver who had woken up in the middle of the desert suddenly didn't seem quite so implausible. In fact, the more I stared through the windscreen at the grey tarmac being endlessly devoured by the snout of the truck, the more it seemed perfectly logical to leave this soul-numbing highway and roll free and unrestricted through the boundless mysteries of the desert. I turned round to tell Hele about it. She was cramped up in a huddle beside the boxes, her head resting on her shoulder and her eyes closed.

'Hele!' I hissed, in a deafening stage whisper. She gave a little moan and opened her eyes dazedly.

'What?'

I couldn't remember what I was going to say.

'How's Mjá?'

She flicked her eyes down to where he lay contentedly in her lap before squinting at me in irritation.

'He's fine... are *you* fine?'

I nodded vigorously. 'He gave me one of those little fucking pills, man, and it's like, fucking *nuts* man, I feel like, *woah*, as if I'm on fucking amphetamine or something.'

'You *are* on amphetamine,' she told me calmly.

'You what?'

'Some form of it, anyway.'

'But – you – what the *fuck?* He bought these at the truck stop! In the shop, not outside. Is that *legal?*'

'Of course it's not legal. It's not legal to give truck drivers such impossibly short times to do long journeys in either. But why would the police do anything about it when they're probably picking up bribes from both sides?'

I gawped dumbly at her, exhaling heavily through my nose. She gave me her best elder-sister look of patient disapprobation.

'Don't worry,' she said, 'it will wear off in a couple of hours. Meanwhile, I'm going to try to get some more sleep. I was going to offer to swap places with you so you could have a turn in the bed, but it doesn't look as if you'll be needing it for a while.'

ψ Ψ ψ

It was mid-morning by the time we arrived on the outskirts of San Luis. Eduardo was driving past the city and left us at a turnoff as he continued round the city bypass, first shaking our hands warmly and brushing off our thanks with the insistence that it had been his pleasure to have such friendly and living company. By this time, however, I was struggling to keep up any attempt at friendliness. I was cranky and under-slept and had a thundering headache. Eduardo had dropped us off next to a truck piled high with crates rammed full of live chickens and the smell of them was making me feel sick. I glared angrily at the unfortunate birds. Bloody chickens.

'It's alright; we're nearly home,' Hele told me soothingly. She patted a box overflowing with kitchen utensils. 'And now I have my coffee maker back, I can make you one of those nice lattes with the frothy milk you like so much. First, though, I think we better hitch a ride to the other side of the road. He's gone and left us on the wrong side of the highway, and we'll never manage to cross it with all this stuff. Never mind. I'm sure someone will help us out.'

An hour and two pickup rides later, we were sitting in her living room, surrounded by boxes, mugs in hands.

'Well,' she announced, looking around in satisfaction. 'I think that trip was quite a success.'

Now that I had my nice latte with the frothy milk, I was inclined to agree.

19
The Letter Z

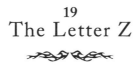

I was washing up in Elvira's courtyard when I heard the first shots. My curiosity had already been piqued by a hubbub of shouting and barking dogs in the street outside, but it was the shots that froze me, plate and sponge in hand, straining to catch some meaning in the confused and increasingly frantic noise. A couple of screams cut through the shouting. Slamming doors. Then more shots.

Trico crashed through the door from the kitchen, Oscar and Chino close behind him. We had just finished lunch, and they had been preparing *micheladas* while I washed the pans and crockery. Elvira was visiting one of her sisters; Don Margaro was away on a journey.

'Get inside, Cat,' Trico barked.

'What the – '

'Get *inside.*'

He pushed me, almost roughly, through the open door to the bedroom, then blocked the exit with his body as he stood in the doorway, peering towards the rooftop. Oscar and Chino appeared behind me, having come through from the adjoining living room, which also faced onto the courtyard.

'It's on the street, isn't it?' Oscar asked.

The shouting on the street continued but there were now also closer noises, seeming to come from above, from the rooftop. Trico stood rigid, like an animal sniffing the air.

'I'm going to see.'

He crept up the concrete steps which led to Elvira and Margaro's bedroom, stopping halfway to crane his neck, trying to see onto the level of the rooftop. Then he climbed a few steps further, almost to the top. Oscar pushed past me and went up to join him. I made as if to follow, but Chino held me back.

'Careful. Wait until we know what's going on.'

The shouts were fewer now, less confused but more urgent, sharp voices from the rooftop as well as more muffled ones from the street. Thuds. Another few shots. Trico and Oscar jumped down and came hurriedly back inside.

'What the fuck are they doing?' Trico exclaimed.

'What?'

'They're on the roof, throwing stones, bricks... they're firing at them from the street... what the *fuck* – '

'Who's firing? Firing at who?'

Before he could answer the tone of the noise changed again, the shouts welling into a panicked crescendo and then fading out, replaced by scuffling, running feet. Suddenly two of the drunk uncles lurched into view, almost throwing themselves down the steps into the courtyard.

'Trico, man, they're coming onto the roof, you have to help us – '

'What the *fuck* – '

The residents of the barrio had all known each other since childhood, and their loyalty was unfailing. Even as he swore at them through clenched teeth, Trico was already pulling them inside and clicking the door closed behind them. He dropped to his knees and I followed, spurred by his urgency to copy him without asking questions. Together, we pulled out the bags and other bits and pieces we stored under the bed. The two drunk uncles wriggled underneath, the last foot barely out of sight before we were frantically shoving the bags back in place to hide them from view. Then Trico hurried me into the living room along with Oscar and Chino. The four of us sat rigidly on the sofas. Doors closed. Television on.

Time is fickle in moments like this. How long did we sit there? Was it half an hour? An hour? Two hours? I couldn't say. There was a clock on the wall, but no one was watching it. Nor did we watch the television. We looked at each other. The walls. The floor. It barely mattered, as our eyes were sightless. All of our energy was focussed on listening, straining to pick up any clue from outside. My chest felt frozen and my head throbbed. The slightest rattle would give me a surge of nausea, in case it proved to be the precursor to the sequence of sounds I dreaded more than all others: the opening of the gate onto the road, purposeful footsteps across the entrance passage, and then a furious banging on the iron front door.

However long that lapse of time was, I felt as if it had aged me several years.

Eventually, Trico got slowly to his feet and walked softly over to the living room window. He tweaked the very edge of the net curtain and stood there in silence for several minutes. Then he crossed the room, cautiously opened the door to the courtyard and slipped outside. I assumed he must have crept up the steps to check the rooftop. I sat, rooted to the sofa. Even with the door open, it was deathly quiet outside. I pictured the whole neighbourhood, tense and listening just as we were.

I didn't stand up until I heard Trico pulling bags out from under the bed. I went through into the bedroom just as the two men were crawling out. Trico glared at them coldly.

'I think they've gone,' he said in a low voice. 'They're not on the rooftop anymore. But I wouldn't go onto the street for a while, just in case. What the fuck did you think you were doing?'

The two men, too tawny-skinned to go pale, were nevertheless looking distinctly grey.

'They must have been Zetas, man.'

'Of course they were fucking Zetas,' Trico hissed. 'And you go throwing fucking bricks at them and then expect me to hide you. What do you think they would have done to us if they'd found you? What do you think they would have done to Cat?'

I had never seen him so enraged. I had seen him angry, of course – frequently with me. But usually it was a hot-blooded, hysterical anger that seemed almost pantomime in its melodrama and could be laughed about in retrospect. Now I saw icy fury. The men looked cowed. They had nothing to say.

'Get out.'

They didn't need telling twice. They fled up the steps to the roof, pausing at the top to check the coast was clear before running across it and disappearing from sight, crouched over as if in a warzone.

It was another hour before we felt safe to talk in normal voices, and several hours before we dared go onto the street. It turned out that the latter fear was not wholly unfounded. The only person who was 'taken' in the whole incident was a boy in his late teens who had been naive enough to go out to see what all the noise was about. He returned a short while later, badly beaten but at least alive. The overwhelming emotion on the street was one of relief. It could have been a lot worse.

I still don't really know what happened that day. No one seemed to know, except possibly the drunk uncles, and they were keeping quiet. The men firing had been dressed as police. Were they police? Were they Zetas masquerading as police? Were they police infiltrated by Zetas, or acting on their commands? All of these scenarios were completely plausible.

From that day on, the cartel wars lost the soothing fog of abstraction that had previously surrounded them in my mind. I had been appalled by the stories, of course. But they had maintained the unreality of things happening to someone else, somewhere else. They had aroused many emotions in me – shock, anger, sadness, pity – but never the wrenching terror that throws you face to face with your own mortality and turns abstract horror into something sickeningly, viscerally real. It wasn't until that day that I truly understood what it felt like to think 'it could have been me'. And it was that thought that led inexorably to the still more chilling realisation: it could be anyone. Not, as the government would have had people believe, only those foolish enough (or, in the case of some journalists and honourable members of the authorities, brave enough) to get directly involved, but ordinary people living ordinary lives in ordinary streets. The rooftop where bricks had been thrown and shots fired was the same rooftop where Elvira hung her washing. The bed under which two men had cowered in fear for their lives was the same bed where I hugged Trico before going to sleep at night. The living room where we had sat for what seemed like eternity, rigid with fear as we waited for the bang on the door we felt sure was coming, was the same living room where two-year-old Jacky watched *Dora La Exploradora* on afternoon television.

It wasn't far away any more.

ψ Ψ ψ

San Luis had changed: a frost had settled over its once cheerful atmosphere. The street vendors seemed to shout a little less loudly and smile a little less. People moved with more purpose and did not stop to exchange pleasantries with strangers on street corners. For the first time since the arrival of Flaca, Trico and I could walk straight through the centre of town without being greeted by a single cry of, '*Oye chavo, que onda con la biciclota, a poco sí te subes?*' 'Hey kid, what's with the big bicycle, do you really ride it?' Some people still looked, but did so furtively through lowered eyelashes, and looked away again quickly to avoid eye contact.

'Reminds me of England,' I told Trico, trying to make light of it. But he was frowning as he looked around and showed no sign of having heard. I wondered if he was thinking of the other comparison that had occurred to me, though I'd chosen not to voice it – the sullen grey streets of Nuevo Laredo. This comparison was much more apt. San Luis's fear was Nuevo Laredo's fear. *La Letra*, they called it. The Letter, an export from Tamaulipas.

The rise of Los Zetas (the letter 'Z' in Spanish is pronounced 'zeta') is one of the most dispiriting stories in the whole dispiriting history of the Mexican drug wars. Their founding members were elite paramilitaries in the GAFE – a Special Forces unit of the Mexican army at the forefront of the fight against the cartels. Its members were selected for exceptional ability, and trained and armed at the School of the Americas. They were among Mexico's greatest hopes for winning the war against drugs – that is until 1999, when drug lord Osiel Cárdenas Guillén offered them higher salaries and 31 of them promptly deserted to become the mercenary wing for his Gulf Cartel, taking much of their world-class arsenal with them. The group grew rapidly, recruiting members from the army and police force as well as ordinary wannabe narcos. Their reputation was based both on terrifying efficiency and utter disregard for civilian life. For the next decade, they used their sophisticated weaponry and knowledge of military tactics to secure the Gulf Cartel's dominance across the east of Mexico.

By 2010, however, they had become more ambitious. After declaring their independence from the Gulf Cartel in February, they had unleashed a wave of unprecedented brutality across eastern Mexico, starting in their home state of Tamaulipas and spreading south. In some places, such as

Torreón, the carnage was due to the bitter turf war raging between the now-rival gangs. In others, such as San Luis Potosí, the Gulf Cartel had barely put up a resistance. The violence we were witnessing was not principally a struggle for territory, but deliberate intimidation calculated to ensure that the citizens were in no doubt who their new masters were, that they feared and obeyed them.

It worked. Day by day, the sense of menace grew heavier and more oppressive, until people felt suffocated beneath it. Until recently, San Luis had been considered one of the safest regions in Mexico, and its residents had not yet developed the coping strategies – the bravado and the black humour – that had struck me in Chihuahua. They would have to learn fast what the people of the borderlands and the western Sierra had known for several long years already: what it felt like to live in fear.

There were several bomb threats in the city centre and a couple of gun fights. Some shooting out by the *periférico* (ring road) caught a bus in the crossfire, killing both the driver and a seven-year-old girl. It was the same bus that I had taken when I went to visit Hele and Alvaro. The house of a small-time weed dealer was raided by the Zetas, who would not tolerate competition. A boy Trico knew was shot in the arm during the raid as he passed by with a friend to buy a couple of joints. The friend was killed. A malabarista was 'lifted' from a semáforo, as part of a string of random kidnappings intended to intimidate the town into submission. He was one of only two to be released alive. A trance party we had nearly gone to was broken up by the arrival of several pickups full of armed men, who lined up the partygoers at gunpoint and systematically relieved them of their money and valuables. Two girls were raped. One of their boyfriends objected, so they put a gun in his arse and made him watch. There were no more parties after that. One of our friends told us how he had sat and listened as his neighbour was dragged out of his house and beaten to a bloody pulp on the pavement outside while his wife and children screamed and sobbed. It reached the stage when every visitor to the house seemed to bring with the caguamas fresh rumours of fresh horrors, told with widened eyes and in furtive voices as if, even behind concrete walls and closed doors, you could never be sure of who might be listening.

Trico went to the semáforo less and less. He was, after all, pretty conspicuous with his two-metre tall unicycle and outlandish appearance. Before, exuberance had been part of the circus lifestyle. Being noticeable got you money. Now, being noticeable could get you killed.

The proof of this came a couple of weeks later. Trico had gone out to a gig with Oscar and Chino. Nowhere dodgy, he assured me, just a little gig in the yard outside a bar. I didn't go. The last time we had gone out, to a small party in the house of a friend, the guy had received an anonymous call at about 1 a.m., telling him to expect 'visitors'. Within seconds, the music had been turned off and conversation reduced to barely audible whispers – mostly on the topic of whether it was possible to exit over the roofs to the back of the building rather than out the front, which could easily be being watched. In the end, no 'visitors' turned up, and we slipped off into the darkened streets unmolested. Probably, they had never intended to turn up. Maybe they hadn't even been Zetas, but just kids with a grudge against the party-holder and an idea for a prank. There was no way of knowing, but we had no choice but to assume the worst. We had all read of the recent massacre at a birthday party in Torreón. Most of the articles had been illustrated with the same photo: a single bloody handprint, smeared across a white wall.

So I was in no mood for a gig. I stayed in the house reading and writing, and around midnight I went to sleep. I was woken at about 4 a.m. by voices, thuds and uneven footsteps in the passage outside. I recognised the voices as Trico's and Oscar's, and wondered how drunk they must be if they couldn't even walk down the passage without stumbling and crashing into the walls. I turned the light on and opened the door between the bedroom and the living room, feeling sure that they would make too much noise for me to sleep anyway, and looking forward to teasing them mercilessly for the state they were in.

As soon as they entered, however, my smile fell away. Trico's T-shirt was covered in blood, one eye was swollen and his lip was split. Although the blood had been cleaned from his face, there were still dried traces of it around his hairline, ear and the corner of his mouth. He was being supported by Oscar who, although in a better state than Trico, had clearly also taken a beating. They both collapsed on the sofa, breathing heavily. I ran to Trico.

'What – *no mames...* What happened?'

It wasn't easy to get the story out of them. Oscar told me some of it, but he seemed only marginally less confused than I was. Trico was finding it painful to move his face enough to talk, and I soon urged him to stop. It wasn't until the next day, when we had all got a bit more sleep and Elvira had tended their wounds with ointments and soothing fingers, that I found out what had happened.

During the afternoon of the previous day, Trico had committed the cardinal error of getting drawn into a conversation with a guy he didn't know very well. He had run into him on the street, vaguely recognised him, and they had gone for a beer together. Such things were Not Done in San Luis these days. But Trico was as defiant in his sociability as he was in everything else.

Later that evening, Trico's drinking partner had mugged a man at gunpoint. Unfortunately for him, the man he mugged was the brother of someone Connected – not with the Zetas, but with La Familia Michoacana, a rival cartel who at the time were fighting the tail-end of a losing battle to maintain some presence in San Luis. (The group fragmented after the killing of their leader Nazario Moreno González in December 2010, and is now considered to be extinct.)

La Familia were a strange cartel. Deeply religious, they claimed to uphold 'family values' and forbade any of their members to partake in the drugs they trafficked. They gained support by giving financial assistance and protection to the poor in their home state of Michoacán, and even went so far as to describe themselves as 'a necessary evil'. Beneath the rhetoric, however, was a vicious streak. Previously allied to the Gulf Cartel, they had announced their independence in 2006 by throwing five severed heads onto the dance floor of a crowded disco in the town of Uruapan. As with all their killings, they declared this to be an act of 'divine justice'. Whatever else their God may have been, he was certainly not merciful.

Determined to get revenge for the mugging of his brother, the Connected man had started to make inquiries with the help of his Connections. Nobody knew where the mugger could be found. But hadn't he been seen having a beer earlier with that *malabarista* with the really big bicycle who was often in the semáforos? Maybe he would know where the mugger was? And surely someone like that couldn't be too hard to find?

He wasn't too hard to find. When Trico insisted that he barely knew the mugger and had no idea where was, the beating started. Oscar tried to defend him, so they beat him as well. When still no information had been forthcoming the attackers finally left, but not without delivering that dreaded final shot: 'You've messed with the wrong people now, *puto*'.

Trico had his head in his hands by the end of the story. Elvira looked grave, and begged him not to tell his father. 'Why not?' I asked him later, and he gave me that impatient look.

'Because then *he'll* have to get revenge, of course. And he doesn't have any connections to protect him.'

He sought advice from one of the younger drunk uncles. They were pretty streetwise. They knew the deal in these situations. The guy took us for a drive in his rusty old car so as to be out of earshot of Elvira or anyone else.

'What should I do?' Trico asked, when we parked up in a back street somewhere. 'How worried should I be? I think they believed me in the end that I had no information to give them. They probably just said that last thing out of spite. It seems crazy to leave town over something so stupid.'

The drunk uncle grimaced.

'I know it does. But you don't want to push your luck with these people. You know what happened to your Tio Loco.'

We did know what had happened to Tio Loco. He had been caught buying crack from the wrong people and been beaten, tortured and left for dead under a bridge, covered in cigarette burns and with several broken ribs.

'That was the Zetas, though. La Familia isn't usually that brutal. Besides, I haven't done anything against them. They must know that. Why wouldn't I have told them where the guy was if I knew? He's clearly a *culero* anyway; why would I want to protect him that much? I don't think they'll take this any further.'

The drunk uncle sighed, and shook his head.

'You're right, man, they probably won't. But why would you risk it? They know who you are. I bet they know who your girlfriend is as well.' I realised with a jolt that he was probably right. I was often with Trico in public, and as a European girl doing street circus, I was fairly conspicuous myself. 'If I were you, man, I'd say it was better to be too careful than not careful enough. It's not a big thing, and I'm sure that in a few months they'll have forgotten all about it. But until then, take Cat and go somewhere else. You're lucky to have your lifestyle. Do you think any of us would still be here, if we were free to leave?'

20
A Delicate Equilibrium

W e left. Although we never discussed it, I think we both felt secretly ashamed, even disloyal, like rats fleeing a sinking ship. But it seemed clear that we would be doing no one any favours by staying.

Turning our backs on the weary and bloodstained north, we headed south towards DF. We stopped just east of it, in Texcoco, not far from Teotihuacán. On the fringe of Texcoco was a house and in the house were some malabaristas. And as usual among any malabaristas we met anywhere across the country, we could stay for as long as we wanted.

It was a concrete bungalow in a yard of peach-coloured dirt where a few baffled chickens scratched among the bushes. The door was turquoise, with four panes of clouded glass. The one nearest the internal handle had been missing for as long as anyone could remember and would never be replaced, as one never knew when a homeless friend might drop by and need to let themselves in. Outside was a concrete washing station shared by several such bungalows, and a view over terracotta fields sprinkled with faded green shoots. It was an hour and a half on a minibus from the outskirts of DF, but even here the fog of pollution that envelops the capital still hung on the air and erased the horizon. Occasionally, though, in the early morning with the wind in the right direction, you could come outside and be greeted by the faint ghost of Popocatépetl: a perfect cone tipped with snow.

Rent-payer-in-chief at the bungalow was a chisel-faced boy named Iván with a ponytail of fine black hair and a single, remarkably central front tooth. Few people can pull off a missing front tooth without looking either thuggish or scheming, but the intriguing symmetry of Iván's gave it an odd sort of dignity. This struck me as appropriate, as he was an oddly dignified person. He wasn't shy, but he took words too seriously to waste them on trivialities. He spoke softly, in a thinly nasal voice, but when he did even Tricopsycho listened, knowing that nothing came out of Iván's mouth that had not been carefully considered. His hands, however, were never still. Beneath his long pianist's fingers old car tyres and scraps of leather would blossom unexpectedly into pairs of sandals, a scattering of tiny beads would coalesce into intricate Huichol-style jewellery, and broken things would fix themselves before anyone else even worked out what was wrong with them.

Iván slept in one of the house's two beds, and everyone else took turns in the other. Failing that, the short-legged could claim a place on one of the two sofas leaking yellow stuffing, and for the long-legged there was the floor. In the living room and the spare room there were rarely fewer than five people sleeping, and occasionally up to 15. A poster in the kitchen listing house rules switched to capital letters to conclude on the point: 'IF YOU FEEL YOURSELF GETTING ANGRY, GO OUTSIDE UNTIL YOU HAVE CALMED DOWN.' Other decorations included a couple of coloured throws, a poster of Frida Kahlo and a framed photo of Iván as a little boy, on which someone had carefully erased one tooth with black pen, and added a moustache for good measure.

After the brooding tension of San Luis, arriving in Iván's house felt like sliding into a warm bath and feeling every muscle relax. The weeks we spent there slipped by in a dreamy haze. Vendors would appear at the door selling *tamales*, *tortas* or other such goodies. My favourite were the *raspado* sellers who would push round a cart containing an enormous block of ice, and for 10 pesos shave off a cupful of snow, to be flavoured with a syrup from one of their array of rainbow bottles. Every *raspado* seller I ever met was desperately proud of his syrups, which were never the same as anyone else's and were always, of course, the best. They were family recipes, passed down for generations, and no amount of cajoling could persuade any of them to disclose the secret ingredients.

Children from the neighbouring bungalows squealed in the yard, chasing the chickens or the tiny orange kitten which darted in and out of every house and had earned the name 'Sincolita' (Little Tail-less) after an accident with a door. Five minutes' walk from the house was a semáforo where one could catch all the traffic between DF and Texcoco, without having to go to either.

Even so, we spent more time practising than performing. Each day would start, after a communal breakfast, with what was supposed to be a half-hour warm-up, which never lasted less than two hours and would frequently go on until mid-afternoon before someone remembered that if we did exactly the same thing 400 metres up the road people would give us money for it. The standard of performance in Texcoco was exceptionally high and this, combined with Iván's ever-open door, had established the house as a gathering point for some of the most skilled malabaristas in the country.

They came to swap tricks and develop new passing patterns, not to make money. Texcoco must be one of the least profitable places in Mexico to be a malabarista. Such is the concentration of talented performers that the population has become rather jaded. Fewer than five clubs? Amateur. Juggling knives on a unicycle? Boring. Poi? Get out. I once saw Trico and a friend play passes with six knives between two giraffe unicycles with another boy dressed as a clown riding a normal unicycle in a figure of eight around them underneath the flying knives, and after half an hour they'd barely raised enough for lunch. The only things that make it possible to survive long in Texcoco as a circus performer are cramped communal living and pulque.

Pulque, it was explained to me, is a magical drink. The maguey cactus from which it is fermented is full of essential vitamins. Pulque is so filling that if you drink a couple of litres of it a day, you have no need for beer and little need for food. And if you go out to the small villages around Texcoco where it is made, you can buy a litre for seven pesos. It's a bit of an acquired taste, pulque. There are two broad interpretations of it: the San Luis version, which is thin and has a very slight fizz on the tongue, and the version sold around DF, which is viscous and almost slimy in its texture. Both have a flavour reminiscent of rotten fruit.

Pulque has to be fresh. Its fermentation process is continuous, and it sours very quickly if not consumed. It is even said to continue fermenting in the stomach, explaining the stomach cramps it often gives to those unused to it. As it cannot be stored or transported long distances, there is no sense in mass-producing it. It has no labels or brand names. Proper pulque is to be found only in dingy cantinas in maguey-growing regions, where it is poured straight from the barrel into clay mugs to be drunk on the spot, or unmarked plastic bottles if you wish to take it away. The man pouring it is very likely to be the man who made it, or one of his relatives. Like the *raspado* sellers, he is desperately proud of his pulque. It is never the same as anyone else's and is always, of course, the best.

Although there were a few decent *pulquerías* in Texcoco, we always preferred to cram into the little white minibuses which rattled out to the villages, where the pulque was fresher, cheaper, and still wrapped in centuries-old tradition. These village pulquerías had a warm, damp smell of baked corn and old wood, men in hats solemnly playing drinking games outside, a heavy-built patroness rolling her eyes and intoning the name of the Virgin every five minutes, and a wizened old man in the corner who knew everything that had happened in the village since 1900-and-something. Often there was a garden, unkempt but pretty, where people poured the first drops of their pulque on the ground as a gift to Mother Earth. Sometimes you overheard them conversing in Nahuatl, one of the most beautiful languages I had ever heard. It sounded like a tiny brook bubbling over pebbles, making them click softly together.

It was on one of these pulque missions that Trico and Iván first took me to Tetzcotzingo, the ruined palace of Nezahualcóyotl, king of Texcoco during the 1400s and still revered in Mexico as a philosopher, an unusually benevolent ruler and, above all, a poet.

We had come to one of our favourite pulquerías on the edge of a nearby village, where the garden at the back was full of stooped trees spilling over tangled grass. That day it was packed with bustling people and smells of meat for the celebration of a village saint's day. After playing a show for the children and accepting a few tacos pressed on us by their mothers, we bought 10 litres of pulque and set out to climb the hill above the village.

There was no gate marking the entrance to the site, no signs to tell us where we were. But as we climbed we started to come across growing piles of fallen stones, until we emerged on the top where the king's palace, gardens and swimming baths had once stood. Although now so weathered as to blend into the rocks of the hillside amidst tufts of coarse grass, its grandeur was still unmistakable, not only in the dignity of its architecture, but in the sweeping view it commanded across the surrounding valley.

Once, this hill would have been one of the few points on which it was possible to build, rising out of the lakes and marshes that filled the Valley of Mexico. Back then, the people lived in a delicate equilibrium with their wetland habitat. They constructed dikes and aqueducts that not only allowed them to overcome the difficulties of their environment but to build cities that made even the conquistadores marvel at their beauty. They grew their food on raised agricultural plots called *chinampas* in the shallower waters and used their own sewage as fertiliser. Most Aztec poetry is laden with references to the flowers and birds that lived there.

When the Spanish arrived, they didn't understand this balance. They destroyed the *chinampas*, and dumped waste in the waterways. Thousands died of waterborne diseases, conquerors and conquered alike. Then, they started to drain the lakes. The first of the drainage canals was started in 1605, and they continued to be built until the early 1900s. Now, the dried out valley is entirely covered by the houses, slums and factories of DF and its satellites, all of which are sinking with alarming rapidity and whose 30 million inhabitants are struggling with a severe water deficit.

We wandered around the deserted ruins of what was described by 17th-century historian Lorenzo Boturini Benaduci as 'The Athens of the Western World'. We brushed hands over time-smoothed stones, warm in the afternoon sun. We juggled passes across the empty pool known as 'the bath of the king'. And when we got tired, we sat on a crumbled wall on the edge of the hill and looked out at the view.

We were drunk by then, but pulque drunk, which is a completely different type of intoxication from any other I've experienced. The drink is so heavy that it lines the stomach at the same time as it spices the blood, causing a heavy, reflective drunkenness rather like those swollen hours following a hearty Christmas dinner. There's something else as well: that bubbling fermentation in the stomach, that fecund rottenness in its flavour, which conjures up a world of its own. Time slows down. Colours waver and lines blur, but in an enchanted, otherworldly way, like being led into a dream. I could understand why it was sacred to the Aztecs – how it inspired poetic, half-formed thoughts of nature, mystery and death.

A memory came back to me – a poem I had found whilst browsing through an old illustrated history of Mesoamerica in Elvira's house in San Luis. I had copied it down, translated it, and reread it so many times that I knew it by heart, both in Spanish and in English, though sadly not in the original Nahuatl. It had been credited to one of the Aztec kings, and as I remembered it I suddenly felt painfully close to those defeated, long-lost people. As the only fitting tribute I could think of, I leant my head on Trico's shoulder and began to recite.

'*Tendré que pasar, como las flores se marchitan...*'

> Will I have to pass
> Like the flowers wither?
> Nothing will remain of my name?
> Nothing of my fame on the Earth?
> At least flowers! At least songs!
> What will my heart be able to do?
> For nothing, we have come;
> For nothing, passed through this world.
> Enjoy, friends, embrace!
> Now we tread the blossoming earth.
> The flowers, and the birdsongs
> Shall not truly die
> But continue living
> In the dwelling of the giver of life.
> Here, on the Earth, is the region
> Of the fleeting moment.
> Does a place follow it
> In which you live in some way?
> There, can you enjoy?
> There, can you know friendship?
> Or have we only known our faces upon this Earth?

Trico put an arm around me, and we gazed out at what had once been the great lake of Texcoco. Now the only lake to be seen was one of murky yellow smog smothering the city below. Raising my eyes upwards from the indistinct jumble of rooftops, I watched the taint of pollution gradually fade until finally, almost directly above me, a couple of birds circled in a milky blue sky.

ψ Ψ ψ

Around the middle of 2010, two things happened that changed everything. Both of them happened many thousands of kilometres away from me.

The first was that 13,000 kilometres away in Sydney, my grandmother died. Although I mourned for her, I had grown up on the other side of the world from her and never known her as well as I would have liked. She was a reserved person whose heart, though generous and loyal, was kept packed away carefully somewhere it could be difficult for a clumsy child to find. She was a mystery to me back then, and I had been a mystery to her as a teenager. Consequently, my most vivid memories of her were of a comforting smell of cardigan and a sincere, though slightly damp, peck on the cheek. I have a feeling she never quite approved of me. She did, however, love me. And remembered me in her will.

The inheritance was not a vast amount but, though gratefully received, it put me in a quandary. If it had been morally dubious to be playing semáforos when I didn't have money, how could I possibly justify it now that I did? Could I really look someone in the eye and take their two-peso coin, knowing that I was probably in a position to pay their rent for a year? Yet if I didn't play semáforos, what was I? Just Trico's *fresa* tourist girlfriend.

It's not a comfortable feeling to come face to face with the lie you've been living, be introduced to it and obliged to shake its hand. What to do with these unexpected riches? The malabarista part of my brain told me that the only honourable thing to do was to spend it all as fast as possible on communal caguamas. I could guess what my grandmother would have thought of that. I could, of course, have given it all away to some charitable cause, or to Trico's family. But I'm not *that* good. Besides, I knew that Trico's family would be insulted by such a gesture.

The second thing was that 9,000 kilometres away in London, the powers-that-be decided that it was high time my generation started paying through the nose for the mess their generation had created. As of 2012, university tuition fees would go up from £3,000 a year to £9,000.

Part of me had always wanted to study, simply for the joy of acquiring knowledge. But I had never known what university or course to choose, or what I wanted to do with a degree, or if I really wanted to join that particular rat race at all. There are many different kinds of knowledge, and the more I travelled, the more I questioned whether I could learn as much about humanity from books and papers as I could learn from humanity itself. As my one socially acceptable gap year slipped into multiple, progressively less socially acceptable years, I kept vaguely promising relatives that I would go to university *one* day, maybe *next* year, and some part of me really meant it. Now, waiting just one more year would be an expensive decision. My bluff had been called.

In a way, the first and the second things – the money from my grandmother and my need to decide about university – were linked in my mind. My grandmother was of that generation of women – the last (at least in her country) – whose brains and talents were wasted due to the misfortune of their gender. Although she had a mind that would have blossomed in and done credit to any university, her parents never encouraged her to pursue her academic ambitions. Her confidence crippled, she had turned down an offer of a university scholarship: a decision she had regretted all her life (though she did eventually, in her fifties, graduate with a degree in environmental sciences that had taken her nearly 10 years of part-time study). Her experiences had given her a reverence for higher education and she put a lot of her considerable determination into ensuring that her six children (five of them daughters) would have the opportunity she had missed.

In contrast there was I, funnelled inexorably towards university since birth and wondering whether to reject it in the name of 'freedom'. It was only now that I recognised the irony – that the younger generation's idea of freedom should be to reject the freedom that the older generation dreamt of in vain.

I began to spend increasing amounts of time wandering in the fields around Texcoco, struggling to make out the forms of the mountains through the haze and struggling to come to some resolution. When I was honest with myself, I realised that those two far-off events that seemed to be forcing me to reassess my life were merely catalysts. A restlessness had been brewing in me for some time. I loved the malabarista lifestyle, but by now it was familiar enough to have lost its intrigue, and I lacked the natural flair for circus that allowed Trico and the banda to pursue it with such love and dedication. I was ready for a new story. Perhaps I would already have moved on, if it hadn't been for Trico.

But Trico couldn't bind me forever, any more than I could bind him. As I had seen long before, the union was always going to fly apart. Ever since we left San Luis, Trico and I had been communicating less with each other: he was spending more time with the banda; I was spending more time alone. The bond between us had changed, the focus switched from the union to the individual. But I knew that neither of us was ready to let go yet.

Eventually, I decided on a compromise. I would use my grandmother's bequest to enrol for a month in a Spanish school in Mexico City and try to knock my anarchic grammar into a shape that would make it recognisable in places other than street corners. I would send some presents to Trico's parents and rent a room in Mexico City where, while studying, I could offer hospitality to passing street performers and drink lots of communal caguamas. Trico could split his time between my apartment and Iván's house or further travel, as he wished. It was October 2010. I would apply for a university place starting in a year's time – to enrol in the last year before the fees went up. When I had finished my Spanish course I would still have several months before I needed to return to Europe. Here, the plan became vague. Where I would spend those months – or who with – I couldn't say. Those questions I left for mañana.

21
The Layered City

My room was a windowless box on the second floor of an apartment block in Narvarte, just south of the centre of Mexico City. When the door was closed, so absolute was its blackness that one unaccustomed to it could easily sleep until three in the afternoon. After several of my friends did exactly this, it earned itself the nickname La Cueva: The Cave.

The Cave was in a flat that I shared with three girls, to whom I apologise unreservedly. I was unceremoniously evicted after two months with the words: 'THIS IS NOT A HOSTEL, THIS IS NOT A SQUAT, AND THIS IS NOT A HOMELESS SHELTER', bellowed into my cave at about one in the morning. Until then, I was extremely happy there.

Mexico City surprised me. Mexico City always surprises me. It surprised me the first time I set foot in it and has surprised me ever since. I never expected to like it. You always hear of the dirt, the pollution, the crime, the kidnappings, the overpopulation... When I first boarded a plane to fly there, its only redeeming feature in my mind was its international airport.

It's true. It is dirty, polluted and overpopulated, and I assume the crime and kidnapping stories must come from somewhere, although in the months that I spent there I was never once given cause to feel afraid. But the dirt is cut through by waterfalls of red and purple flowers spilling from the poinciana and jacaranda trees, the acrid burn of pollution is soothed by smells of magnolia, coffee, lime or sizzling meat, and there is always a moment's respite from the crush of people and traffic to be found in the many tree-lined parks or sculpted gardens of Chapultepec. Besides, the worst thing about the overpopulation is also the best – every corner explodes with life, in a myriad of different styles and settings. The indoor markets where you search for your vegetables in a warren of fragrant tunnels, bumping your head on piñatas and pushing past flowers, sacks of spices and canaries in cages as you go. The sprawling *tianguis* (open-air markets) such as those of Tepito or Santa Marta, cluttered with snaggle-toothed vendors and pirate goods. The quaint bohemian elegance of Coyoacán – one of those places that turn dilapidation into an art form. The packed metro carriages, always filled with music by valiant buskers or CD-sellers with speakers sewn into their backpacks. El Cerro de la Estrella (the Hill of the Star), with its half-forgotten ruins and ramshackle pulquería, popping its head above the seething city as if searching for a lost friend. The free open-air salsa dancing sessions in various parks and plazas, where elderly couples sway in long-practised unison and little girls spin pirouettes on the arms of their pint-sized suitors. The bars, the museums, the squats, the galleries... There's barely a corner that doesn't captivate me in DF.

But what captivates me most about it – about all cities, but DF in particular – is the layers. Any city of reasonable age is composed of great mouldering slabs of history piled one on top of the other, each bearing its own tragedy, beauty and stories. I have never been anywhere where the layers are more in evidence than in DF.

The conquering Spaniards tried to suffocate the Aztec capital of Tenochtitlán under mansions, government buildings and churches, only to have them sink under their own weight on the marshy soil, causing them to slip and crack as if cursed by the ruins beneath. In the centre of the city, imposing cathedrals tilt at drunken angles over the rubble of temples on which carved serpents are still visible, while the officious post-independence architecture struggles to keep control. Although the Zócalo is the most famous of these schizophrenic plazas, the most compelling is surely the Plaza de las Tres Culturas in the district of Tlatelolco. The square is framed by a fallen temple, a smog-blackened cathedral and a utilitarian 1960s housing complex – the three cultures that trapped 10,000 people between them during the 1968 student massacre, when an unknown number died under the guns of the Mexican army. (There is no accurate record of the death toll, as the massacre was covered up by the ruling PRI and shamefully ignored by the world in the run-up to the 1968 Mexico City Olympics; estimates of the number who died range between 45 and 300, with countless more attendees of the peaceful demonstration injured and/or arrested.)

Towards the outskirts the layers are still clear – Xochimilco, for instance, where families and tourists come to picnic and listen to mariachi music whilst floating on gaily painted barges around the remnants of the *chinampas* of Tenochtitlán, the waterways now rancid and black as peat. There are more modern layers too, such as the walled compound in Coyoacán where León Trotsky lived in exile until assassinated with an ice pick in 1940. Though its interior is preserved in sparse 1930s precision (apart from the bullet holes in the walls), the wall outside is daubed in modern political graffiti in which something of his spirit lives on.

My own district was an apparent monolayer composed of greying streets sandwiched between apartment blocks and supermarkets. But even here, within sight of McDonald's, a deeper layer was constantly bursting through. I rarely ate breakfast in my apartment because early morning was the one time of day when the grimy pavements bubbled with colour, brought in from the surrounding villages by women who had to wake up at 4 a.m. every day to get there. They sat on blankets between pyramids of fruit like illustrations in a child's counting book, or stooped over charred hotplates, flipping quesadillas of blue *maíz* filled with squash flowers or the nutty-flavoured corn fungus known as *huitlacochtli*. They chattered together in Nahuatl and smiled with gold-capped teeth. In those few hours each day, indigenous Mexico blossomed like flowers through the cracks in a pavement.

ψ Ψ ψ

My Spanish school also surprised me. Walking into class for the first time, I was unsure whether the teacher had arrived. Two people sat on opposite sides of a small table: one a platinum-blonde girl with a tightly curved figure and immense blue eyes, the other a morose-looking boy with black hair and a nose ring. Both looked in their early twenties; both fiddled intently with mobile phones. I entered a little awkwardly, unsure whether to greet them in Spanish or English. The boy looked up without smiling.

'Advanced?' he demanded, in Spanish.

'Yes.'

'You're late.'

'Sorry. I was watching a really good acrobat in a semáforo.'

'Huh. Are you more interested in grammar, or conversation practice?'

'Oh, definitely grammar. I get plenty of conversation practice. But my grammar is awful.'

'Well I like to do half and half. Two hours in the classroom for grammar exercises. Then a fifteen-minute break. Then we usually go out to a café for two hours of conversation. On Fridays we go to the pulquería. I think it's important to be able to talk in natural settings, so I always structure my lessons like that. *Some* people complain.'

His expression left no doubt exactly what he thought of *those* people.

'That's fine by me, as long as you correct my conversation when I make mistakes.'

'Well, first off, you needed to use subjunctive there. *Cuando haga fallas,* not *cuando hago fallas.* You're talking about an uncertain future event.'

'Oh, I think I'm talking about a fairly certain future event.'

He allowed himself a little sniff, but not a laugh.

'Shall we start then? I'm Julio, by the way. This is Cindy.' The blonde girl gave me a warm smile.

'*Mucho gusto.* I'm Cat.'

He looked me up and down distastefully.

'Are you a hippie?'

'You can be the judge of that. Why do you ask?'

'The dreadlocks.'

'They're more convenient to travel with. No need to look after your hair. Are you a hippie?'

'Why do you ask?'

'The nose ring.'

His lips twitched slightly.

'Recovering hippie.'

'Right,' I said, not sure what game we were playing but determined to play along. 'Me too. In a way.'

Julio behaved himself reasonably well that first lesson. Although he looked barely older than me, he had just turned 30 and had a master's degree in linguistics. He approached Spanish grammar with the fanatical earnestness and bad temper one might expect from a retired drill sergeant. I meekly took notes and completed my exercises. This was, after all, what I had signed up for.

In the afternoon, we walked out into the leafy boulevards of Colonia Roma. The splashes of warm sunlight along the pavements made me feel like skipping, so I skipped. Julio glared at me.

La Roma (along with neighbouring Condesa) was once the district of choice for the Mexico City aristocracy, before they migrated out to newer suburbs and left it to be divvied up among expats and the trendier class of chilango bohemians. Its gracious mansions are now mostly divided into apartments, but retain their air of refined superiority. Wrought-iron balconies and Art Deco door frames are common. Beggars and street hawkers are not. Low box hedges and stately trees line the pavements, the latter casting feathered shadows over streets remarkably clean and free of traffic. Colours are cheerful, while just muted enough to remain tasteful. It's the sort of district that is made for cafés, and its cafés are made for intellectual conversations and slender cigarettes.

Over an overpriced coffee, we went through the obligatory 'getting to know you' motions. As I spoke, I gradually noticed that Julio was pursing his lips, and appeared to be repressing a snigger.

'Why are you laughing?' I demanded.

'Just about every word in your last sentence was slang,' he said.

'But that's how people talk!'

'Maybe it's how *hippies* talk. It's not how polite people talk.'

'You know what I meant though, right?'

'Of course I know what you meant. But I thought you wanted to learn how to talk properly? You can't be using those words in polite society – you sound like a street kid. And your subjunctive is all over the place.'

'How should I be using it, then?'

'Well, the subjunctive is an indicator of uncertainty. So you should be using it after '*talvez...*' ('maybe...') and '*no sé si...*' ('I don't know if...'), not only to express a wish.'

'But nobody actually talks like that! It sounds so *mamón*!'

He sneered, presumably at my use of '*mamón*', (which literally means 'big suck', but colloquially means 'stuck up') before retorting: 'They most certainly do.'

'Maybe linguistics graduates do, but most people don't. Not the normal people, the people you meet on the street. Not where I learnt they didn't.'

Julio looked taken aback. He was by no means 'high society', but a world where people failed to use the subjunctive after '*talvez...*' was clearly unfamiliar to him.

'Where did you learn?' he asked.

'Well, all over the north, really. Mostly in San Luis Potosí.'

'Ah,' he said, comprehension dawning. '*Un pueblo.*' A village.

'*Un pueblo?!* It's got a population of nearly three million!'

'Exactly. *Un pueblo.*'

'*Pinche* chilango. You guys think that anywhere with less than 20 million people is a village.'

He laughed a rare laugh, before checking it hurriedly.

'No, seriously,' he explained. 'I don't say that because of its population; I say that because of its attitudes. You must have noticed that everywhere else in Mexico is quite... backward compared to DF. This is the only state in Mexico where abortion is legal, or gay marriage. It's even the only state where you can find a decent magazine! The rest of Mexico is stuck in a time warp of outdated beliefs and machismo. Places like San Luis Potosí... They may be cities in terms of population and economy, but in terms of culture and attitudes... *Pueblos.* In that respect, Mexico has only one city: DF.' He thought about it for a moment before conceding: 'Well, maybe one and a half. Guadalajara is *trying.*'

I was tempted to dismiss this as typical chilango snobbery (indeed, typical snobbery of capital dwellers worldwide), but the more I wandered around DF, the more I had to admit that he had a point. Women wore less traditionally feminine clothes, and seemed to walk with more confidence. In buses, parks or the metro, it was much more common to see people reading books. Book stalls were set up outside markets or in metro stations, the volumes stacked in neat piles across trestle tables. Even Julio's comment about the magazines seemed to be true. In the centre of the city, practically every street corner boasted a chaotically overflowing newsstand selling magazines for every interest or political persuasion. By far the best (for my tastes) was *Proceso*, which showcases a truly impressive standard of investigative journalism in the country that is currently rated the most dangerous in the world for journalists. It made an invigorating change from the limited scope, shaky accuracy and often blatant bias of the mainstream newspapers that are the sole source of print journalism for most of Mexico.

Perhaps even more noticeable was the difference in attitude towards gay people. The first time I saw two young men passionately kissing on a metro platform, I was momentarily shocked. Not from any distaste or disapproval, simply from surprise. Without realising it, I had become unaccustomed to a world where gay men (or women) could show affection in public without shame or fear. In DF, it was not uncommon to see same-sex couples walking hand in hand, or canoodling on park benches under the jacaranda trees. One of my flatmates was lesbian, and had a girlfriend with a smoker's voice and baggy jeans. She was also a recent convert to a branch of reform Islam, and went to cook at the mosque every Thursday. A Mexican lesbian Muslim is the sort of delightfully improbable hybrid you would only be likely to find in DF.

I added it to an ever-growing list of things I loved about DF. It felt both older than the colonial and modern industrial cities to the north, and at the same time younger: a city in a continual process of discovery and liberation.

ψ Ψ ψ

Over my time in Mexico City, Julio, Cindy and I, somewhat to our surprise, became close friends. Cindy was German, but had moved to the city with her Mexican boyfriend and was in the process of honing her Spanish to a level where it would not hamper her employment prospects. Beneath her Barbie-girl good looks, she was down-to-earth and easy company.

With Julio, on the other hand, there was so much to dislike that I barely knew where to start and, while deliberating the problem, found myself liking him by accident. He was surly, persistently critical and (as Cindy and I discovered very shortly into our conversation classes) still deeply bitter that his girlfriend of 10 years had left him almost a year previously. The breakup itself he seemed philosophical about; what really irked him was that, at the age of 30, he felt that he had not had nearly enough sex – or at least, not nearly enough sexual partners. If uninterrupted, he could maintain a an almost indefinite monologue on this topic, spoken in exactly the same tone of intense seriousness with which he discussed his other great (though secondary) fascinations: structural linguistics and Mexican politics.

'It's not that I regret the time I spent with her,' he would begin, stirring sugar into his coffee with an air of tragic stoicism. 'But you do know that a woman's sexual peak is at thirty-five, right? And a man's at eighteen? So she took my best years and left me already on the downward slope, when she still had six years to go. I ask you: does that strike you as reasonable? Does that strike you as *fair*?'

Julio had been doggedly making up for lost time ever since, but the wound inflicted by the theft of his golden years had scarred him deeply and, as he reminded us frequently, made him painfully aware of the passing of time.

It was, I reflected, not an easy life being a Mexican intellectual.

Another Mexican intellectual who did not have an easy life was Pablo, the teacher of the beginner group, a plump and eager boy in his early twenties who would join us in the pulquería after Friday classes and of whom Cindy and I became extremely fond. His air of cherubic innocence was the perfect antidote to Julio, and only slightly belied by his passion for homoerotic poetry and participation in some eye-wateringly explicit theatrical endeavours in the Zona Rosa ('the Pink Zone' – Mexico City's gay district). Once, when the staging of one of these productions clashed with a beginner Spanish class, he solved the problem by inviting the whole Spanish school to come along for a 'cultural outing'. His class, who understood not a word of the lyrical and sensitive dialogue (that is not sarcasm; I was genuinely impressed), but could not have failed to understand the artistically stylised sex sequences, were completely nonplussed by the experience.

I soon learnt why Julio was so disappointed by my knowledge of Mexican slang. One of his favourite ways to shock his students was to devote whole lessons to the etymology of swearing. Most of it I already knew, and I would shout at him to get back to the seemingly infinite complexities of the subjunctive, but some of it was new to me.

'*Pinche*', for instance, came from an old word for a kitchen helper, evolved to denote anything small and insignificant, and gradually took on a life of its own to mean something akin to 'bloody', as in '*pinche hippie*': 'bloody hippie' – Julio's preferred means of addressing me. '*Güey*' (correct spelling '*huey*', but almost invariably misspelt '*guey*', and pronounced 'way'), was another interesting one. Its original meaning was 'ox', before it started to be used to deride a cuckolded husband, due to a legend that the unfaithfulness of his wife would cause horns to grow on his head that only he could not see. It eventually became a slightly jocular way to say 'guy' or 'dude', or simply to pepper sentences at random.

Apart from slang and swearing, another favourite lesson topic of Julio's was *albures*. The basic principle of an *albur* is to fool someone into saying something explicit they didn't intend to say.

For instance: What is the most dangerous place in DF?

To which one might well answer: '*Es Tepito*' or, even better, '*Es Tepito en la noche*'. It's Tepito at night. Tepito is a district just north of the Zócalo, renowned for its drug dealers, pickpockets and other shady goings-on. The point of the *albur*, however, is that '*es Tepito*' spoken aloud sounds identical to '*este pito*': this penis.

As a sex-obsessed linguistics graduate, Julio considered *albures* to be just about the highest conceivable form of wit, and devoted large proportions of his free time to devising them. It was a passion that his friends and cousins shared. They often came down to the pulquería with us after they got out of work, and were frequently the most enthusiastic in dragging us all to other bars, clubs and houses after it closed. Julio had introduced me to his two cousins in inimitable Julio style.

'Guys, this is Hippie. Don't worry; she isn't as stupid as she looks. Hippie, this is Primo Guapo (handsome cousin) and Primo Feo (ugly cousin).'

They were expansive, extrovert, and heavy drinkers. By now they were all thoroughly alert to the ever-present threat of *albur*, and rarely caught each other out. I was a godsend, particularly when made careless by alcohol.

'Hey, Hippie!' they asked me, several caguamas and half a bottle of tequila into an evening at one of their houses. 'How do you say in Spanish: "I want to see gas?"'

'Why do you want to know that?'

'We heard it on a television programme, but we don't know what it means.'

'You probably heard it wrong. It doesn't really make sense.'

'But what does it mean?'

'*Quiero ver gas.*'

They fell about laughing. I stared at them in bewilderment for a few seconds, replaying the sentence in my head before I finally twigged. *Quiero vergas.* I want dicks.

Albures aside, they were all good company, in a rowdy sort of way. But my favourite times were when Julio, Cindy, Pablo and I were alone in the pulquería. It was a dingy room full of dark wood furniture and self-consciously rustic decor, with a jukebox that veered between cumbias, heavy metal and 1990s pop. As my month of classes went on, we spent more and more time there – both in and out of lesson hours. At first, I would urge Trico to come and join us when he visited from Texcoco. But after one attempt he refused to come again, declaring that Julio was a *pendejo*, the pulque was poor quality and way overpriced, and the whole place was full of *fresas*.

ψ Ψ ψ

After finishing my Spanish course and being evicted from my flat, I accepted a very generous invitation to live for a few weeks with some new friends of mine in an apartment near the university. I could have gone back to Iván's house in Texcoco. But everything had changed and somehow, I didn't feel that I belonged there anymore. Although we had been ignoring it and both pretended it wasn't there, a gulf had opened between me and Trico which was widening by the day. He had been supportive of my sudden change of lifestyle, and during my Spanish course he divided his time roughly half-and-half between Iván's house and my apartment. But even so, from the moment I moved in, I think we both felt it was the beginning of the end. The two lifestyles do not mix, however much you want them to. When I told Trico I had bought my return ticket for July 2011, his reaction bore no trace of melodrama.

'So you *are* going to leave me, Cat,' he said. It was not a reproach. It was simply a clarification. I didn't know what to say.

'It's not that I *want* to leave you. It's just... I love your lifestyle; you know I do. I love Mexico. I love you. But what future is there for me here? I enjoy circus and I've improved a lot, but you know as well as I do that I don't have enough natural ability to ever be a great performer. I've been lying to myself, Trico. I was trying to live your life. But I'm not you. I need to live my own life, develop what *I'm* good at. Otherwise I'll always be incomplete.'

He nodded, without saying anything, and looked at the floor.

'I'm sorry,' I said.

He shrugged and turned away, without making eye contact.

'You have to do what's right for you, Loquita,' he said, with the forced nonchalance that was one of his specialities. 'Don't worry about me. I'll be OK. I have my Flaca. What more do I need?'

I knew, even while I watched his hair fall over his face as he rooted in his bag for something he had no use for at that moment, that he would be OK. He would be sad for a while, of course. But Trico had a heart like a rubber ball. Impressionable, and prone to wild leaps up, down and side-to-side, but ultimately unbreakable. He had proven himself resilient through innumerable trials and tragedies, and he would find himself resilient now. Resilient, impetuous, volatile, colourful, unpredictable, generous, histrionic, enigmatic... Trico, Mexico, Mexico, Trico... Between the two of them they had swept me head over heels into their circus, and I had all but forgotten what the world looked or felt like outside of it.

There could only be one way to remember. Over the next few days I said some thank yous, and wrote a tear-stained letter. And then I went to Acatitla, in the far south of the city, from where cheap pirate buses leave for all corners of the southern states, carrying market sellers and huge bulk buys of goods from DF. The bus was crammed with people and their wares, and through the night I was woken up at every bump or sharp turn when several plastic babies with staring blue eyes fell on my head from a sack squashed into the luggage rack above me. I disembarked in Tapachula, on the frontier with Guatemala. And as I strode through the border posts, bag on back and passport in hand, trying to fake a conviction

I didn't feel, I wondered how long it would be before I saw either of them –
Trico or Mexico – again.

22
Three Mornings

~~~~~~~~~~

Three months – until I saw one of them, anyway. Three months so crammed with places and people and their stories that they deserve a book in themselves. But this one isn't it. So I will reduce three months to three mornings. Three snapshots of three worlds.

ψ Ψ ψ

I am woken by Jaz calling good morning outside my window. Unfortunately, he is calling it so loudly that his voice is curdling with the effort, and it would have been a much better morning if he had waited a couple of hours, at least until the sun was fully up. By the oblique angle of the sunlight through my bamboo walls and the crispness lingering at the edges of the air, I imagine it is about 6 a.m. There should be a sparkling chorus of bird calls at about this time, but they have been startled into silence by the arrival of Jaz.

'*BUENOS DÍAS!*' Jaz screams. '*BUENOS DÍAS A TODA LA CALLE! BUENOS DÍAS A TODOS USTEDES! BUENOS DÍAAAAA –*'

His voice splits and he chokes on the final syllable. There is a volley of furious bangs as doors and window shutters are thrown open along the street, followed by an eruption of swearing in three different languages – Creole, Spanish, and Garifuna. Jaz falls silent, whether from obedience or sore throat is hard to say. I roll over and go back to sleep.

When I next wake the air is already heavy and saturated with heat, and the sun stabs through the gaps in the window shutters. There is a medley of car horns blaring outside and people shouting. People in Livingston are always shouting. They don't usually honk car horns though. I'm sure they would if they could, but they don't usually have cars. I didn't realise there were enough vehicles *in* Livingston to cause a traffic jam. Although it's not actually an island, it may as well be. There's a swathe of dense jungle between it and the nearest town, and the only way to reach it is by boat – either the ferry from Rio Dulce, the smaller *lanchas* from Puerto Barrios and the Mayan villages along the river, or the vast Caribbean cruise liners. It's a tiny place, and the few roads there are serve more to keep the houses in line than anything else.

'Cat!' Amanda shouts through the floorboards from the room below. 'The baby's crying, and I think Jaz is holding up the traffic. Can you go and see what he's doing, please?'

I pull a dress on and pad down the wooden stairs. There are no doors or windows in this half of the ground floor, so I go straight out onto the street. I see immediately what has caused the traffic jam. Jaz has dragged his sofa into the middle of the road and is lying sprawled across it, unconscious. Jaz is very attached to his sofa, and takes it with him most places within dragging-distance of his house. One never knows when one might have to pass out, after all. It's the first time I've seen him put it in the road though. A line of three vehicles has built up behind it – quite a queue by Livingston standards.

Livingston is one of those places that drive me up the wall when I'm there, but that I miss desperately when I'm not. Despite all its infuriating madness, it was the one place in Guatemala that I knew I had to come back to: the one place where, after a year and a half away, I still felt like I had family. Very dysfunctional family, sure, but isn't that the nature of family? They're the only people who you love unconditionally, however fucked up they (or you) may be.

I go into the road and look down at Jaz. He is wearing baggy shorts and a string vest and has wiry, muscled arms and mahogany skin. Livingston and Puerto Barrios are the only settlements of any reasonable size on Guatemala's tiny window of Caribbean coast, and unlike the rest of the country, the population is largely Garifuna – the mixed-race descendants of African slaves and indigenous Caribbean islanders. Their culture is a jumble of traditions and superstitions from three different continents, including considerable influence from Rastafarianism. I think this may be partly why they are always so accepting of me – they assume that anyone with dreadlocks must be one of them. Jaz himself has a voluminous crop of very thin dreadlocks in a bowl cut around his head. He looks like a mop. Right now, a very drunk mop.

I look at him with affection, feeling uncharacteristically maternal. It is rare to see Jaz so peaceful. His lips are pouted, and blow little bubbles when he exhales. It seems a shame to wake him. But the drivers are getting more irate, and I'm not strong enough to move the sofa with him on it. So I reach down and shake his shoulder.

'Jaz! Jaz, wake up! Your sofa's in the road, man. You're holding up the traffic.'

He groans, grimaces, then squints up at me through one bloodshot eye. He reaches for my hand, and grasps it in both of his.

'You gonna marry me, Rasta?' he asks. This proposal would be more surprising and/or flattering if Jaz hadn't proposed to me, and every other woman in town between the ages of 15 and 50, at least 20 times before. I sigh.

'Jaz, we've already been through this. I'm actually not looking for a husband at the moment.'

He looks sceptical, as well he might. Every girl in Livingston is looking for a husband. Even the ones who have husbands are looking for husbands – either the current one, in various bars, gutters and beds around town, or a new and improved model. It doesn't particularly matter which.

'Why you come back here if you don't wanna marry me?' he demands.

'To see you, Jaz. To see all of you. I'm not looking for a husband, but you're still my friends. I missed you.'

He thinks about this.

'I mek you good husband,' he offers at last. 'I catch you fish *every* day.'

Before I can reply, the driver of the first pickup leans on his horn, sending a wave of honking down the line of waiting vehicles (now numbering four), and I remember what I am supposed to be doing.

'Look, Jaz, we can discuss this in the house. But let's get your sofa out of the road first, OK?'

It takes another 10 minutes of coaxing, but finally we get the sofa into the back yard, next to the washing station, where Jaz promptly passes out on it again. Sabrina is standing on a crate to reach the water in the concrete trough, scrubbing furiously at a T-shirt, all lithe glossy limbs in her mini-shorts and flip-flops.

'Out washing already, Sabrina?' I ask her.

'*Ay!*' she exclaims, rolling her black eyes theatrically but pursing her lips in the struggle to keep a straight face. 'So much work, and so little time! I am going to die young from so much work!' I laugh at her. Sabrina has taken on considerable graces since I last saw her. She's 12 now and expected to help with chores like an adult, a development she has taken with resentment and glee in equal measures.

The yard is of dense red mud, invaded by weeds and banana palms in boisterous shades of green. It's a vivid, fecund place, brewing in the clammy air and unruly colours of the tropics. Fat blackish tree roots nibble at the walls of the houses and thin sun-bleached chickens run in and out of doors. A few mangy dogs slink around, chewing on the fish bones that people throw outside. The mangiest of the lot answers to the name of 'Sexy'. A man with waist-length dreadlocks is standing barefoot in his doorway, a joint in one hand, talking severely to one of them.

'You ate ma fish de udda day!' he scolds it, wagging a finger with his free hand. 'Ah vex wid you! Ah vex wid you real bad!'

Pauly is wandering vacantly around in his stained trousers and tattered straw hat. I say good morning, and he thinks about it for a minute before raising a limp hand. I don't think he recognises me. He's always like this, they say, ever since an accident on the banana plantations some 30 years ago. The only times I ever see him look fully connected to this world are when all the men gather to drum together and the women dance *punta*, the slender girls and their voluptuous mothers and obese grandmothers shaking their varied behinds in ways I have never come close to achieving, however hard they try to teach me. Pauly sometimes plays *maracas*, sometimes a drum made out of a tortoise shell, which he beats with wooden sticks. His rhythm never falters. None of their rhythms ever falter.

'Cat!' Amanda calls from the house. 'If Jaz has been on the *gifiti* all night, we won't have any fish! Could you go and get some, please?'

I take some coins and set off down the path to the beach. The older women are all out on their rickety verandas, overflowing their armchairs in polka-dotted dresses with pleated skirts and puffed sleeves straight out of 1950s Americana. They are all enormous. Every woman over 50 here is enormous – they pay in their latter years for the sensuality of their youth. And for all the banana bread and coconut, I guess. They wave at me as I pass.

The beach is quiet by this time – you have to come early to get the best fish. Usually we don't bother. We have Jaz for that. He sets off at 2 a.m. every day to paddle his canoe out to sea with his net and his spear. Up to seven kilometres, he tells me. There used to be fish closer to shore, but the water is warmer now, and cloudier, so you have to go further out. Leave earlier. Jaz is a good fisherman, though, and he never comes back empty-handed. When he goes, that is. Sometimes he gets on the *gifiti* (a lethal sort of white rum, in which grasses are soaked to add flavour), and we have no fish the next day and have to come down to the beach to buy it. Luckily there are still a couple of men standing by their canoes, so I know there's still some left.

The beach is no paradise by this time of morning. The pink glow of sunrise hides a multitude of sins, when the canoes glide in over the golden water and the fishermen pull them up under the palm trees. But by 9 a.m. the light is not so romantic, and it's no longer possible to ignore the tidemark of rubbish and the odd corpse of a stray dog. The fish are scrawnier as well, the rejects of the town's housewives. I still love buying them, though. I choose the ones I want from the bottom of the nearest canoe, and the fisherman plucks a frond from one of the palm trees and threads it through their gills, tying a knot in each end so the fish don't fall off and I have a handle to carry them home.

On the way back, I pause to look down the mud track that leads into the jungle towards Wolanda's shack. '*Wolanda*' in Garifuna means 'friend to all'. Wolanda knows every single person in town – not only by names and faces, but by lives and souls. He greets everyone he passes with a shout and a beaming smile and would do anything for any one of them. He has a room in his brother's house, but prefers to live mostly in the shack he built himself. It has no running water, no gas, and no electricity. When I was first in Livingston I used to spend hours sitting there with him, brewing tea from fresh papayas over a metal wheelbarrow full of hot charcoals and trawling through stacks of photocopied papers about Garifuna history. Wolanda loves history but nobody ever taught him to read, so I would read the Spanish words aloud and then he would talk to me about them to see if I had understood. Often I hadn't.

'Wolanda, it's too hard,' I would tell him sometimes, in English. 'I'm never going to learn this language.'

'Of course you are,' he would tell me, in Spanish. Like most of the older Garifuna community, Wolanda is fluent in Creole, English, Spanish and Garifuna. 'You just have to keep trying.'

Wolanda takes languages very seriously. Many of the kids in Livingston don't learn Garifuna anymore. They don't see the point. Wolanda is as strict with them as he is with me. He won't speak to them in Spanish or English, however much they moan.

'Wolanda, it's too hard,' they tell him, in Spanish or English. 'Why do you make us learn this? None of the tourists understand Garifuna. What good does it do us?'

Apart from fishing (and cocaine), tourism is the only economy in Livingston. And the fishing is all but dead.

'This is your heritage,' Wolanda tells them, in Garifuna. (At least, I assume this is what he tells them. This is what he tells me, when I ask him about it.) 'This is part of your culture. You should not forget where you come from.'

Amidst the drifts of paper in Wolanda's shack are photos of his wife and children. Sometimes, if I come round unexpected, I catch him looking at them. They emigrated to the United States many years ago, and now his wife has a new husband. Wolanda doesn't blame her for leaving; he knows there was no future for them here. He misses them – more than he will admit, I think. But this place is in his blood, and his soul is in this place. He would be only half a person anywhere else, and he knows it. He's lonely, though. Funny, that a friend to all should be lonely. But maybe lonely people are the only people who can be friends to all, without a heavier love to skew their priorities. Sometimes I think that Wolanda is one of the happiest people I've ever met. Sometimes I think he is one of the saddest.

I promise myself that I will come and visit him later, but for now I must get back with the fish. Mega was planning to prepare *hudut* tonight – a traditional fish and coconut stew, served with plantain which he mashes in a giant wooden mortar with a pestle the size of a tree branch. There will be drumming, and dancing. Hopefully some tourists will come. Rasta Mesa is one of the few Garifuna-owned businesses in town – a cultural centre and restaurant. The vision is to use the profits from the restaurant to fund the cultural centre, but it's an uphill struggle. They've come a long way since I was last here, but their location at the far end of the wrong road has proved an all but insurmountable barrier. There are really only two roads in Livingston as far as business is concerned: the right road and the wrong road. The lucrative shops and restaurants are the ones along the main road between the two piers. They're mostly Hispanic-owned, and do little to dispel the idea that the road that leads up into the Garifuna end of town is dangerous. 'Full of drunks and crack-heads,' say the whispers on the street. 'You can go there, sure. But not after dark. And watch your valuables.' So people come to town, stay for a couple of days, look at the gift shops and the dirty beach, make a quick trip up to the waterfall where the first Tarzan movie was filmed, then leave saying, 'There's not much to do in Livingston'.

I leave the fish in a plastic tub in the kitchen, covering it against the flies. Coming back out into the yard I run into Jaz, looking belligerent and a little worse for wear but at least now vertical.

'You see dis?' he demands, shoving a large, evil-looking fish under my nose, wrapped in a plastic bag.

'Er, yes. So you do have fish after all! Did you catch that?'

'I catch dis! I catch dis fish for YOU!'

'Thank you. It's a very nice one.'

'Dis is second fish I catch for you! But first fish EVEN BIGGER and you no want!'

'What fish?'

'I cooking all yesterday for you! But you no want!'

'I didn't know you were cooking for me.'

'You see me! You see me yesterday in de morning cooking for you!'

'I saw you cooking over the fire outside. But you never said it was for me.'

'You can feel?'

'Um... yes...'

'You cannot FEEL when I is cooking for you?'

'I can feel, Jaz, but I'm not telepathic.'

'Your MIND is your SOUL?'

'Er...' I laugh awkwardly.

'WHY YOU SMILING, GIRL? I SERIOUS!'

I am about to defend myself, when I remember the thing it took me weeks to learn the first time I was here – the lesson I have learnt over and over again around the world, but somehow still have to re-learn in every place I travel to. Resistance is futile. People work according to their own unique system of logic, and trying to respond to them with your own is as frustrating and pointless as trying to go up the down escalator. All you can do is go with the flow. The trouble is, sometimes the logic seems so alien that you can't even begin to figure out which direction it's flowing in. That's when you just have to let go altogether. This is definitely one of those moments.

I let my eyes roll until both my pupils are focussed on my nose. Then I puff out my cheeks before releasing the air in a long raspberry. I refocus my eyes, and widen them. I bare my teeth. I make a noise like a chipmunk. Then I scrunch up my nose and start gnawing on my lower lip.

Jaz stares at me with an expression of utter bewilderment, gradually morphing into nervous distaste as I continue making faces at him.

'You crazy, Rasta,' he decides at last. 'Mebbe I don't wanna marry you. I don't wanna wife who is crazy.'

ψ ψ ψ

The bus shudders into Guatemala City in a colourless early-morning light and finds no colour to greet it. This is the filthiest city I have ever seen. No, perhaps I have seen Indian cities which are filthier, but theirs is a living, dying, rotting, breeding filth. This is a peculiarly soulless filth. Every building is clad in an armour of black grime, with iron bars across the windows. Even the graffiti is colourless – angry black scribbles on bleak walls. I see '*Colom y Rector CORRUPTOS*' and '*Educación es un derecho*' (Education is a right). Fifteen years after the 1996 Peace Accords, the city still doesn't seem to have shaken off the horror of nearly four decades of civil war. A few blocks along, we pass another piece of graffiti: '*Los jovenes queremos paz y amor*'. The young people want peace and love.

I have mostly avoided this city in the past – every traveller, local and newspaper in the rest of Guatemala confirms its reputation. But tomorrow is the first day of the annual Guatemalan circus convention, and I knew I couldn't miss that. I heard of it by word of mouth and didn't think to ask where it would be held, but was naively assuming that it couldn't be too hard to find. Now I'm not so sure.

It's both liberating and daunting to travel alone again. When alone, you have to go through a delicate courting ritual with each new place, like learning the steps of an unfamiliar dance. The most delicate phase of all is first arrival, when it's all too easy to allow yourself to be confused, and then cowed, and then irritated, and then angry. And you never come out of that looking or feeling good. As we pull into the bus station, the taxi drivers are clustering around my window before the bus has even stopped moving, mouthing unintelligible words and pointing at their chests and then their taxis. I steel myself.

After years of hitchhiking almost everywhere, there are few things I find more intimidating than arriving at foreign bus stations. In general, when you are hitchhiking, people pick you up out of humanity and respond to you as they would to any other human. At a bus station people pick you up out of necessity and respond to you as they would to a banknote dropped on a crowded pavement. And in a new place, where you don't know the distances or the prices (or even, in this case, where you're going), you know that they have the upper hand. The trick is not to let them know it. I used to have a whole arsenal of bluffs to make it look as if I knew what I was doing when I didn't. They're a bit rusty by now. But it is clearly time to get them out and polish them up again.

I wait until everyone is off the bus. This has the disadvantage of ensuring that all the remaining taxi drivers are crowded round the door waiting for me, but the advantage of allowing me to make the descent in my own time, rather than being pushed into the mêlée and won by tug-of-war.

'Taxi, taxi!' they clamour, grabbing at my sleeves. 'Where are you going, señorita? Come, come, I take you! Taxi, taxi, taxi!'

I learnt my first bluff from nature documentaries: make yourself look as big as possible. I adopt a piratical stance, throw my arms wide and give them a toothy smile – the one that says: 'I am probably friendly, but there is a slight chance that I may be a psychopath.' (This differs subtly from the smile I would go for if I didn't want a taxi – the one that says: 'I am probably a psychopath, although there is a slight chance that I may be friendly.') I hold the pose and wait.

'MALABARISTAS,' I announce, once I have relative quiet. They look at me uncertainly, and then glance at each other.

'Taxi?' one suggests, a little tentatively.

'I am looking for malabaristas,' I inform them. 'Where can I find MALABARISTAS?'

There is a moment's hush, before one pipes up: 'Pensión Meza! In Pensión Meza there are many malabaristas!'

'*Sí! Sí!*' they chorus. 'Pensión Meza! Many malabaristas!'

'How much to take me there?' I ask the first one, indicating him with a sweep of the hand so everyone turns to look at him. He looks slightly intimidated. He knows that the other drivers won't let him get away with anything too outrageous. There is a certain amount of solidarity, but it has its limits.

'Forty quetzales!'

'Twenty!' If in doubt, half it and gauge the reaction.

'Thirty!'

'Twenty-five!'

'Thirty is a good price, señorita. You will find many, *many* malabaristas!'

'Then I will give you one quetzal for every malabarista we find.'

I can almost see the cogs turning as he calculates whether or not he is prepared to gamble on current malabarista density in Pensión Meza.

'OK, twenty-five. *Vámonos!*'

'*Vámonos!*'

I allow him to take my arm and sweep me through the throng to our waiting chariot. And once we are alone in the quiet bubble of the cab, and Mr Taxi-Taxi has a name (Juan Luis) and children (three) and a birthplace (in a village in Petén), he stops being a Mr Taxi-Taxi and becomes a fibre in the great fabric of stories that make up this world, and I start to feel more at ease. We arrive at Pensión Meza; I thank him and give him 30 quetzales.

Pensión Meza turns out to be a guest house of glorious, decrepit elegance: a selection of rooms and dormitories with lumpy mattresses and stained sheets arranged in a quadrangle around a courtyard which once upon a time must have been beautiful. There are cracked black-and-white tiles, a jungle of plants, mismatched patio furniture and carvings in the walls eroded by time and acid rain. And, I am pleased to note, three Latino-looking boys with scruffy clothes and juggling clubs. Mr Juan Luis Taxi-Taxi didn't let me down. I dump my bag in a dormitory and come out to talk to them. Their names are Orenato, Pedro and René, from Panama, El Salvador and Honduras, respectively.

'Plenty of people here for the convention,' they assure me. 'And more should be arriving today. Are you hungry? We were about to head to the *comedor solidario* for breakfast.'

They lead me several blocks, past drifts of rubbish and beggars in doorways, to a more modern looking single-storey building set back a little from the road. A queue stretches all the way out the door and along the outside wall. We join the back of it.

'Shouldn't take too long,' René says. 'They serve pretty quickly. And you get breakfast for one quetzal! They do lunches as well, for three quetzales. Subsidised government project, set up for school children. The children eat first, of course. But there's loads of food, and workers and beggars get whatever's left.'

Inside, a huge photograph of President Colom and his wife looms over the queue, both smiling down beatifically, looking happy and united. This is a joke, because you can't open a newspaper at the moment without reading of their impending divorce. Which is also a joke, because nobody in Guatemala believes that the divorce is genuine, but rather a ruse to circumvent the rule in Guatemala's constitution which states that no president can serve more than one term, nor can his family members stand for election. It is common knowledge that Sandra Colom wants the presidency. There are grim predictions that the Coloms are seeking to create a political dynasty. The couple spout all the right rhetoric about indigenous rights and helping the poor, but in the wake of 36 years of civil war and a seemingly endless procession of repressive military regimes, the people are understandably suspicious. (In the end, Guatemala's Supreme Court ruled that, despite the divorce, the terms of the constitution still prohibited Sandra Colom – now Sandra Torres – from running for president. As a result, the Coloms' UNE party [National Unity of Hope] was unable to field a candidate in the 2012 election and the presidency was won by Otto Pérez Molina of the Patriotic Party. As Molina is a retired military officer and has been accused of various atrocities, including torture and genocide during the civil war, it is hard not to feel that in this case, the people's demands for justice may have backfired.)

Breakfast is served school dinner-style on vacuum-formed plastic trays. We get eggs, beans, two bread rolls and a cup of achingly sweet coffee. For one quetzal, I am impressed. The canteen is a vast white hall, full of identikit cream tables and mealtime clamour. We find one of the few free tables and sit down to eat. 'You should come and play some street shows with us later,' Pedro tells me. 'Always helps to have a girl. And we need to raise some money to pay for workshops at the convention. I have a programme here somewhere.'

He fumbles in his pocket and pulls out a folded and crumpled photocopied sheet, which he opens and smoothes out on the table. We all crane over to look.

'There are no workshops I want to do on the first day,' I say, disappointed. 'I don't really like ball-juggling. And what the hell is "construction of character"?'

Pedro looks at me in surprise.

"You must do construction of character," he says. 'It's the most important workshop on here. They teach you tricks for creating your stage persona, your alter-ego. Fundamental for clowning.'

'I'm not really into clowning. I prefer malabares.'

He shakes his head severely.

'If you cannot clown, you are missing the point of circus.'

'What do you mean?'

'If you only do malabares, however good you are, you can only be successful within the reality defined by your audience. Even if you juggle seven clubs, as soon as you drop one, that's a failure. It can still be a good show, but it's not perfect – you know it and they know it. But if you know how to clown, you create the reality, and you define your own success. Orenato! Tell her how we end our street shows!'

Orenato laughs.

'*Nueve clavas en el aire.*' Nine clubs in the air.

'We build up to it all show,' Pedro explains. 'Promising that after just one more act, we will show them nine clubs in the air. Then finally – drum rolls. I count the clubs very slowly, picking them up one by one. The drums build. And then... I throw all of them as high as I can and run for cover.'

'I wouldn't dare to do that! Isn't it a massive let-down?'

'Not if you know how to clown! It's all about the psychology. Throughout the show, you are creating your persona. You have distinctive facial expressions, postures, catchphrases, ways of reacting to things. All hugely exaggerated, of course. For every successful trick, you have a particular reaction. By the end of the show, the audience has built a subconscious link between that reaction and success. So at the end, after the nine clubs fall to the ground, I come out from hiding and run around in triumph making that posture, that facial expression, but now even more exaggerated. If I've built it up properly, the audience goes wild.'

'Does it ever go wrong?'

'Hardly ever. Occasionally you get catcalls. Usually from people who haven't watched the show from the beginning, so haven't internalised the cues. Part of clowning is knowing how to respond to that. When someone catcalls, they are trying to drag you back to their reality. You have to develop responses that will reassert the reality that you have created.'

He thinks about it for a moment before continuing.

'I think this might be why some people are scared of clowns – because they know that, with a good clown, they are no longer in control. The clown is king of his own universe; the clown sets the rules. These are the tricks they will teach you in this workshop. Not how to be absurd – as a clown, you are automatically absurd. What they will teach you is how to be in total control of your absurdity.'

I remember my earlier taxi incident, and the incident with Jaz in Livingston, and I have to laugh. Travellers, clowns – the bluffs are nearly identical. You are automatically absurd. The trick is to be in total control of your absurdity.

ψ Ψ ψ

Lake Atitlán is another place where it pays to be an early riser. Hemingway once described it as the most beautiful lake in the world – and he doesn't strike me as a person who would give a compliment lightly. It has the sort of beauty that makes you possessive, wanting it all to yourself and muttering darkly about *tourists* while refusing to acknowledge that you are one of them – especially in a gringo-trail village like San Pedro where, although the buildings aren't too obtrusive compared to, say, the high-rise hotels of nearby Panajachel, the thumping rock music and tour-agency adverts definitely are.

The lake is cradled by volcanic hills as if between two cupped hands. Letting your eyes slide down from their peaked tips, you watch their dark wooded fingers drop into the dusty jade of the coffee plantations before brightening to emerald in the banana palms at the water's edge. At a particular hour of the morning, when the sun first peeks over the eastern ridge to scatter the surface with a million droplets of light, it looks as if the mountains are drinking their colour from the lake itself. At this hour, the shore is quiet. Up in the market there is chatter, and Mayan women arriving with covered baskets, and men exchanging pleasantries in Tz'utujil – the Mayan language that is spoken in this region – over cups of *atole* (a hot maize drink), but by the lakeside you hear only the birds, and perhaps the rhythmic brush of a broom against cobbles.

I am up at this hour every day to walk down to a hostel on the lakeside. It's a kitsch sort of place with a bar and a private pool, but at 7 a.m. the bargirl teaches a yoga class in the golden morning stillness and I am addicted. If there's one thing I need more of, it's calm. The teacher is a girl called Sofia with a nature born in Australian sunshine and honed in Indian ashrams. Like me, she was lured to San Pedro by an anaemic bank balance and the hope of earning just enough quetzales to live for a while next to the most beautiful lake in the world. We have an exchange going – she teaches me calm and I teach her circus.

By the end of the class, my whole body tingles and my mind feels weightless. I jump down from the raised deck into the patch of garden between the hostel and the lake, and pick my way through the rows of herbs to the beach. An old man is pulling up a canoe amidst the reeds and I stop to see what he's caught. He shows me a handful of tiny spiral shells.

'Water snails,' he says. 'Good for *ceviche*.' His Spanish, though fluent, has the same touch of awkwardness that mine does. Round here, those of his generation tend to be more comfortable in Tz'utujil.

'Do you catch anything else in the lake?' I ask.

'Of course. Big freshwater crabs, over by the rocks. And fish as well. But this year the water is colder than normal, so there are fewer fish.'

'Do you know why the water is colder?' I ask.

He shrugs and looks out over the lake, but there is reverence in his eyes rather than despondency.

'The lake has many secrets,' he tells me.

I push through the bushes to the rocks and dive into this lake of many secrets. The water feels fresh, but is clogged with algae. I swim out to where it clears and takes on glints of sapphire. The encircling mountains seem to focus the whole sky onto the point where I tread water, a tiny speck on a sheet of stained glass, framed in concentric ripples. Among the many secrets in the depths below me, so I've heard, are the skeletons of guerrilla fighters from the Mayan villages around the lake. For 36 years they held out against the Guatemalan state as a succession of military regimes orchestrated what is now acknowledged as a near-genocide of Guatemala's indigenous people. Around 200,000 people are thought to have died during the war, including countless 'disappeared'. Almost everyone in the villages knows at least one person who disappeared. Many of their bodies were weighed down with stones and dropped into the cool dark water.

I swim back to shore, and climb out to sit on a rock by the lakeside. I can hear the laughter of women as they wash their clothes and children's hair in the shallows further down the bank. They are hidden by bushes and a rocky hillside, but I see a milky cloud of soap suds float over the indigo water from the direction of their voices. I cross my legs and close my eyes, feeling trickles of water run down my back from my wet hair. The sun shines through my eyelids, tinting the darkness with pink. I breathe deeply and smile. Anyone watching would think I was meditating.

But in my head, Hele's crisp tones cut through the calm, speaking aloud the words of the message she sent me yesterday. She is now living in a small rented house in Real de Catorce, doing her online research work and finishing a master's thesis that has been on the boil (or more often on the back-burner) since before I met her. Work has been going well, enabling her to invest in a combi van. This brings her to the point of the message:

'The plan is to drive up to the Torreón circus convention with a group of performers from Matehuala. If you can get here in the next two weeks there's definitely a space for you! You should really be at this convention – loads of the banda of the north will be there. Don't you miss us?'

23
Barbed Wire and Scissors

I left San Pedro with four quetzales, no bank card (stolen), a week left to get to Real de Catorce, and my yoga teacher. It seemed like the logical next step of our exchange that, after I had brought circus to her calm, she would now bring calm to my circus.

The addition of Sofia to the mission made it all seem much less daunting. Materially she was in no better position than I was, and possibly in a worse one – although she did have a bank card, her account was empty, and her Spanish and circus skills were basic – but spiritually she floated on some higher plane where everything was always going to be fine. Her Zen was infectious. With my four quetzales and the last of her pay from the hostel we got onto a proudly decrepit and enthusiastically decorated bus headed for the Mexican border.

The Guatemalan side of the border was a nasty, dirty, sleazy place – a corridor of boxy stalls lining a mud-slicked street ridden with potholes. The men who grabbed our arms had a rat-like hunger about them and hustled with a ruthless lack of humour. The Mexican side, by contrast, had such a relaxed and friendly vibe that the cynical part of me wondered if they did it as a deliberate snub to their more desperate southern neighbours. A man pedalling a little yellow rickshaw insisted on giving us a lift, despite our insistences that we had no money, and dropped us off on the main road with a cheerful wave.

A short ride took us to an almost empty petrol station on an almost empty road, by which time it was getting dark. We sat on the curb outside the shop and I started to teach Sofia how to make aluminium flowers with the cans we'd found in the bins. Before long two petrol station attendants spotted us and, seeming glad of entertainment to help while away the night shift, sat down to chat. Ten minutes later they were bringing out six-packs of beer ('so you have more materials!') and insisting on buying everything either of us produced for their mothers, wives, sisters, daughters, nieces, grandmothers and distant cousins.

The men spoke to me in Spanish, but also demonstrated an impressive level of English with Sofia.

'Have you lived in the States?' I asked one of them.

'Yes,' he told me. 'For two years. But then I couldn't stand it anymore.'

'Why not?'

'It's no life. So many people here watch US TV and Hollywood movies and think life over there is all like that. But it never is. You can earn more money, but you work like a dog to get it, far away from your friends and family, and people treat you like shit. It's so hard to make American friends. You can't afford to live in their communities and the only jobs you can get are working with other Latinos, so you struggle to learn the language... and then they say that you won't integrate, that you're just another scrounging wetback. I stuck it out for two years, hoping it would get better, but it didn't. So I came home. I'm poor here, but I'm much happier than I was there.'

'At least you learned something from the experience, then – to appreciate the good in your life here.'

'That's true. But it's sad I had to suffer so much to learn it. Not only in my time there, but in the journey. I paid all my money to a *coyote* to guide me overland, but he abandoned my group while we were sleeping, and after that we lost our way in the desert and the group got split up. There were twenty of us, but I heard that only eight made it alive. The others – mostly women and children – died of thirst.'

I was silenced for a while by the petrol station attendant's tale and marvelled, for the millionth time, at how many stories there are in this world. How many ordinary extraordinary people.

We spent a sweaty and uncomfortable night in a storage room full of oil drips and ants, bought *tamales* for breakfast from a woman who arrived with a whole batch of them steamed in what looked like a metal rubbish bin, and soon after found a ride in a truck heading north. It had a partner truck in convoy and a ferocious amount of barbed wire wrapped around the metal bar you use to pull yourself up to the door, making the process of getting in much more difficult and perilous than usual.

'Why all the barbed wire?' I asked, once we were safely inside.

'Oh,' the driver told me casually, 'there are a lot of bandits on this road. They wait by speed bumps where they know you have to slow down, and if you don't have the barbed wire they grab the bar, pull themselves up, and swing round to shoot you through the windscreen.'

'Shit... does that happen a lot?'

'Not so much anymore. We all have barbed wire.'

The road undulated through verdant forest between banks of red mud before climbing into cooler, more barren country. Every so often we would pass settlements cobbled together from concrete, brick and wood, slowing down for the speed bumps as we approached. We saw no bandits though, only women with cakes or *empanadas* (stuffed pastries) in covered baskets and children with buckets of soft drinks. Around midday we stopped by one of these settlements, and the drivers of the two trucks announced that they had a job for us.

'What is it?'

'We were carrying corn, but now we're going to pick up new loads of sugar. We need to sweep out all the stray kernels and corn dust from the inside of the trucks. Could you help?'

'We'd be happy to.'

They unlocked the backs of the trucks and provided us with brooms, but stopped us after only a couple of minutes, looking shocked.

'You know how to sweep!'

'Um, yes.'

'You have done it before?'

'Of course.'

They laughed incredulously.

'We didn't think people knew how to sweep in your countries.'

Apparently we had been supposed to provide entertainment with our charming incompetence rather than genuine help. We had to laugh – although it was a little sobering to realise quite how useless we are considered by the rest of the world. We finished the job though, leaving the drivers so distracted with guilt that they insisted on buying us lunch in a wood-walled *comedor*, heavily decorated with icons of the saints and Looney Tunes postcards.

Our luck was smooth throughout the journey. We got a few hours' sleep in the bed of another truck during the night and woke in time for the long ascent into Puebla that sees the humidity relax its grip, the vegetation darken, and the trucks struggle and pant as they drag themselves up towards the capital. We were briefly swallowed by the grey and smog of the DF bypass before being spat out again into faded fields. We passed a turning with a sign to Texcoco and I nearly, very nearly, shouted to our driver to stop and let me out.

But I didn't.

I wasn't even sure if he was still there.

ψ Ψ ψ

We were already some way up the highway towards Querétaro when Sofia made an unexpected decision. I was in the passenger seat, chatting with the truck driver, and she was sitting on the bed with a book. Suddenly she leaned forward, poking her tousled golden head between the front seats. Her brow was slightly furrowed, but she looked happy.

'Cat,' she said slowly. 'I've been thinking. I think I want to go home.'

'Home? What, like *home* home? Australia? When? Now?'

'I think it's time. I'm sorry. I did really want to come with you. But I suddenly have this feeling, you know, that I'm needed there. It's been a year since I last saw my family. And this has been such an amazing journey to end it on. I don't know... it just feels right.'

This was Sofia all over. She did things on instinct, guided by whatever happy spirit it was that she channelled. The announcement, though sudden, didn't seem impetuous. I saw the serenity on her face and realised that her mind was made up. It was time.

'I'll come with you until the end of this ride, of course,' she assured me. 'But then, if we can find an internet café, I'll use my credit card to get a flight. Once I'm home, I can work and pay it off. And I'll buy us both a nice meal.

What do you say? Will you be alright?'

I nodded, still slightly stunned.

'I'll be alright.'

I translated her decision to the truck driver, who nodded approvingly. Going home to the family was, of course, a good thing. He went out of his way to drop us off at a large service station with a restaurant and an internet café, just on the outskirts of San Juan del Rio. It was dark by the time we arrived there. Sofia booked a flight. We ate a nice meal. Then she curled up to sleep on the floor of the service station. I tried to do the same, but my brain was whirring. After half an hour I gave up and sat back at the table, staring out the huge plate-glass windows at the forecourt of the petrol station.

I kept staring until sunrise.

In the morning I made a call and organised a taxi to take Sofia to the central bus station, from where she could get a bus to DF. She left me with a long, warm hug, all the change left over from the meal, and one of the most beautiful letters anyone's ever written me. After she'd gone, I read it and I cried.

So now I had a bit of money, but I still had no bank card, I no longer had a yoga teacher, and I was starting to feel distinctly less calm.

I hadn't been entirely truthful when I promised Sofia I'd be alright. I hadn't hitchhiked alone in Mexico for nearly two years, and after the last time I'd resolved not to do it again if I could help it. It wasn't that anything terrible had happened, but you quickly get tired of solicitations. Even when your refusal is immediately accepted and respected, it puts a dirty spin on the journey that means you can never feel entirely comfortable. Worse still are the indirect approaches, the sleazy compliments, the wandering hands and sliding eyes. There's a reason why there aren't many great hitchhiking epics written by women. There's nothing glamorous about the surge of nausea as you realise where a conversation is going, or the flicker of panic as you see that leer and know, as you almost always do, that your strength would be no match for his. There's nothing romantic about feeling like a piece of meat.

But fuck it – I only had 500 kilometres or so left to go. On my last journey to Central America, before I met Trico, I had hitchhiked alone from

Nicaragua to DF with elementary Spanish at the time of the Honduran military coup. If I had been alright then, surely I would be alright now?

I walked to the exit on to the motorway and stuck out a thumb.

Within a minute, a pickup pulled over. It was silver and gleaming with a five-seat cab and a metal lid locked down over the back. As I bundled in with my bag, I realised that it was quite crowded. There were already five men inside it, and the three in the back had to squeeze over to make room for me. They were middle-aged and portly with slick hair and shiny shirts. The dashboard was high-tech, with a full-colour sat-nav screen that could also become a music player or a TV at the touch of an icon. The men immediately started to bombard me with jovial questions and, although I endeavoured to answer with a smile, my stomach was lurching. Five men travelling together? Clearly well off? Fuelled by exhaustion, my paranoia spiralled. The bulge in that guy's pocket... could that be a gun? What was in the back of the pickup? I remembered a chain email I'd received from a friend a few months previously, with the subject line '*CHICAS – NO ANDEN CON NARCOS*' (girls – don't go with narcos). The photo inside had made me retch and stayed burnt onto my retinas for several days afterwards. Would that be my fate? I turned and looked out of my window at the blur of tarmac beside the wheels. We were now doing over 100 kilometres per hour in the middle of several lanes of traffic. There was no way I would survive bailing out.

Barely had these thoughts had time to flash through my mind when we started to slow and pulled up in a grassy car-park next to a low white building. The man driving turned round and beamed at me.

'*Ya llegamos, güerita!* (We've arrived, little white girl!) Sorry we can't take you any further, but this is where we work! The best *barbacoa* restaurant in all of Querétaro! Come in, come in! Order whatever you want! All on the house! We saw you standing there and we liked your vibe! Everything is free for you today!'

As I stumbled out of the pickup, two of the men were already opening the back and unloading sacks of onions, bags of coals, and great armfuls of coriander.

Barbacoa meat is slow-cooked, traditionally by wrapping it in maguey leaves and steaming it over a cauldron of stock in a covered pit full of hot coals. It is rich in flavour and so tender you barely need to chew it. I ate until my stomach hurt – soup, tacos of every different cut of meat, brimming cups of fresh orange juice. Every time my plate was empty, one of the men would appear at my shoulder urging me to eat more. Finally, when I felt that even one more mouthful might make me explode, I thanked all of them, was showered with fervent wishes for good luck on my journey, and dragged my swollen stomach and guilty conscience back onto the highway, resolving to be less suspicious in future.

The next vehicle to stop for me was a truck. The driver looked about 50, slender and soft-spoken, with silver hair and a fatherly manner.

'*Ay, mi hija,*' he said. 'So far to go? And you look so tired!'

'I am tired,' I admitted. Glancing at myself in the wing-mirror I realised I looked haggard, with great bruise-like circles under my eyes. I felt dizzy and could hardly focus my eyes. My head kept lolling involuntarily.

'We have some way to go,' the man said. 'Why don't you lie down in the bed, get some sleep? I'll wake you when we arrive.'

I looked round at the bed. The blankets. The pillows. It looked like the most comfortable place in the entire world. I knew I shouldn't actually sleep... but my body was aching from the strain of the last days and surely I would feel better if I rested my muscles a little?

'Thank you so much,' I said. 'You're so kind.'

'It's nothing, *mi hija.* Don't worry. Sleep well.'

I lay down. The mattress seemed to engulf me in a warm, soft embrace, like Sofia's parting hug a few hours earlier. The vibrations of the engine massaged my body until every joint relaxed. I remembered the head massages Sofia used to give everyone during meditation at the end of the yoga session. Sunshine on my face. The breeze off the lake. Pure bliss. Pure calm...

When I woke there was a weight next to me, a heavy awkward presence. Stiff fingers probing my waist, lifting my dress to find the top of my trousers, a hand on my stomach, a palm running upwards...

I sat bolt upright with a sharp elbow backwards.

'What the fuck are you doing?'

'*Ay, mi hija.*' He shook his head sadly, as if hurt by the unreasonableness of his disobedient daughter.

'Don't call me that. I'm not your daughter. And don't touch me. While I'm sleeping! You sick pervert.'

'Look,' he said, in a long-suffering tone. 'If you have sex with me I'll take you wherever you want to go.'

I was struggling for words, rendered speechless by shock and disgust. All I could manage was a single choked affirmation.

'I am not a prostitute.'

'A blowjob...?'

But I was already grabbing my bag, throwing the door open and jumping down from the cab. We were in the middle of absolutely nowhere. Nowhere and nothing. There were no vehicles in sight. No people. No buildings. No animals. Not even a fucking cactus. Just grey dust, a broken wire fence, and a thin worm of tarmac. If I ever make a film and I need a location for Purgatory, I'm going back to find it. If not, I never want to see the place again.

The truck waited for a moment, as if hoping that I might still see reason. Then, with a snort of air like an exasperated sigh, it grumbled into life and pulled off into the wasted landscape. As soon as it was gone, I remembered every swear word I had forgotten when I most needed them, and screamed all of them in both Spanish and English, throwing my bag on the ground and kicking it. I felt tears threaten so I slapped myself in the face, then sat down on top of the bag and pulled my hair over my eyes, taking deep, shuddering breaths until I calmed down.

I had never hitchhiked with a weapon, in accordance with some wishful idea that the energy you put into the world tends to be the energy you get back. But this logic, however nice it sounds, only gets you so far. As Pepe might have put it: 'With some people you can't afford to be nice.'

So I opened my bag and took out the pair of scissors that I used for making aluminium flowers. They were fairly blunt by now but they were large and glinting, and I figured they'd make most people think twice before trying to come too near me. I shoved them into the waistband of my trousers and pulled my dress down over the top to hide the handles. Then I walked to the edge of the road, looked down the empty grey strip to where it disappeared in the heat haze hanging on the dust, and waited for a vehicle.

After 10 minutes a car pulled over, and its driver promptly set about restoring my faith in humanity. This is the beautiful thing about hitchhiking – for every one person who dents that faith, there are another 99 ready to mend it. My benefactor was a professional man of about 40, fair-minded and intelligent. He tutted sadly when I told him what had happened.

'You're a long way off track,' he said. 'About a hundred kilometres. I'm afraid that where I drop you off will be more or less where you started.'

'It's still a great help,' I said. 'Thank you so much.'

'You shouldn't be hitchhiking alone,' he told me. 'It's just not done here.'

'It's not really done in my country either, but I never have any problems. In fact, in my country it's done less than it is here. Here I see loads of people hitchhiking. Whole families, sometimes. People coming home from work. It's much more accepted than it is in England.'

'Not for a woman on her own, though. The only women who hitchhike alone here are prostitutes. That's why you'll find that many drivers will treat you like a prostitute. That's what they're used to.'

'But if the only women who hitchhike alone are prostitutes, and therefore drivers treat all women who hitchhike alone as prostitutes, and therefore women who aren't prostitutes won't hitchhike alone… Does it make sense in Spanish to say it's "*un circulo vicioso*"?'

He nodded vigorously. Mexicans, of all people, understand vicious circles.

ψ Ψ ψ

My luck was patchy for the rest of the day, and by nightfall I was still only just north of Querétaro, about halfway between DF and San Luis Potosí. I was dropped off at a truck stop and decided to make just one round of the vehicles at the pumps before giving up and sleeping there.

I found a truck driver willing to take me another hour north. He was fairly young, but his face looked puffy and his eyes were very red. I hesitated, but there was something about the indifference with which he offered me the lift that made me trust him.

A short way up the road, we pulled into a dark lay-by.

'What are we doing here?'

'I need a break. I'll be about twenty minutes. You can get out and find another lift if you don't want to wait.'

I dithered. What was this all about? Hadn't he just been in a truck stop? Why stop here for a break? But why would he suggest I get out if he wanted anything from me? Or was that a bluff?

He clambered between the seats and sat down on the bed.

'Come back here,' he said.

'No. No, I'm getting out.'

'Fine, get out then. But don't just sit there in full view. You can sit on that if you don't want to sit on the bed.' He pointed at a crate next to the bed. I was baffled, and very reluctant to leave my seat – in either direction. He sighed with exasperation at the delay.

'Look, I need to smoke, OK? I can't have you sitting there attracting attention. You can get out or sit on the crate, whichever you prefer, but you can't stay there.'

I was still unsure – many truck drivers in Mexico smoke weed openly whilst driving and I had never seen anyone be so secretive about it. But it was pitch dark outside, and I knew I would struggle to get another lift from there. I moved round and sat on the crate.

He fumbled in a pocket over the head of the bed and pulled out a light bulb, mottled black on the outside and with the end removed. With a further rummage he extracted a small bag of a white substance, opened it, and tapped the contents into the light bulb. I watched, intrigued. I had never seen anyone smoke crack before.

'I'm not an addict,' he said, defensively. 'I only do this to keep awake on these long journeys. At home, with my family, I don't touch it.'

'Don't you take those little pills that most of the truck drivers take?'

'I used to take those, yeah. But you get a tolerance to them so fast, and when you need three for every journey... well, it's cheaper to smoke this. Besides, I find this much smoother. I'm less tense; I can concentrate better. Safer for driving.'

It was the first time I'd met someone who smokes crack cocaine for reasons of road safety, and I hope it's the last.

24

The Sacred Mountain

It is a dramatic moment when, after hours of following the monotony of the highway, you turn off and head straight towards Real de Catorce, nestled in the top of one of those strange clumps of mountains which rise from the *altiplano* like the knuckles of a giant fist. At first it appears as no more than a heap of pale brown rock scored by rivulets of purple shadow, but as you draw nearer its cliffs, thickets of scrub and tiny villages start to take form and soon it dominates your whole horizon, as immense and majestic as a desert Mount Olympus. After the long approach the ascent takes you by surprise and the road starts to crumble and fall away on one side as it writhes its way upwards. You pass a couple of hamlets whose sand-coloured buildings camouflage with the landscape, distinguished only by the brighter colours of flower beds and window boxes. On the final leg the road hugs tight to the cliff and you look out over the drop to the barren plateau below, as flat and endless as the sea.

At the end of this stretch, usually, you wait. Since the old road fell into disrepair, all traffic to and from Real must pass through two kilometres of tunnel bored through the mountainside. As it is over 100 years old and too narrow to allow two cars to pass, the tunnel requires a man with a walkie-talkie on either entrance, signalling to the waiting vehicles when it is safe to enter. When your turn comes you are plunged into a claustrophobic catacomb of hewn rock, lit only by pale yellowish bulbs. Local drivers take this at what feels to a newcomer like terrifying speed. In the back of the pickups used to shuttle pedestrians you feel the temperature drop and your teeth rattle as you fly over the cobbled road round subterranean curves, shrinking from the sides and convinced that the top of the cab will never clear the low tunnel ceiling. But it always does, and you burst out the other end into bright sunlight and what could almost be the 19th century – if it weren't for the queue of vehicles waiting to head back the other way.

Founded in the late 1700s after the discovery of rich silver seams in the surrounding mountains, Real de Catorce is an old mining village of exceptional beauty. The town centre is built entirely from the pale stone of the mountain, with narrow cobbled streets emerging onto sudden, breathtaking views. All but abandoned in the early 1900s when a sharp drop in the price of silver led to the closure of the mines, it now exists as a sparsely populated ghost town subsisting off the revenue from tourism and pilgrimage. The village is flooded with Catholic worshippers during the holy seasons of Christmas, Easter and the feast day of San Francisco de Asís in October, but also attracts visitors of a more shamanist inclination by virtue of its proximity to El Cerro Quemado (The Burnt Hill) – the sacred mountain of the Huichol people. This hill is the site of the Huichol's annual pilgrimage and represents the spiritual heart of their ancestral lands and culture.

Real de Catorce manages to depend on tourism without succumbing to it. It knows that rustic charm is its principal attraction, and it has taken good care to preserve it. Visitors are welcomed, but they must be content to stay in quaint, cramped guesthouses, because they'll find no deluxe hotels. Gift shops are ubiquitous but tasteful, adding a tapestry of colour to the stone streets. Restaurants are furnished in dark wood and emit spiced smells of *café de olla* (fresh coffee brewed with cinnamon and piloncillo). The artesanos around the plaza are a mixture of white-clad Huicholes, young itinerants and older local hippies, but all see themselves as artists rather than businessmen and are usually too focussed on their latest creation to bother with anything but the most peremptory hustling. The men touting horseback rides on the edge of the town look far from out of place when you realise that plenty of the local residents use horses or mules as their own preferred method of transport; there are notices saying 'Please do not tether animals here' where 'No Parking' signs would usually be. Outside of holy seasons the village is a relaxed, friendly place, where everybody knows everybody and nobody moves any faster than is strictly necessary. I could see why Hele had chosen it as the ideal place to get some peace and finish her thesis.

Hele was living in a one-roomed stone cottage on the edge of town. Its back windows looked out on two cactus-strewn mountainsides parting over the deep cleft of a valley as it fell from their embrace onto the plains below. On my first night there, as we sat on the rocky hillside to the back of the house and watched the falling sun spread rivers of orange and gold up the sides of the canyon, Hele raised her mug of coffee in a silent salute.

'My family think I'm mad to be living in one room in a ghost village in northern Mexico when I had a nice apartment and a career back home,' she said. 'But come on... There are millionaires who would rip their hearts out for that view.'

I had arrived a few days early, giving me time to explore before our journey north. Having been there for several months, Hele proved an enthusiastic and knowledgeable guide.

The town is dominated by a white-domed cathedral, memorable for the ex-votos that line the walls of the sacristy to the left of the altar: pictorial representations of miracles attributed to San Francisco, offered in thanks by the recipient of the favour. Often moving and sometimes exquisitely painted, they cover almost a century of folk art and history. A few have an unmistakably Mexican flavour. My personal favourite, now several decades old and complete with a most fetching illustration, offers a father's devout thanks 'for allowing my daughter to recover after I shot her'.

Real's inhabited buildings cluster around the cathedral and central plaza as if seeking warmth around a fire, while further out the town crumbles into the cold loneliness of abandoned stone: an old bullfighting ring; a little-used church surrounded by cacti and weathered tombstones. Further out still, up the hill above the town, lies a true ghost village, its stark walls and collapsed ceilings now smothered by weeds. Here are the entrances to the old mines. A heavy stone dropped into the pit can be heard bouncing off rocks into the heart of the mountain with an echoing roar that makes the ground shiver. Past the village there are further ruins, smaller and all but forgotten, scattered amongst the maguey. Below Real lie tiny half-empty hamlets buried in the valleys, poorer and more rustic, but some with little streams feeding hidden oases of trees and grass.

El Quemado lies at the western extremity of the huddle of mountains, a hulking form said to resemble an elephant. It is a few hours' walk across ridges and hillsides and a steep scramble up a winding path to the summit, from where a sheer rock face plunges almost vertically down to the desert of Wirikuta, and the boundless horizon and God-like sense of height make it easy to see why Huichol legend holds this to be the birthplace of the sun. In a cleared space amidst the cacti in a fireplace ringed by concentric circles of stones, the most sacred of the Huichol peyote ceremonies take place. A tiny hut nearby houses a jumble of ritual offerings, such as decorated bowls and *sikuli* – concentric diamonds of coloured yarn woven around a wooden cross. The atmosphere is both wild and desolate, and intensely peaceful.

UNESCO has designated this area a Natural Sacred Site and, along with the Wirikuta desert, an Ecological Reserve and a Natural Protected Area. Its protected status has not prevented extraction rights to its remaining silver seams being sold off to foreign mining companies. In 2009, extensive mining concessions, 70 per cent of which fall within the area of Wirikuta and El Quemado, were granted to the Canadian First Majestic Silver Corporation. It is feared that the proposed mines will not only destroy the ambience of the site, but also drain meagre aquifers and allow chemical residues to poison the lands of Wirikuta. The potential effect on its delicate ecosystem, including the revered and endangered peyote cactus, is severe.

'What do people here think of it?' I asked Hele.

'The Huichol will resist it every step of the way,' she said. 'But for all the high sounding governmental rhetoric, there is still plenty of institutional discrimination against indigenous peoples and the Huichol are hardly experienced lobbyists. And of course, it's never simple. Beneath the beauty of this place there's a lot of poverty, and the effect of the cartel wars on tourist revenue isn't helping. A lot of people really struggle to get by, and there is a fair bit of support for the mine in the hope that it will bring jobs. But the support is also symptomatic of the fact that many people here regard indigenous culture as worthless. This place has been central to Huichol tradition since time immemorial. With their sacred lands destroyed and the peyote gone, what would they have left? To them, that would represent the death of their gods and the end of their history. They see this as a war of extermination. They ask for so little, have lost so much, and now face losing the most precious thing they have.'

It's a conflict which must be played out daily across the world: the needs of progress and an ever-growing population versus an older and gentler world view. Who knows how long Real will remain the way I saw it? I am grateful for those beautiful, tranquil days of long walks, good food and bottles of red wine under constellations embroidered on black velvet flecked by shooting stars. Hele generously supported me, assuring me that I could pay her back from semáforo earnings in Torreón.

'How is the situation in Torreón these days?' I asked.

'I think a little calmer than it was before, now that the territories are more settled,' she said. 'Still not great, but when is it ever?'

On the final evening before Hele's friends arrived for the drive north, as we sat with our coffees and our millionaire's view, Hele took her eyes off the sunset to slip me one of her searching looks under her eyelashes.

'Do you know if Trico will be in Torreón?' she asked.

'I'm not sure. Last time I heard from him he said he might go. But you know what Trico's like. He could be all packed and ready and then be invited to share a bottle of mescal with someone he'd just met and end up in Chiapas. I have no expectations either way.'

'Do you want him to be there?'

'I... I don't know. Of course it would be wonderful to see him. But I'm leaving in three months, aren't I? And I've spent the last few months coming to terms with it, reminding myself how much I love the freedom of being alone. I imagine he has too. Maybe it's better for both of us if we don't see each other again.'

Hele laughed. She had always found me amusingly transparent.

'You'll see each other again,' she said. 'I'm sure of it.'

ψ Ψ ψ

With her eyes shaded by a fetching straw hat and her face set in a tolerant half-smile as she focussed on the road, Hele approached the mission with characteristic businesslike zeal. She had always impressed me with her ability to make everything she ever did, however eccentric, feel like not just the most sensible thing to do, but the *only* sensible thing to do. Perhaps this is the highest form of clown – so in control of their absurdity that they cease to be absurd and instead create a new standard for normality.

Hele's friends, who I'd met the previous night in a blur of mescal and fire on the mountaintop under the stars, were now a tangle of limbs in the back of the combi, from which a hand would occasionally emerge to pass a caguama to Hele and me in the front. Hele had decided to dispense with the tolls and tedium of the Saltillo highway, and instead elected to go by a back road through the barren heart of the desert.

'Stock up on caguamas,' she instructed the tangle, as we stopped in the last dusty village on the edge of the vacuum. 'We only pass one Oxxo in the next 400 kilometres.'

For a country with around 9,000 Oxxo outlets, this was wilderness indeed.

Throughout the day and into the dusk the road unfurled before us, barely distinguishable from the pale dirt stretching to the horizon on either side. For miles the skyline was crisp and smooth, unbroken even by mountains or rock formations, with nothing in sight but scrub and cacti whose muted tones of green and brown blurred together on the distant slopes into one endless, changeless carpet of grey. With a cloudless sky echoing above us, it felt as if we'd entered the virtual landscape of a computer program, a hypothetical empty world waiting to be filled with objects of our own imagination. Even road-signs displayed a level of creativity that I felt sure would struggle to find approval on a major highway. A huge metal cutout of a dinosaur, for instance. And further on, a very official-looking blue square with white border, at the centre of which was a single white question mark. I imagined the workers who placed it there, beavering away at the side of the road.

'*Ay, no mames*…Where the fuck are we?'

That inimitable Mexican shrug.

'*Quién sabe, güey. Quién sabe.*'

ψ Ψ ψ

From the outside, Casa Morelos in Torreón is a gently sagging building of peach-coloured brick. The ground floor is obscured by garish shop fronts, but the first floor displays a row of dark red French doors, each facing onto a narrow wrought-iron balcony. The entrance is sandwiched between two shops, easy to overlook, and guarded by the windscreen-washers in the semáforo opposite in return for use of its outside tap. Its location is not advertised, but nor is it secret. It was squatted with the full knowledge and permission of the owner, an elderly woman who had spent the last few years worrying about how to stop it falling down and was more than happy to pass the brunt of the worry to someone else. Whether she's aware of the aerial circus equipment now rigged from the ceiling I'm not sure, but it's been there a few years and the building hasn't fallen down yet.

The rooms that face the street are lent an air of grandeur by high ceilings, tiled floors and columns of sunlight falling through the French doors. From the narrow stairwell, dingy and disorientating with its swirls of coloured graffiti, it comes as a surprise to enter into the first of these rooms and see people lounging on threadbare sofas around the walls and mixing drinks or rolling cigarettes on a long counter that might once have been a reception desk. The walls are covered in brightly painted murals, with empty picture frames at strange angles and newspaper articles and bicycle wheels glued on for added decoration. The second of these front-facing rooms is the main practice area. It has red-painted walls, crash mats on the floor, trapezes and aerial silks hanging from the ceiling, and trunks of circus toys and unicycles piled in the corners. There are always at least five people practising there at any hour of the day, and the air is charged with concentration. All ages are welcome and it is not uncommon to see tattooed and dreadlocked youths swapping tricks with the children of local street vendors, who often come up to visit while their parents are at work and seem delighted to find adults who take the business of playing with toys with the seriousness it deserves.

At the back, the building loses all pretence to elegance, but the shabby courtyard and the abandoned building site behind it still manage to house a spacious practice hall, two art rooms, a full-height aerial circus rig and an open space for fire performance. During the convention, tents fill the courtyard.

As Hele had promised, banda had come from all across the northern states, and even a few from the south. I saw faces I recognised from San Luis, Texcoco, Durango, Chihuahua, Zacatecas – a human collage of memories from a year and a half that had changed and taught me so much I could barely remember a time before it. Jorge had come from Chihuahua, although he was a quieter and more forlorn Jorge than the brazen Señor Talón of my memory. His sister Gabriela was dead, killed by kidney disease, shortly after finishing the qualification she had worked so hard for. I remembered her pale face and constant tiredness and wondered sadly whether in a more fortunate family she might have been diagnosed and treated early enough to save her. I offered Jorge my condolences, and asked him for news of Javi.

'He's almost recovered now,' he said. 'But it took him months to regain full use of his arms. It was hard for them with the new baby and Javi unable to work, but Lupita kept teaching classes and their family and friends helped them pull through.'

'Did they ever find out who did it?'

'Javi knows, but he won't say.'

There was a hint of relief in his voice. Javi, ever the loyal friend, had spared his friends the masculine obligation of avenging him. This time, at least, a vicious circle had been averted. They were free to move on.

'How is the new baby?' I asked.

For the first time in the conversation, Jorge smiled.

'Very well. He looks just like his dad.'

I recognised another face, from my first days with the banda in Creel: Luis, with his devastating good looks and alleged violent streak. I was still wary of him. But Hele, who had got to know him back in Chihuahua, greeted him warmly.

'Don't trust him,' I warned her.

'Why not?'

'I heard that he stabbed someone, after a party in a town near Creel. Almost two years ago now.'

'I know,' she said.

'Really? Did you ever hear what happened?'

'At the party, one of his friends was raped. He found out who did it, went to the guy's house and stabbed him.' She shrugged and pulled a face. 'I know it's not a nice thought. But that's how it works round here, especially in the Sierra. Rape cases never get investigated. The only justice is revenge.'

I fell silent, remembering how Luis had lost his mother. In a region where the rape and murder of women routinely go unpunished, can you blame people for taking the law into their own hands? The pacifist in me still recoiled at the idea of cold-blooded violence. But now, at least, I understood.

The next day, I played passes with Luis. He seemed to laugh more freely these days, and had lost his wolfish air. There was still an arrogance about him, but now it struck me as playful cockiness, without the underlying coldness I remembered. Maybe I had misjudged him before. Or maybe he too had found a way to move on.

Amidst the old faces were new faces also – faces I got to know and share caguamas with over the riotous first night and the days that followed. Paula, so beautiful it hurt to look at her, still playing four hula hoops even with her delicate figure distorted by the tight globe of a seven-month pregnancy. Primaveras, one of the founders of the circus school, with the heavily muscled torso of a trapeze artist and the permanent smile of a born clown. Picudo, a 19-year-old fire-breather from Ciudad Juárez, wide-eyed and irresponsible (he'd left two kids behind him), on the run from a life in the *maquiladoras*, the huge factories that provide almost the only employment in the ravaged border states of the north. And many more from across the country, who continued to arrive in bunches over the following day with their bags of toys and latest hitchhiking stories, filling the squat with raucous laughter and flying coloured objects. Every time a new bunch emerged from the stairwell to throw down their bags and be greeted by slaps on the back and caguamas thrust in hands, my eyes would flash quickly over each one of them. But it was never the one I was looking for. Each time, I couldn't decide if I was disappointed or relieved.

ψ Ψ ψ

Like Chihuahua, Torreón/Gómez is another hideous north Mexican city that I can't help liking. I think it's because it strikes me as a glorious example of optimism over logic. Undeterred by the fact that it is a crime-torn industrial wasteland of no historical interest in the middle of the desert, the city seems never to have lost faith that it can still become one of the world's great tourist capitals. (After all, Las Vegas managed it.) What it lacks in imagination, it compensates for in ambition. Residents will proudly tell you that the statue of Jesus watching over the city is second only in size to that of Rio de Janeiro. (Sadly untrue, but I wouldn't tell them that. At 21.9 metres high, it's definitely a good effort.) And I would love to have been a fly on the wall in the town council meeting when it was decided that what Gómez Palacio most needed was a 58-metre-high scale replica of the Eiffel Tower. I can only assume that, with such unfortunate material to work with, it was decided that the best strategy was to cunningly disguise the city as somewhere else.

Torreón was in a good mood that spring. Violence continued, but the murder rate was down from the previous year and there were fewer armoured cars on the streets. The epicentre of the drug war is continually moving and although its tremors are felt almost everywhere, for now Torreón was simply grateful not to be its focus. It was scorching hot, ice cream and balloon vendors were out in force, and in the semáforos all the car windows were open. For all its problems, Torreón is a prosperous city of wide streets and modern architecture, and the heaving four-lane semáforo 20 minutes' walk from the squat proved extremely lucrative for two güeras with a drum and some juggling clubs. Hele and I were averaging about 700 pesos between us in two-hour sessions, making our individual earning power at least double that of any of the boys – almost embarrassing considering I was one of the least proficient jugglers of all of them. They grumbled amongst themselves, but didn't complain when we came back with armfuls of caguamas and bottles of mescal.

Torreón wasn't the only north Mexican city in a good mood. As we sat in the sun and passed drinks around, much of the conversation revolved around the latest rumour from Juárez – that Chapo had finally won the long struggle for control of the city, and the rival Juárez Cartel was in retreat. The city whose morgues had been overflowing for much of the previous two years was finally seeing a drop in its murder rate. In the east of the country the cartel wars continued to escalate but the battle for Juárez, at least, appeared to be over. (A year and a half later, Juárez is no longer the most violent city in the world, and some of the people who fled are tentatively returning. The Sinaloa Cartel's trafficking routes are free and unobstructed from the Sierra Madre to the US border. The authorities have declared it a triumph of Mexican law enforcement.)

Although we toasted the news, grateful for anything that would bring some relief to the beleaguered city, the aftertaste was bitter. There's only so much enthusiasm one can feel for the victory of a brutal gang lord responsible for the devastation of a vast tract of his own country and unknown thousands of deaths. When the result of national and international policy is the gradual dismemberment of a whole country, limb by limb, and the only 'hope' left for the terrorised population is that one criminal group should consolidate control, it is surely time to think again. Don't take my word for it. Take the words of, among many others, three former Latin American presidents (Gaviria, Zedillo and Cardoso, of Colombia, Mexico and Brazil respectively), Latin American writer-intellectuals Carlos Fuentes and Mario Vargas Llosa, former UN High Commissioner for Human Rights Louise Arbour, former US Secretary of State George Shultz, and former Secretary General of the UN Kofi Annan, who were all signatories to the 2011 report by the Global Commission on Drug Policy. The first paragraph is unequivocal:

> The global war on drugs has failed, with devastating consequences for individuals and societies around the world. Fifty years after the UN Single Convention on Narcotic Drugs, and forty years after President Nixon launched the US government's war on drugs, fundamental reforms in national and global drug control policies are urgently needed...

ψ Ψ ψ

Workshops at Casa Morelos were held in the afternoon, as most participants depended on a morning semáforo session in order to pay for them. Half of the main practice hall was given over to juggling, the standard so high I was forced to give up after the first day and simply watch in awe, trying to commit to memory the odd pattern or manipulation for future practice.

In the other half of the room, participants took turns to climb the aerial silks (two wide strips of fabric hung from the ceiling) and twist themselves into gymnastic poses in the air. In the second practice hall, the percussion collective layered complex rhythms over reverberating bass drums while girls drilled in hula hoop and African dance. Each workshop charged 200 pesos for four sessions, all of which went back into running the squat and purchasing new equipment.

After dusk, the arid heat of the day softened into a balmy night air that brushed like silk against the skin. Every evening there was a show – either a private gala night or a public performance. The main source of funding for the circus school was the weekly street show played by the Torreón collective – a fusion of fire performance, unicycle acts and clowning. On Sunday night, we all trooped down to the plaza to watch.

Primaveras took centre stage, his hair in a topknot, the muscles of his chest straining against a tight red T-shirt and a pair of absurdly narrow black braces. The children sat cross-legged in front of him, giggling in anticipation, many clutching sticks of chocolate-dipped strawberries bought from the stands around the plaza. Parents and passersby stood cross-armed behind. Primaveras cleared his throat theatrically and spread his arms and smile wide.

'*DAMAS Y CABALLEROS!*' (Ladies and gentlemen!)

A second boy pranced behind him, bleating an echo.

'*...lleros ...lleros ...lleros*'

'*BIENVENIDOS!*' (Welcome!')

'*...idos ...idos ...idos*'

'*A NUESTRO...*' (To our...)

'*...estro ...estro ...estro*'

'*SPECTACULO-O-O!!!*' (Show!)

The children saw the joke coming and were squealing with laughter before it was even completed. Primaveras rushed to silence his echo, his face an exaggerated grimace of panic. Deprived of a punch line, the bolder children provided it for him, a dozen soprano voices gleefully shouting '*CULO-O-O!*' (ARSE!).

Primaveras was an expert at softening up the crowd and they uncrossed arms and delved in pockets as the show proceeded, delighted to see the banda's normal repertoire of clowning, fire and unicycle acts expanded with a host of extra performers from the convention. An aerial circus rig was erected in the plaza for performances of trapeze and aerial silks. Donations overflowed the hats and were siphoned into separate bags after every round.

Yet the show I remember most was one that earned no money at all. A private gala night and party in a second squat in Gómez Palacio spilled out onto the road for a group fire-spinning session. It was a quiet residential neighbourhood and after midnight but, unconcerned by the disruption to their sleep, families came out of their houses to cheer and clap as their street was lit up with whirling patterns of flame.

25
The People Who Love You

From Torreón to Matehuala, from Matehuala to Real, from Real to DF. I shed friends along the way, eventually finding myself standing on a grimy DF pavement, coughing up the last truck's exhaust fumes with only Picudo for company. He was a limp and pale boy with an obstinate clinginess that never failed to evoke feelings of profound irritation in those he clung to, made still more piquant by guilt. He had claimed to have friends in DF he could stay with, but when we arrived it was painfully obvious from the droop on his mouth that the friends had been either a lie or a wishful delusion and he was more alone in that vast crush of concrete and humanity than I was. I felt bad leaving him on a corner by a metro station, feeling his baleful eyes watching me go, but I had no sanctuary to offer him.

I spent much of the next month staying with friends in the city, earning some money and trying (and failing) to learn Nahuatl from a fly swat vendor in my regular semáforo. But I was moody and tense, feeling the impending date of my return ticket drawing ever closer. Instead of inspiring me to make the best use of the time I had left, it seemed to paralyse me.

There was only one date left in my mental calendar before that one: the Mexican national circus convention. It was to be held just outside Guadalajara in June, just one month before I had to be in Cancún to catch my flight. All my remaining energy was focussed on it. This, I felt sure, would be the answer to... something. I just wasn't quite sure what.

The day it was due to start I took a bus north to Guadalajara. From there an older and clunkier local bus carried me out towards the site of the convention. The sun was dying, the clouds shot with purple and orange. Under that violent sky the landscape, ravaged by brushfires a few weeks previously, looked post-apocalyptic, all charred earth and blackened skeletons of trees. I was apprehensive, in the mood to see omens.

The bus was uncomfortably crowded, so I sat on an upturned bucket beside the driver, who chatted happily to me throughout the journey. I answered perfunctorily, only hearing half of it. As I gazed through the windscreen I saw that we were starting to pass silhouettes – silhouettes with staffs and unicycles, stooped under the weight of heavy backpacks but still striding purposefully along the side of the road, occasionally waving a thumb in the idle hope of a lift. A little further on, they started to turn off down a narrow path.

'Here,' I told the driver.

'Here?' he looked doubtfully out at the barren hills and twisted trees.

'Yes. Thank you.'

He shrugged and pulled over.

I jumped down and joined one of the groups of silhouettes, exchanging names and kissing cheeks before trekking together off the road, following the path for 20 minutes or so before it turned down a rocky hillside towards a full-size blue and yellow circus top erected in the burnt field at the bottom. As we approached we merged with other groups, the crowd thickening as we neared the tent, which was now emitting booming shouts and drum-rolls. The opening show was about to begin. I allowed myself to be swept along by the tide of people until suddenly, between the backs of heads, I saw the flow disrupted by one lone figure coming the other way. It too was in silhouette, with a battered trilby hat squashed down over its hair, but I would have recognised it anywhere.

We came face to face, and stopped walking.

'Hello, Trico.'

He looked at me, his face furrowing in all sorts of surprising places, and I wondered again at the elasticity of his features. He was one of those people who can tell a story without having to say a single word. Sometimes it was a story I was incapable of reading, but it had never lost its hold over me. Trico, Mexico, Mexico, Trico... It is possible to love something you don't fully understand. Maybe those are the things you love most desperately of all – the elusive things that are always just beyond your reach.

Without a word, he pulled me into a hug. It was a stiff, uncomfortable hug, obstructed by my bag and jostled by groups of people pushing past us on either side. We withdrew awkwardly, the question still unanswered. But our hands knew us better than our heads did. I looked down, and realised they had found their way into the binding spiral of the *Hunab Ku*. He noticed it too, and I saw the dimples cut into his cheeks in the first flicker of a smile.

'Where are you sleeping?' he asked.

'I don't know. I just arrived. I don't have a tent.'

'You never did come properly prepared for anything.'

'Don't start.'

We were both making faces now, crinkling eyes and pursing lips, trying to honour the seriousness of the occasion and refrain from inappropriate giggling. I had spent six months thinking about this moment, trying to imagine where we would be, how it would feel, what we would say. Agonising over how it should end. In my head, I had rehearsed a thousand different movie moments. Now, I couldn't remember any of them. The conclusion had always been obvious. The formalities were just another act of clowns.

'There's room in my tent. I mean – if you *want*...'

'That would be – that would be perfect.'

'Come on; I'll show you where it is. You should leave your bag there before the show.'

We turned and pushed our way back through the throng, leaving the crowds and noise behind us and heading towards the campsite, which now lay silent and deserted.

We never did see the show. I am told it was very impressive.

ψ Ψ ψ

The whole five days of the convention were enveloped in a choking haze of ash. Baked to furnace heat by the sun, it billowed up in scorching mushroom clouds around every footfall or dropped club. Once, a tendril of wind even whipped it into a small tornado, which snatched a couple of tents before dissolving over an adjoining field. Everybody was shrouded in a permanent grey film.

A water tanker drove round twice a day, hosing down dust and jugglers alike. The workshops in aerial circus were held in the big top, those in malabares outside. Classes were conducted in a mixture of languages and mime as, unlike the one in Torreón, this gathering was international. Although the vast majority of participants were Mexican, performers had also come from across South America, Europe and the United States. Circus, like music, is a universal language. Playing passes, in particular, is a silent conversation. As you synchronise your rhythms, observe each other's style and mimic each other's tricks, a bond of friendship and understanding is formed without having to exchange a single word. There was no trace of antagonism between the Mexicans and the gringos as they played together, high-fived successful exchanges, and patted each other on the back. At night, as everyone spun fire together under a hazy moon, it wasn't even possible to tell which was which.

The shows, held every night, were spectacular: a Chilean who did a Charlie Chaplin-style act riding a unicycle along a tightrope; a couple who performed aerial ballet, their bodies striking impossible shapes, flowing around each other like liquid whilst suspended three metres in the air by a rope looped around the man's ankle; two teenagers on unicycles who could not only ride them with balletic grace but also use them like pogo sticks to jump over five prostrate bodies, do spins off the stage and then bounce back up the steps. Competition was ferocious in the *olimpiadas* (resistance competitions) and even more so in the tournament of *volley-clava* – a fusion of juggling and volleyball in which the aim is to defeat the other team with uncatchable passes.

Nowhere was the Mexican macho streak allowed fuller rein, however, than in the *renegada*. The atmosphere of a *renegada* is gala-night-meets-gladiators. The stage is opened up to anyone brave enough to perform, the acts the audience declares worthy are rewarded in alcohol, and those that are considered substandard are viciously jeered and bottled off. Typically, the audience becomes more unforgiving the drunker it gets, and by the end anyone daring to face the crowd needs a crash helmet and unhealthy levels of adrenaline and/or testosterone to even consider it.

By the next morning, the crowd that had been howling for destruction the night before were as generous and easy-going as ever, milling around the campsite sharing caguamas and catching up with old friends. The circus network is a tight one, and conventions feel more like family reunions than commercial events. When not in shows or workshops, a large proportion of my friends from the last two years were to be found clustered around Hele's combi, cooking spiced stews and soups in clay *ollas* over an open fire and serving portions in cut-off plastic bottles to anyone who wandered over. I was even reunited with two friends I'd met in Guatemala – a Swiss girl called Sophie with blonde dreadlocks and effervescent energy and her Guatemalan boyfriend Diego. I hugged them both and asked how their journey up from the border had been.

'Interesting,' Sophie told me. 'We got a ride from a Zeta on the way here.'

'How did you know he was a Zeta?'

'He told us. He was just a young guy; I doubt he was very high up. We didn't ask many questions, obviously. It was funny, though. We were talking about our lifestyle – about hitchhiking and doing street performance – and he said, "You know, sometimes I wish I were as free as you."'

'Maybe you inspired him to try something different,' I said. 'We can always hope.'

Sophie laughed. 'For a moment, I thought he was considering it. He looked a bit wistful, anyway. But then he brightened up and asked Diego "But what can *you* buy your woman? I bought *mine* a Mini Cooper!"'

ψ Ψ ψ

We left the convention with the undercarriage of the combi threatening to scrape the ground, weighed down by every malabarista that would physically fit and all the backpacks plus two crash mats and four unicycles (two normal, two giraffe) piled on the roof. One of the giraffes was Flaca. The other belonged to an old friend of Trico's named Victor. Victor was an amiable drunk with a thick mat of hair on the back of his head, rather like the tail of a platypus. He owned only one outfit: a shirt patterned with red, black and white diamonds, a pair of brown corduroy trousers, and a grey pork-pie hat. With his unkempt black beard, calloused bare feet and caguama permanently in hand, he had the aura of a happy old hobo beyond any possibility of sophistication and proud of it. His dopey, donkey-toothed grin and unshakeable good humour gave the impression that he must be rather simple, but beneath it he was surprisingly knowledgeable and a dedicated malabarista and drummer. 'Where are we going?' his strangled voice inquired from the depths of the tangle, once we'd finally managed to close the doors.

'I'm giving a couple of people a lift into Guadalajara,' Hele announced, pushing the straw hat down over her curls. 'And then I figured we'd just head west until we he hit the sea.'

The road uncoiled through crumpled mountains towards the coast of Nayarit, bringing the overloaded combi within a short skid of a tragic end on a couple of cliff-hugging switchbacks. We hit the sea at Sayulita, about 40 kilometres north of Puerto Vallarta. Following directions from locals we parked up in front of La Playa de los Muertos (The Beach of the Dead), a secluded cove tucked behind a cemetery on the very edge of town. The beach was deserted, with sand that sparkled like salt crystals. The sun was setting and the humidity felt more soothing than cloying after a week of breathing scorched ash. We set up our tents under the palm trees, gathered wood for the small brick barbecue left by unknown picnickers, and declared ourselves home.

For me, these were golden days. They would start when the glare of the sun turned the tent into a greenhouse and the first action of the morning would be to throw the tent flap open and sprint across the burning sand to the sea. Within half an hour we'd all be there, either splashing and shrieking in the shallows or grouped in pairs, murmuring nose to nose.

The morning swim would be followed, of course, by circus practice. One of the boys had even rigged up aerial silks from a tree overhanging the beach, with the result that I was covered in bruises and friction burns for days as I struggled to master the basics. The minor injuries resulting from my incompetence seemed a small price to pay for the experience of dangling in a web of fabric over golden sands. From upside down, the Pacific Ocean takes on whole new levels of majesty.

Hunger would eventually be our cue to start ambling towards the centre of town, playing mini shows outside houses or street stalls on the way in exchange for breakfast. The sun-drenched concrete blistered our feet so we would skip between patches of shade, pausing under trees to allow the stinging to die down and laughing at the enormous emerald and blue iguanas eyeballing us from amidst the branches.

Sayulita is quietly touristy, the ideal place for foreign holidaymakers who want to experience the beautiful beaches of Puerto Vallarta in a less garish setting. The beach and main plaza are lined with restaurants, all with neat and politely smiling waiters promising to serve up a slice of 'the *real* Mexico'. This, Trico was convinced, was a gold mine.

'Because,' he declared the first morning, as eight of us sat on a curb sharing a caguama and formulating a plan of action, '*we* are the real Mexico.'

'I'm English,' I pointed out. 'And Hele's Estonian. And Sophie's Swiss. And Diego's Guatemalan.'

'But we have the Mexican *spirit*,' Trico insisted. 'Besides, half of us are Mexican. And Diego is honorary Mexican. You girls can be translators.'

Trico approached Operation Mexican Spirit with fanatical seriousness, and was frequently goaded into explosions of frustration at the shambolic nature of his team.

'*No mames*, can we please have a little professionalism?!' he would snap. 'Concentrate, all of you! I want a clean show, no drops! Enter together! Victor – PUT THAT CAGUAMA DOWN! You lot make me despair; you are all good performers, but you have *no focus!*'

It was tempting to point out that a group of energetic and talented people with a lax approach to organisation was, in my experience, a fairly accurate representation of the Mexican spirit. But I had learnt that it was better to humour Trico when he was in one of these moods. Victor, however, had not. He would greet these bursts of temper with a sharp drum roll and the bellowed announcement:

'*Damas y caballeros! Les presentoooo... CAPITÁN ENOJO!!!*'

(Ladies and gentlemen! I present you... CAPTAIN ANGER!)

Roughly half the time this would make Captain Anger even angrier and occasionally he would storm off in an exasperated rage. The other half, his face would go through a most intriguing series of contortions before the repressed laughter burst out through the frown and we would all end up in helpless fits of giggles, with Captain Anger the most helpless of the lot.

When we managed to obey orders and maintain some semblance of professionalism, however, the show was usually well received. We varied the order of acts according to our mood, but the finale was always Trico's entrance on Flaca to play his own solo show followed by three-way passes with two jugglers on the ground. Hele and Victor accompanied the show on djembes and announced each act. Victor – whether in a deliberate attempt to embody the *real* Mexico or from pure high spirits – took to ending the show by staggering around the spectators with his pork-pie hat held out for donations, blowing extravagant kisses and yelling '*Aplausos, aplausos, aplausos! MEXICO SOMOS TUYOS!!!*' After a good show, with a positive audience, this would be met with laughter, claps, and a rain of coins. But sometimes we would play shows to a more sedate class of tourist, who would look nervous and recoil slightly at the vision of this strange barefoot donkey platypus creature in a filthy diamond-print shirt stumbling towards them shouting and making kissing faces. This would be when Trico would nudge me sharply and hiss: 'Come on, Cat; you're supposed to be translating!'

I often had a suspicion that the language barrier was the least of the problems our esteemed audience had with Victor. But just in case, I would dutifully stagger, and blow kisses, and call out to the bemused diners:

'Applause, applause, applause! MEXICO, WE ARE YOURS!!!'

ψ Ψ ψ

One afternoon I was with Trico in the tent, enjoying the few daylight hours when it fell under the shade of the palm trees. We had just come out of the sea and we tasted of salt, our skin tightening and tingling as it dried. The sun had baked us into a state of languid dreaminess and we lay blinking at each other slowly without saying very much.

'Are you really leaving, Cat?' he asked. The question caught me off guard, right in the raw side of the heart. Tears came – the sort that sit plumply on the eye-rims without falling.

'I have to leave. I already have my flight. I already have my university place.'

'But do you really want to leave all this?'

This was the closest Trico would ever come to trying to persuade me to stay. One of my tears wobbled, and then dropped. The other one followed.

'Of course I don't. How could I want to leave? But...'

'...But?'

'Don't you ever think about it? The future, I mean. Surely you can't go on living like this forever. What will you do when you have children, or you get too old? What then?'

He stroked my arm absently, gazing up at the roof of the tent as he pondered the question. It genuinely didn't seem to be something he'd given much thought to.

'I will be a truck driver, I suppose. Like my father. I already know how to fix trucks. Even to drive them. I only need a licence.'

'Wouldn't you be bored? Frustrated? When you're used to having so much freedom?'

'I don't think so. I would still get to travel, to see the country. And I would pick up every hitchhiker I saw and listen to their stories. Maybe tell them some of mine.'

I hugged him and buried my head in his chest, struggling to come to terms with this life plan. I wondered if it would be him one day destroying his health with amphetamines or crack, just to meet ludicrous deadlines in order to maximise profits for people who didn't know a thing about him and didn't care. I pictured him staring at the road with puffy face and bloodshot eyes, his wiry body bloated by endless sedentary hours, his taut juggler's biceps softened to flab. The thought was more than I could bear.

'How can he accept that?' I asked Hele later, despairingly. 'When he's so talented, so charismatic, so intelligent? Surely he's deluding himself thinking he could be happy in that life? How can he want so little for himself?'

'I suppose he doesn't see it that way,' she replied. 'One of the things I like about Mexico is that most people work to live, not live to work. They don't have this fixation that what you do for a living should be central to who you *are*. Who you are is defined by your family, your friends, your community. The people who love you.'

I sat on the beach of the dead and stared out to sea. I didn't know who was deluded anymore.

ψ Ψ ψ

We were forced to leave Sayulita when a car was broken into nearby.

'I believe it wasn't you,' a sympathetic local told us. 'But very few others do. The men here make their own justice; they will come for you in the night, perhaps beat you or break into your van. It is better for you to leave.'

We drove to the next beach along the coast, arriving after dark in a holiday town frequented only by Mexicans. Here there were no candlelit restaurants with murmured conversations and the delicate chink of cutlery on plates. Instead, the street was lined with trestle tables under makeshift awnings, serviced by taco stands spitting oil and rich savoury aromas from heaps of unidentifiable meat scraps sizzling on the hotplates. Many had a speaker erected on a tripod next to them, blasting a wildly clashing mixture of cumbia and *reggaetón*. The men behind them wielded machetes and wiped greasy hands on their aprons, shouting jokes and banter to each other across the heads of their customers. Every stand blazed with lights and noise, vying with all the others to be the brightest, noisiest and busiest. Over-excited children ran around the street, occasionally being subjected to an energetic scolding from their mothers when they shrieked too loudly, only to re-enter the game just as shrilly as before. Youths passed caguamas over the tables and entreated the *taqueros* to accept a swig. Trico beamed.

'These people look like they want a show,' he declared. 'Let's give them a good one!'

It took no effort to grab attention. People were shouting at us before we even set our equipment down.

'Here! Here! One for the children!'

'*Ay, mamacitas güeritas,* do you do malabares as well?'

'*Oye chavo, que onda con la biciclota, a poco sí te subes?!*'

We flung ourselves into the show, with no plan except never to let the fire go out, passing it to the next set of petrol-soaked toys as soon as it started to waver, each person in turn stepping forward to light up and weave themselves in fire. Gradually we moved the show along the parade of stalls, Trico leading the way atop Flaca, Hele and Victor heralding his approach, Sophie and I passing behind with the hat.

'*Una sonrisa es el regalo más bonito,*' Trico would tell the children sitting with their families around the food stands, dripping grease from their tacos. '*No nos deja pobres y no nos hace ricos!*' A smile is the most beautiful gift – it doesn't leave us poor, and it doesn't make us rich!

We all had food pushed into our hands by so many stallholders that by the time we reached the end of the row and stopped to draw breath, we were already full. But we bought more food anyway, and countless caguamas, and sat on the pavement gathering curious crowds until well into the night.

The next day we rolled back across the country, swept up by terracotta hills from the tropical sweat of the coast into the arid highland plains. We set a course for Guanajuato, only stopping when we ran out of petrol or beer and had to play emergency shows. In the small towns we passed these would cause quite a sensation. In one, we played to a whole plaza packed with spectators, collected over 500 pesos, and spent it all on refuelling (the combi and ourselves) before we'd even left town. When we got hungry we would play passes in the aisles of covered markets, disoriented by the tumult of colours and smells: baked corn, lilies, overripe avocados, coriander, fried meat, oranges, smoked chilli, scented candles and a thousand other fragrances all laced together in an intricately textured symphony of sharp, rich and sweet notes. We would be rewarded in vegetables, meat scraps and stacks of warm tortillas wrapped in paper, which we ate sitting on the pavement outside, throwing morsels to the dogs.

It is one of Mexico's many paradoxes that, in a country torn apart by greed, one is constantly surrounded by effusive generosity. As always, Mexico seems to revel in the contradiction, almost teases you with it. If you look carefully at the blood-coloured face of the 100-peso note, you will find, in letters almost too tiny to read, a poem by the pre-Hispanic philosopher king Nezahualcóyotl.

Amo el canto del zentzontle
Pájaro de cuatrocientas voces
Amo el color del jade
Y el enervante perfume de las flores
Pero amo más a mi hermano el hombre.

I love the song of the mockingbird
Bird of four hundred voices
I love the colour of the jade-stone
And the intoxicating scent of flowers
But more than all, I love my brother man.

26
Kinich's Message

All the way to Cancún, Trico said he wasn't coming with me.

He first said it in Matehuala. The combi had dragged itself almost 1,000 kilometres back to Hele's house in Real de Catorce before finally expiring from dust and exhaustion. Hele and a couple of local handymen had managed to coax it into grinding and coughing its way back down the hills to the mechanic's workshop in Matehuala, but its condition was still critical. We had been hoping to make one final trip into the desert together, but I had no time to wait. My flight left from Cancún in a few days. The group splintered, its various members preparing to scatter across the country. New collectives waited to be formed. New shows waited to be played.

Most of the boys intended to stay in Matehuala, where the house of Hele's friends was full of banda from the convention preparing for a cabaret. When we went to drop them off, the banda was sitting cross-legged around one of the back rooms, conducting a meeting about the coming performance. A boy in a wife-beater and a top hat stood at the front of the room, pointing at people with a juggling club.

'And once the two clowns go off that's when *you* enter for your hula hoop number, Fani, and you wanted a tango tune for that, right? And afterwards will be Amado on the trapeze...'

Each person nodded seriously. Trico's eyes shone.

'I'm sorry Loquita, but I want to stay here,' he said outside, after I had said my goodbyes. 'They're really dedicated, this banda; they're doing really cool things. Proper shows like we used to do in Cancún, here in my own state! I've wanted to be part of something like this for years.'

'I understand, Trico,' I assured him. 'I'm the one who's leaving. You're free. You should do whatever feels right.'

'We'll look after her, Trico,' Sophie said. She and Diego were coming down as far as Mexico City, on their way to the south Pacific coast.

He left his bag at the house and walked with us to the big intersection on the ring road. Diego was penniless and wanted to work for an hour before we hitched a ride south. He headed to one of the semáforos with his poi.

'Shall we play some passes, Loquita?' Trico asked, jerking his head at the opposite semáforo. 'One last time?'

We played for 15 minutes, but heavily, clumsily, our thoughts somewhere else. Trico took the coins we had collected and wandered off, muttering something about needing a caguama. I felt no urge to continue playing without him. Hele had lent me some money before we left Real de Catorce, so there was no pressing need to. 'For emergencies,' she had said. 'It's a long way to Cancún, and you don't want to risk missing your plane. Wire me a bank transfer when you get to the UK.' I sat and chatted with Sophie, trying to distract myself from the gnawing feeling behind my ribs.

By the time Diego stopped playing, Trico still hadn't returned. We went to buy some *gorditas*, which we ate sitting on the pavement with the bags, but when we finished them there was still no sign of him. The heat of the day was fading, warning us it would not be many hours until sunset.

'Maybe we should just go,' I said. 'Maybe he's not coming back.' I tried and failed to sound nonchalant.

'We can wait a while longer,' Sophie assured me. 'Can't we, Diego? I'm sure he wouldn't have left without saying goodbye.'

When he finally appeared he was wheeling Flaca before him with his bag on his back and a determined scowl on his face. He seemed irritable and refused to acknowledge his sudden change of plan.

'Come *on*,' he snapped, ignoring our questions and striding impatiently past us as if it was we who had held up the journey. 'I want to get a ride out of here while it's still light.'

ψ Ψ ψ

He said it again in San Luis.

It had never been our intention to stop in San Luis. A truck had dropped us off in a service station just past the city, already after dark. It seemed unlikely we would find another ride until morning, but I was prepared to try. We dumped our bags in a heap and left them with Trico while Sophie, Diego and I went to inquire if any trucks were heading south that night. When we came back (unsuccessful) we found Trico asleep, and my bag gone.

I tend to take a fairly blasé attitude to things getting stolen – easy come, easy go – but there are limits. Apart from a few boxes of books back in England, the bag contained everything I owned. Including my passport.

It took me a while to calm down enough to stop shouting and look at the situation rationally. I was pretty sure who had done it – a slimy drunk with the cauliflower face of a third-rate boxer who I'd taken some verbal abuse from (and given some back to) when I'd mistaken him for a truck driver and asked him for a lift. Luckily, the truck stop was large enough to have a security booth showing screens from several CCTV cameras. Unluckily, the security guard had a screen of his own and was watching telenovelas with his feet on the desk. He deeply resented being interrupted and refused to look at the CCTV footage, or phone the police, or let us use the phone.

'What are you *for* then?' I asked.

He shrugged.

'So you're just a pointless fat *pendejo?*'

'Yes.' He chuckled to himself, apparently quite tickled by the analysis. 'I'm a pointless fat *pendejo.*'

If nothing else, I had to commend his honesty.

We borrowed a phone from a man in the service station to call the police, and sat down to wait. I was apprehensive – I usually went out of my way to avoid contact with the Mexican police – but I didn't know what else to do. I soon became too agitated to sit, paced up and down for a while, then went to stand at the edge of the truck stop and stared out at the streaking lights along the motorway. I was so lost in thought I didn't hear the prostitute approaching until she tapped me on the shoulder. She was on the brink of middle age, with greasy hair in a pony-tail and the blank expression of one so used to being treated like a piece of meat that she'd almost forgotten she might once have been something else.

'You're looking for a bag?' she asked.

'Yes! Did you see who stole it?'

'It was that man in the green T-shirt. He ran that way.' She waved her hand towards a road leading behind the truck stop, in the direction of a small village.

'I thought it was him. Thank you for telling me.'

She shrugged.

'He's a *culero*. He always comes here, drunk with no money, giving me abuse. I hope you find him.'

I've always believed that you can tell a lot about a man's character from his attitude towards prostitutes. There are few things that disgust me more than those who use the service, yet condemn the providers. Rationality went out the window. Blind rage surged back. I ran back to the others, snatched up one of the fire staffs and marched off in the direction she had indicated. Trico and Diego sprinted after me.

'Where are you going?'

'Where do you think I'm going? To find him, of course.'

Trico groaned.

'Are you crazy? The villages round here are fucking rough. You can't just walk in there in the middle of the night, searching for scum like that. Nobody's going to tell you where he is. And even if you find him, he'll be roaring drunk with all his friends by now. What are you going to do? Attack him with a fire staff? You're more likely to get shot than get your bag back.'

'I don't give a shit,' I retorted, with the petulant self-righteousness that tends to accompany monumental stupidity. Trico and Diego looked at each other. If I hadn't been armed, I'm sure they would have rolled their eyes.

I have no idea what would have happened next, if a small miracle hadn't happened first. Shambling back onto the forecourt of the petrol station came none other than the bag thief, flanked by two friends. I can only assume that he was too drunk or too stupid, or both, to have the common sense to keep away for a couple of hours. I ran up to him, waving the staff in his face. Trico and Diego hurriedly grabbed their own weapons and ran after me.

'Where's my bag, *puto*?'

Before he could answer, the second miracle happened. In a triumphant blaze of lights, a police pickup drew up beside us. The policemen swiftly handcuffed the man and his friends (they appeared to recognise them), but then we had a problem.

'I'm afraid we can't arrest him without evidence that he has committed a crime,' they said. 'At least one eyewitness.'

It was tempting to say that I'd never known the Mexican police to concern themselves with such trivialities before, but on reflection decided that it was heartening to find that the rule of law wasn't entirely dead. Finding an eyewitness, however, was problematic. The pointless fat *pendejo* was no use at all. The prostitute had disappeared.

'What we can do,' one of the policemen told me, 'is *pretend* to arrest him, drive him round a bit and see if he confesses. In the meantime, you can look for your eyewitness. If we can get neither a confession nor an eyewitness, I'm afraid there's nothing we can do.'

I agreed. Only after they drove off with the man and his friends handcuffed in the back did it occur to me to wonder what tactics might be used to secure a confession. But there was no time to worry about it. I had a prostitute to find.

I eventually found her jumping down from one of the parked trucks. She was willing to give evidence, but when the police hadn't returned in 10 minutes she started to get impatient.

'I can't wait all night,' she said. 'I need to earn a living. I don't come here for fun, you know.'

Reluctantly, I let her get back to her rounds. At first I tried to keep a watch on her, following her at a discreet distance and peering round parked vehicles to check where she was. But I soon discovered that there is a limit to the amount of time you can stalk a prostitute around a truck stop whilst maintaining a modicum of self-respect, at which point I gave up and went back to sit with the others.

When the policemen returned, the thief was alone in the back of the truck. I peered at him anxiously, but could see no signs of a beating. I have no idea what means were used, but the policemen had managed to unearth my bag. I quickly riffled through it, and found everything still there.

'The only question,' the policeman said, 'is what you want to do now. We could arrest him, but then you would have to come to the station to make a statement. Perhaps, as you have your possessions back, you would prefer to leave it at that?'

I looked at the thief coldly. Red-eyed and handcuffed with his head lolling drunkenly, he looked weak and pathetic. I felt the anger drain out of me. Uncertain, I looked at Trico.

'*No mames*, Cat,' he said. 'Are you going to let him get away with that? If you do, he'll only do it again to someone else.'

I thought about it. Not the theft; now that I had my bag back, it had lost the power to anger me. Instead, I thought of the deadened look in the prostitute's eyes as she told me how she was used to him molesting her. Then I thought of truck drivers who imagined they had the right to touch me while I was sleeping, and men who thought they had the right to beat their wives, and all the unreported and unprosecuted rapes across the country, and the 'systematic sexual feminicide' in Ciudad Juárez: hugely varying degrees of evil, but all the result of the same nauseating misogyny that countless Mexican women still struggle against every day of their lives. There was nothing I could do about any of that, but at least I had the opportunity to give one woman a few nights' (relative) peace.

'I could forgive you for the theft of my bag, *puto*,' I told the man. 'But for your disrespect of women, never.'

It was a small victory, probably forgotten even by the man himself in the grinding headache of the next morning's hangover. But it felt good.

The only downside was that it meant we all had to accompany the thief back to the police station in San Luis to make a statement. It was dawn by the time we made it back to Trico's parents' house, exhausted and desperate for a proper sleep before we continued the journey. Elvira was just waking, and was overjoyed to see Trico.

'Maybe I should stay here, Loquita,' he told me. 'It hasn't been easy in San Luis over the last year. I think my family missed me.'

'Of course they did,' I said. 'I would understand if you wanted to stay.'

But by the time we had rested, he had changed his mind.

'I may as well come with you, at least as far as DF,' he decided. 'I need to get my old unicycle fixed anyway. It's a good model; shame not to use it just because I have Flaca.'

ψ Ψ ψ

He said it again in DF.

As always happened when we came to DF, we drifted in opposite directions: he to Iván's house in Texcoco, I to say my goodbyes to my friends near the university who had put up with me much longer than I deserved. Trico and I arranged to meet the next day in one of my preferred pulquerías, where the walls are covered with vibrant murals and the pulque is served with a complimentary *botana* of spiced stews and beans. (Many Mexican bars have a wonderful habit of plying you with free food as long as you keep drinking.) We would gather my friends from DF and Texcoco for one final farewell and then take a bus to Villa Hermosa in the evening, from where we would find a connection to Cancún.

Julio and Cindy were the first to arrive, and over our first mug of pulque I recounted the bag saga from San Luis. Julio was unimpressed by my defiant stand for Mexican feminism.

'*Podría perdonarte...*' he sneered, repeating the beginning of my triumphant final shot to the misogynist thief. 'What an awkward construction. Have I taught you nothing, hippie?'

But his heart didn't quite seem in the insult, and he smiled more than usual. Proper smiles, that looked like happiness rather than wind.

'What's going on with you, Julio?' I asked. 'You're in a suspiciously good mood.'

He snorted. But he had a gleam in his eyes he couldn't hide.

'Come on, Julio, drop the act for one second and tell me who she is. I know a man in love when I see one.'

'*Pinche hippie.* You and your peace and love and all those *mamadas.* Who's being sexist now? Do I need a woman to make me happy?'

'Not necessarily. But you haven't talked about any of your ex-girlfriends once in this whole conversation. That sounds like love to me.'

He grumbled and evaded for a while longer, but didn't take long to crack. Although he felt obliged to uphold his reputation and maintain an appearance of grouchiness, he was clearly bursting to tell me. Her name was Bea, and she was the most incredible woman in the world.

Sophie and Diego arrived shortly after, followed by Trico and all the current residents of Iván's house in Texcoco. I couldn't have wished for a better set of friends or memories. But although he wheeled Flaca ahead of him and carried the smaller unicycle under one arm, there was obviously something missing.

'Where's your bag?' I asked.

He looked sheepish.

'I'm sorry Loquita, but I'm going to stay with the banda here. They're all going to Xico in a few days, in the forest in the north of Veracruz. I think that's what I need... a natural place, somewhere peaceful. A different journey.'

I looked down, refusing to betray any emotion. The end was coming; whether now or in a few days hardly mattered. There was no sense in spoiling the few hours we had left.

'OK,' I said. 'I understand.'

But I could hardly bear to talk to him as we drank our pulque, afraid I would vent my disappointment in anger. Instead, I chatted with one of the other boys, who sat with a large black wheelie suitcase at his feet. This suitcase was legendary among the banda. Surprisingly, there were no professional-quality circus shops in DF. Juggling clubs had to be ordered from South America (where the street circus scene is said to be even more thriving than in Mexico), and one needed a contact who ordered in bulk to get a good price. This made the process of buying toys a complicated affair, involving a cryptic-sounding phone call followed by a brief meeting in a bar or alleyway to exchange money and goods. The boy with the black suitcase was known to be one of the best toy-dealers in DF.

'What have you got at the moment?' I asked him. 'Anything interesting?'

His eyes lit up.

'Yes, actually. Got these, just in from Chile.' He unzipped the suitcase to reveal, amongst the jumble of clubs and balls, three juggling machetes with curved blades and long wooden handles. They looked like pirates' cutlasses. He heard my intake of breath and looked up at me slyly. 'Top quality. Really well balanced.'

'How much?'

'For you... Three hundred each.'

'I'll give you eight hundred for the three.'

'Deal.'

With that, I had spent most of my getting-to-Cancún money. But, I reassured myself, I still had enough for the bus to Villa Hermosa and from there to Cancún, and it wasn't like getting food was ever a problem. Besides, now I had three juggling machetes. Top quality. Really well balanced. Everything was going to be fine.

As evening approached, we meandered towards the bus stop in Tepito. I said goodbye to most of my friends at the nearest metro station, but Trico, Iván, and a few others announced that they would wait with me for the two hours until my bus left. After all, what's the most dangerous place in DF? *Es Tepito en la noche.*

Tepito in the evening, however, didn't feel threatening. The streets, clogged with bargain hunters by day, were now clogged with vans as the vendors dismantled their stalls and packed away their heaps of lacy underwear and pirate DVDs. Men shouted clearance prices on papayas and dried pig skin. The gutters were slimy with trampled vegetable waste.

I bought my bus ticket from a man sitting in a garage doorway with a clipboard in one hand and a can of beer in the other. We bought our own beers and juggled to pass the time. Trico was in full Tricopsycho mode, pedalling frantically up and down the street on Flaca, slaloming between vans and pedestrians, whistling piercingly, and shying away from any attempt at conversation or gesture of affection. I sat on the ground with Sophie, feeling tense and fragile, talking determinedly about Other Things.

Half an hour before departure, I realised that Trico had suddenly fallen silent. His lips were pouted and the furrows on his brow were doing that little dance they always did when his thoughts were racing. 'What's up, Trico?' I said.

Instead of answering, he addressed the man with the clipboard.

'Is the bus full?' he asked.

The man glanced at his list. 'Not quite.'

Trico turned to me, his face splitting in a triumphant grin. 'What do you think?'

'What, you mean – you want to come? But all your things are in Texcoco.'

He looked round at Iván. Iván rolled his eyes.

'*Pinche Trico*. Didn't I tell you to bring them, in case you changed your mind? But yes, of course I'll look after them for you.'

'But you don't have enough money for the ticket, do you?' I asked. 'I've only got just enough to get me to Cancún, and there's no time to hitchhike. *Ay*, why didn't you say this earlier, before I bought those bloody machetes?'

But once Trico had an idea in his head, he was not one to be dissuaded by such trifles.

'You've got enough for two tickets to Villa Hermosa,' he pointed out. 'The bus will arrive there in the morning, and the connection to Cancún won't leave until that night. We can easily raise the money in that time! That would give us a whole day and night in Cancún together before your plane leaves! I'm sure we can stay with my friend Kinich – you'll like him; he's really cool. Ay, Cancún! I've always wanted to show you the Caribbean! What do you say, Loquita?'

He got more excited with every sentence, his eyes shining as if he'd been dreaming of this for years rather than the last five minutes. *Pinche Trico*. Once again, he made me feel as if it were I who was holding up the journey. For a moment, I was exasperated.

Then I burst out laughing.

ψ Ψ ψ

He said it again in Villa Hermosa.

We arrived at dawn but were already pouring sweat, squashed up between the market sellers returning home with their bundles of goods. 'You know what they call this city?' Trico asked, as we walked out in search of a good semáforo to raise the money for the onward journey.

'What?'

'*La ciudad de las dos mentiras*. [The city of the two lies].' He laughed. 'Because it's not a *villa* [town], and it's not *hermosa* [beautiful].'

It was a sprawling, muggy, sensuous city, full of coffee skin, liquorice eyes, ample bosoms tucked into tops clingy with sweat, smells of drains mingled with flowers mingled with fried food, and seething, fuming traffic. In the semáforo I could hardly see for the perspiration running in my eyes, and when I wiped my brow it left a dirty smear across my face. The street vendors wore shorts and sandals and sold cans of cold drinks from buckets of ice. We had sunstroke and short tempers.

'Catch them, Cat, *no mames!*' Trico shouted, after the third time I'd dropped a club in the same red light. 'You expect people to give us money when you can't even catch the fucking clubs?'

'My hands are sweating! They slip!'

'You're always making excuses.'

'It's a valid excuse. It's fucking hot.'

'Don't be a *fresa*. I don't want to play with someone who can't even stand a bit of sun.'

'Fuck off then. I didn't ask you to come. I would have had enough money to go straight to Cancún if you hadn't.'

He fucked off. I sulked. He returned 15 minutes later, caguama in hand, to inform me he was going to Palenque.

'Fine.'

'There's no point me coming to Cancún. You're leaving anyway.'

'I know.'

'I have friends who will be in Palenque now. And there's a party on tomorrow I want to go to.'

'Go then.'

He went. I sulked. He returned 15 minutes later to ask if I had one of his clubs.

'No.'

He grumbled and swore for a while as he looked for the club. It turned out to be in his bag.

'Look,' he said, 'if I play with you again will you concentrate this time?'

'I was concentrating last time. I can't promise not to sweat.'

'Well, the sun's not quite so high now. We can try.'

We managed to raise the bus fares by evening, with enough left for some fried chicken with tortillas and a caguama before we left.

ψ Ψ ψ

We arrived in Cancún to find Kinich covering the front of his house in polythene. He was a lanky boy with floppy hair, wearing a pair of sunglasses with neon yellow rims and a huge plaster cast on one foot. He greeted us with effusive excitement.

'What did you do to your leg?'Trico asked him, as soon as Kinich stopped talking for long enough for him to get a word in.

'What? Oh, the leg! Yes! Hah! Funny story. Was doing a show in one of the big hotels – great atmosphere, adrenaline got to me! Decided to try a new trick on the trapeze. Hah! Didn't go as planned. Never mind, never mind. Only problem is, it's affected my stilt-walking as well, so I'm temporarily unemployed. Hah! Luckily I had a bit of money saved, but I have to find other ways to spend my time.'

'Is that why you're covering your house in plastic?' I asked.

'Oh – hah! Yes. It's a rented house, you see.' When I failed to make an instantaneous logical connection, he went on. 'They don't allow me to paint it. So I'm covering it in plastic. And then painting it.'

'What are you going to paint on it?'

'Oh, you know. Lots of colours. Motivational messages. Just things to make people smile.'

Trico shouted with laughter and clapped him on the back.

'*Pinche Kinich*. I told you you'd like him, Cat.'

Cancún is a bizarre place. In 1970, it was nothing but a green and gold promontory jutting into the Caribbean, with a total population of three. But it could not go unnoticed forever. It was made a designated tourist development site by the Mexican government in 1974, and has grown exponentially ever since. Forty years after its foundation, it can only be described as Legoland-on-Sea. The Zona Hotelera features giant concrete cubes squatting next to giant white toast racks, draped with neon lighting and set off by regimented clumps of token palm trees. The sand and sea have been kept immaculately clean, but the man-made landscape of roads and hotel developments has taken over to such an extent that it makes the natural landscape look artificial, like a painted backdrop.

More to my tastes was neighbouring Puerto Juárez, with that vibe of sun-bleached shabbiness than I always associate with the Caribbean. The houses were ramshackle and painted in bright colours, with rooftops swarming with auburn-furred racoons. We called in on a few old friends of Trico's, collecting some money he was owed for long-ago shows and sprawling on sagging mattresses with wayward springs, almost catatonic from the heat. The clammy pressure of hurricane season was building over Cancún, when sudden violent storms can sweep out of a pristine sky to hose down the blistering concrete before vanishing as abruptly as they come. We got caught by one of these on the beach in Puerto Juárez and lay spreadeagled on the dirty sand under a stinging massage of raindrops.

On our return we found Kinich sunbathing in his front garden, the clumps of grass between the paving slabs steaming dry in the aftermath of the rain. Behind him, the house appeared to have contracted some form of plastic leprosy. The storm had ripped his carefully painted banners to shreds, leaving only a tattered mess of coloured scraps.

'Bad luck!' I commiserated. 'After all that work!'

But in Kinich's world, there was no such thing as bad luck.

'What? Oh, the painting! Yes, that didn't last long, did it? Hah! Never mind, never mind. It has quite a nice *abstract* effect now, don't you think? And you can still kind of read it, no? If you really focus?'

I squinted. 'Kind of...'

'Maybe it has more *significance* that way. Hah! I mean, you always value things more when you have to work for them, no?'

'Yes,' I said. 'I suppose you do.'

ψ Ψ ψ

Having travelled over 2,000 reluctant kilometres, protesting all the way, Trico definitively refused to come to the airport with me. For the first time, I tried to persuade him, which was probably the reason why he didn't. Trico would do nothing if not on his own volition.

'I hate airports,' he declared.

'Have you ever been to an airport?'

'No, but I've seen pictures; I know what they're like. White and sterile. Like hospitals.'

I laughed.

'Where people arrive and where people leave, Trico. What could be more beautiful than that?'

But, ever sensitive to everyone's bullshit but his own, he was having none of it.

'*No mames*, Cat. I'll come to the bus stop with you. You'll be fine on your own from there.'

Of course, I shouldn't have been surprised. Trico had never been good at arriving or leaving. Trico, who would return home after a silence of six months without telling his parents he was coming. Trico, who would wander down an alleyway and disappear without telling anyone where he was going, leaving his friends to reconstruct their shattered plans in his wake. Maybe after so many years he was desensitised to greetings and goodbyes. Or maybe they became more frightening every time, and he had long since reached the point where he could bear them no longer. I couldn't guess what he was thinking. Two years on, he was as much of an enigma to me as ever.

I had wanted to spend the morning with him, but he slipped off soon after breakfast and was gone so long I started to wonder if he'd walked out to the motorway and thumbed the first ride out of Cancún: maybe a clapped out pickup rolling east towards the sweating jungles of Chiapas, or one of the groaning trucks with drivers heading at desperate, amphetamined speed to the empty spaces of the northern deserts.

But by noon he was back, carrying with him a dismembered body – a gleaming silver seat pole, a worn pair of pedals, a wheel with coloured beads on the spokes, and a tyre round his neck that was thicker and with better grip than the usual. Good for offroad riding. Mountains, deserts, that sort of thing. His old unicycle: the one I had seen him ride, in Creel, that first day nearly two years ago.

'So you can learn to ride, Loquita. So next time I see you we can throw passes between the two unicycles.'

'I... don't you need it Trico? It's been with you a long time.'

He shook his head dismissively.

'I have my Flaca. What more do I need?'

We wrestled the parts into my rucksack, later to cause great consternation at the airport when my hold luggage was found to be too heavy and I had to unpack and rearrange my possessions in the middle of the departure hall, spilling chains, machetes, metal bars and a large tyre across the floor amid the flip-flops of sun-broiled holidaymakers. The weight dragged at my shoulders on the walk to the bus station, and the sweat ran down my face in the merciless Cancún sun. We said very little.

On the steps of the bus, he reached for my hand. Palm met palm, and fingers curled into each other. Thumbs on the outside. A spiral, starting at our linked fingertips and radiating outwards. We held the grip for a long moment. Then slowly, simultaneously, each of us extended our index fingers to point into the solar plexus of the other.

In lak'ech. Tú eres mi otro yo.

One last look. Then the grip loosened.

'Take care, Loquita.'

He turned away.

There was no waving. That wasn't Trico's style. By the time the bus shuddered to life and heaved itself out of its bay, he was already gone. I pictured him walking away, one arm round Flaca, chin up, chest out, carrying the eternal circus to a new street corner, a new semáforo, a new audience of strangers who maybe, just maybe, would take 50 seconds out of this age of movement to watch him, to smile, to wonder who he was and how he came to be there.

And all the while, that other great circus played out across Mexico, and countries and continents beyond. I leaned my forehead against the window, using unshed tears to cloud my vision until the colours outside blurred together like a chalk drawing in the rain. Unanchored from the present, I allowed myself to slip back through two years of memories. Two years of ordinary extraordinary people. Elena, whose kindness still glimmered through a sedated fog, long after beauty had been beaten out of her. Master, who kept sane by remembering the obvious in a mad world. Doña Maria, her eyes glittering at the memory of where the Wheel of Fortune had taken her. Elvira, thinking always of others, as if they were the son she had lost. Javi, his handsome face drained of colour as he staggered out of hospital supported by his friends. Wolanda, friend to all, sitting alone in his shack full of secret history. The banda of Juárez, half drunk but still serious, risking death to bring a flash of colour to their blighted city. And finally, like a ringmaster presiding over the whole chaotic performance, Kinich in neon-rimmed sunglasses set crooked on his nose, grinning at the tattered remains of a sign whose fragments were still just legible in the Cancún sun.

TU ARMA: EL ARTE

QUE CADA ACCIÓN SEA CON

VALOR

AMISTAD

AMOR

LIBERTAD

Y ALEGRIA

Your weapon is art. Let every action be with courage, friendship, love, freedom, and joy.